PRAISE FOR *Number Our Days*

"The veil with which our culture covers the daily affairs of the aged has been pulled aside in *Number Our Days*. We see powerful personages thinking, reflecting, loving, arguing, and, above all, articulating their long experience of living—in splendidly rich language. . . . Being, meaning, and narrative are intimately related in Dr. Myerhoff's vision of the human condition as it is played out among these people." —Victor Turner, from the Introduction

"One of those rare books that leave the reader somehow changed." —Bel Kaufman

"One of the most significant, seeding, sturdy, essential books of years and years." —Tillie Olsen

"A compelling and compassionate account of elderly Jews who have much to teach us about surviving and aging with grace and wisdom." —Maggie Kuhn, Gray Panthers

"Shines with the luminous wit of old age." —Robert Bly

BARBARA MYERHOFF, Ph.D., was chairman of the Department of Anthropology at the University of Southern California until her death in 1985. She was a collaborator on the documentary based on this book, which won an Academy Award. Her 1976 Book, *Peyote Hunt*, was nominated for the National Book Award.

Number Our Days

Culture and Community Among Elderly Jews in an American Ghetto

---

BARBARA MYERHOFF

A MERIDIAN BOOK

MERIDIAN
Published by the Penguin Group
Penguin Books USA Inc., 375 Hudson Street, New York, New York 10014, U.S.A.
Penguin Books Ltd, 27 Wrights Lane, London W8 5TZ, England
Penguin Books Australia Ltd, Ringwood, Victoria, Australia
Penguin Books Canada Ltd, 10 Alcorn Avenue, Toronto, Ontario, Canada M4V 3B2
Penguin Books (N.Z.) Ltd, 182–190 Wairau Road, Auckland 10, New Zealand

Penguin Books Ltd, Registered Offices: Harmondsworth, Middlesex, England

Published by Meridian, an imprint of Dutton Signet, a division of
Penguin Books USA Inc. Previously published in a Dutton edition.

First Meridian Printing, May, 1994
10 9 8 7 6 5 4 3 2 1

LIBRARY OF CONGRESS CATALOGING-IN-PUBLICATION DATA
Myerhoff, Barbara G.
Number our days : culture and community among elderly Jews in an American ghetto / Barbara Myerhoff.
p. cm.
ISBN 0-452-01122-1
1. Jews—California—Los Angeles—Social life and customs.
2. Social work with the aged—California—Los Angeles. 3. Jewish aged—California—Los Angeles. 4. Los Angeles (Calif.)—Social life and customs. 5. Venice (Los Angeles, Calif.)—Social life and customs.
I. Title.
F869.L89J555 1994
305.892'4079494—dc20 93-45422
CIP

Printed in the United States of America

For Ruth Adams
1932–1975
A woman of valor

"... *Give her of the fruit of her hands;*
And let her works praise her in the gates."

PROVERBS 31

ACKNOWLEDGMENTS

I am grateful above all to the Center People who gave themselves to me so fully, and by doing that gave me parts of myself and my heritage. Many other people helped me in various ways throughout this work. Sherrie Wagner assisted with many research tasks, and along with Maggie Starr, typed the manuscript with intelligence and patience. Margie Remar helped with my children, generously and lovingly. Bill Whitehead, my editor, brought extraordinary skill, sensitivity, and devotion to his work and mine. Foremost among those who gave abundant criticism, encouragement, and love from the very beginning are Lee, Nick, and Matthew Myerhoff, Deena Metzger, Morris Rosen, Lynne Littman, Victor Turner, and Riv-Ellen Prell-Foldes. To all these people I wish to express my great appreciation. The National Science Foundation contributed part of the funding for the work, in connection with its grant to the Andrus Gerontology Center of the University of Southern California, and this assistance too I gratefully acknowledge. Naturally I alone am responsible for the interpretation offered here.

CONTENTS

FOREWORD

Although this book celebrates the elderly and an ancient tradition, it is also in the vanguard of anthropological theory. With it anthropology has come of age: Its extremes have touched. Barriers between self and other, head and heart, conscious and unconscious, history and autobiography, have been thrown down and new ways have been found to express the vital interdependence of these and other "mighty opposites." A few years ago M. N. Srinivas, the distinguished Indian anthropologist, foretold this development. A Brahmin, and hence "twice-born," he urged anthropologists—in a lecture delivered at the University of Chicago—to go one stage further. We were to seek to be "thrice-born." The first birth is our natal origin in a particular culture. The second is our move from this familiar to a far place to do fieldwork there. In a way this could be described as a familiarization of the exotic, finding that when we understand the rules and vocabulary of another culture, what had seemed bizarre at first becomes in time part of the daily round. The third birth occurs when we have become comfortable within the other culture—and found the clue to grasping many like it—and turn our gaze again toward our native land. We find that the familiar has become exoticized; we see it with new eyes. The commonplace has become the marvelous. What we took for granted now has power to stir our scientific imaginations. Few anthropologists have gone the full distance. Most of us feel that our professional duty is done when we have "processed" our fieldwork in other cultures in book or article form. Yet our discipline's long-term program has always included the movement of return, the purified look at ourselves. "Thrice-born" anthropologists are perhaps in the best position to become the "reflexivity" of a culture.

Dr. Barbara Myerhoff is one of the few anthropologists whose work attests to this double cultural rebirth. She has written an important book, *Peyote Hunt,* about the sacred journey of the Huichol Indians whose homeland is in the more inaccessible reaches of the Sierra Madre Occidental of Mexico. She accompanied a pilgrim group of Huichol on a journey east to the holy land of Wirikuta where the gods dwell, the place once inhabited by the First People. Her analysis of the myths, rituals, and symbols associated with this quest for a sacred origin broke new ground in the study of cultural dynamics. *Peyote Hunt,* nominated for a National Book Award, may itself be regarded as a protracted metaphor for the human quest for reflexive wisdom, and for the anthropological search for cultural meaning.

Number Our Days is the fruit of Dr. Myerhoff's "third birth." To write it she has returned not only to her nation of birth, but also to her Jewish heritage. A pilgrimage may be as much temporal and interior as overland. It is a venture, history, biography, and autobiography. Anthropologists learn respect for the elders among those they study. It was thus a felicitous chance that brought Barbara Myerhoff among the truly elderly folk of the Aliyah Senior Citizens' Center, a group of former migrants from Eastern Europe now mostly abandoned by their more or less successful and assimilated New World progeny. She was prepared to find wisdom in their memories and found not only wisdom, but also a source of vitality, "survivor's" vitality. For the Center people were survivors twice over: By emigration they had escaped the Holocaust and by extreme old age many had "survived their peers, families, and often children." Wisdom comes through in the many autobiographies Dr. Myerhoff collected, vitality informs the sociocultural dramas of living she observed and took part in.

Dr. Myerhoff demonstrates with full documentation that the very old can remain in command of the basic human faculties of insight and imagination until the very end. The veil with which our culture covers the daily affairs of the aged has been pulled aside in *Number Our Days*. We see powerful personages thinking, reflecting, loving, arguing and, above all, articulating their long experience of living—in splendidly rich language. Dr.

Myerhoff mostly lets them tell their stories and present their cases in their own words, bringing us the very ring and savor of what is elsewhere a fading Yiddishkeit.

Being, meaning, and narrative are intimately related in Dr. Myerhoff's vision of the human condition as it is played out among these people. In her conclusion, she characterizes our species as *Homo narrans,* humankind as story-teller, implying that culture in general—specific cultures, and the fabric of meaning that constitutes any single human existence—is the "story" we tell about ourselves. Her use of narrative and dialogue gives the work its distinctive flavor, at once deep and rich, full of subtlety and surprise. The process of going from the familiar to the far and then back again involves movement in depth as well as distance. Dr. Myerhoff constantly goes beneath the surface of events, relationships and personal statements to the many underlying levels of Jewish culture, seeking to discover how people assign meaning to their own and to other people's lives. Her approach to her subjects is consistently probing as well as affectionate. The anthropological perspective is omnipresent but not intrusive, always made to serve the purpose of presenting specific people and events.

New theoretical wine requires new presentational bottles. It is not simply to give an "impression" of the original, pungent quality of her subjects' speech and thought that Dr. Myerhoff introduces so many verbatim transcriptions of the "bobbe-myseh," or "grandmothers' tales," nor does she cite people's narratives merely for introducing "rattling good yarns," or "edifying stories," though often they are. She uses this material to show us the very processes through which her subjects weave meaning and identity out of their memories and experiences. As she writes, "The tale certifies the fact of being and gives sense at the same time." And such tales, marvelous tales, spun from the plain strong wool of ordinary human life. The book brims with comedy as well as tears: true to the many-layered complexity of the human tragicomedy, sometimes in bristling, bustling crowd scenes, sometimes in a portrait gallery full of Rembrandtesque chiaroscuro characters. If there is a hero, it is Shmuel the tailor, one of those rare spirits that a culture occasionally produces, ample and strong enough to contain all the complexities and paradoxes of the human condition and his own tradition. Though thoroughly rooted in Judaism, he transcends it; he is a timeless, placeless man whose insights and courage do not belong only to any specific epoch or social form.

William Blake has urged us to "labour well the Minute Particulars," for "General Forms have their vitality in Particulars. And every Particular is a Man." In this book, the Minute Particulars are Jewish culture and its bearers, the vital aged of the Center. In Dr. Myerhoff's analysis, "Being a Jew . . . is a dense and sacred symbol . . . with many inflections," all of them in complex interplay—in casual conversations, internal, private reflections, and in the major ceremonies and sociocultural dramas where the lifelong quest for identity and meaning are pursued to the last stage of human and cultural history. The people are continually engaged with the problem of what it is to be Jewish, which among them amounts to what it is to be human. It is a passionately disputed problem, dramatized, contemplated, and fought over. We are reminded of Thomas Hardy's poem, "An Ancient to Ancients," where he speaks of the elderly who "burnt brightlier toward their setting day. . . ." In the struggles of the Center elderly with themselves and each other, we see them in their "brightlier burning," making visible the hidden things of the heart. They are seen enacting their identity in what Dr. Myerhoff calls "Definitional Ceremonies," public performances that often shade into dramatized myth. But these are boisterous often disorderly events, not the solemn, formal rites we usually associate with religious ritual and symbols. This troubles even the Center members. At one point Olga laments the conflicts in their interchanges and asks why it is that Jews have to argue all the time. Basha—practical, calm, and strong—replies with a quotation: "We fight to keep warm. That's how we survive." The word *warm* is used in both senses here, including the physical state and the heart that is never allowed to grow cold, despite the temptations and pressures. Dr. Myerhoff presents us with a study of what she calls "Domestic Religion," the "local usages sanctified by long practice and their embeddedness in culture, located in the first experiences of family, home, and community." Linking ethnic experience, family ritual, and Yiddishkeit, Domestic Religion is also a matter of the heart, circumventing cognitive processes and formal training: ineradicable, and even among these extremely verbal people, often ineffable.

Because Barbara Myerhoff "keeps [her] wits warm to the things that are" in Center life and records them with perceptiveness, fidelity, and compassion, the theoretical structures she discovers have a lambency seldom found in the literature of the social sciences. While her work is always informed by her anthropological training, it goes beyond the usual reports from the field. It can perhaps best be characterized as compassionate objectivity, or better yet, as realistic humankindness.

1978 VICTOR TURNER

Lord, what is man, that Thou hast
regard for him?
Or the son of man, that Thou takest
account of him?

Man is like a breath,
His days are as a fleeting shadow.

In the morning he flourishes and grows up
like grass,
In the evening he is cut down and withers.

So teach us to number our days,
That we may get us a heart of wisdom.

This prayer, read at the Koved funeral described in Chapter 5, is adapted from Psalms 144 and 90.

CHAPTER ONE

"So what do you want from us here?"

Every morning I wake up in pain. I wiggle my toes. Good. They still obey. I open my eyes. Good. I can see. Everything hurts but I get dressed. I walk down to the ocean. Good. It's still there. Now my day can start. About tomorrow I never know. After all, I'm eighty-nine. I can't live forever.

Death and the ocean are protagonists in Basha's life. They provide points of orientation, comforting in their certitude. One visible, the other invisible, neither hostile nor friendly, they accompany her as she walks down the boardwalk to the Aliyah Senior Citizens' Center.

Basha wants to remain independent above all. Her life at the beach depends on her ability to perform a minimum number of basic tasks. She must shop and cook, dress herself, care for her body and her one-room apartment, walk, take the bus to the market and the doctor, be able to make a telephone call in case of emergency. Her arthritic hands have a difficult time with the buttons on her dress. Some days her fingers ache and swell so that she cannot fit them into the holes of the telephone dial. Her hands shake as she puts in her eyedrops for glaucoma. Fortunately, she no longer has to give herself injections for her diabetes. Now it is controlled by pills, if she is careful about what she eats. In the neighborhood there are no large markets within walking distance. She must take the bus to shop. The bus steps are very high and sometimes the driver objects when she tries to bring her little wheeled cart aboard. A small boy whom she has befriended and occasionally pays often waits for her at the bus stop to help her up. When she cannot bring her cart onto the bus or isn't helped up the steps, she must walk to the market. Then shopping takes the better part of the day and exhausts her. Her feet, thank God, give her less trouble since she figured out how to cut and sew a pair of cloth shoes so as to leave room for her callouses and bunions.

Basha's daughter calls her once a week and worries about her mother living alone and in a deteriorated neighborhood. "Don't worry about me, darling. This morning I put the garbage in the oven and the bagels in the trash. But I'm feeling fine." Basha enjoys teasing her daughter whose distant concern she finds somewhat embarrassing. "She says to me, 'Mamaleh, you're sweet but you're so *stupid*.' What else could a greenhorn mother expect from a daughter who is a lawyer?" The statement conveys Basha's simultaneous pride and grief in having produced an educated, successful child whose very accomplishments drastically separate her from her mother. The daughter has often invited Basha to come and live with her, but she refuses.

> What would I do with myself there in her big house, alone all day, when the children are at work? No one to talk to. No place to walk. Nobody talks Yiddish. My daughter's husband doesn't like my cooking, so I can't even help with meals. Who needs an old lady around, somebody else for my daughter to take care of? They don't keep the house warm like I like it. When I go to the bathroom at night, I'm afraid to flush, I shouldn't wake anybody up. Here I have lived for thirty-one years. I have my friends. I have the fresh air. Always there are people to talk to on the benches. I can go to the Center whenever I like and always there's something doing there. As long as I can manage for myself, I'll stay here.

Managing means three things: taking care of herself, stretching her monthly pension of three hundred and twenty dollars to cover expenses, and filling her time in ways that have meaning for her. The first two are increasingly hard and she knows that they are battles she will eventually lose. But her free time does not weigh on her. She is never bored and rarely depressed. In many ways, life is not different from before. She has never been well-off, and she never expected things to be easy. When asked if she is happy, she shrugs and laughs. "Happiness by me is a hot cup of tea on a cold day. When you don't get a broken leg, you could call yourself happy."

Basha, like many of the three hundred or so elderly members of the Aliyah Center, was born and spent much of her childhood in one of the small, predominately Jewish, Yiddish-speaking villages known as *shtetls,* located within the Pale of Settlement of Czarist Russia, an area to which almost half the world's Jewish population was confined in the nineteenth century.[1] Desperately poor, regularly terrorized by outbreaks of anti-Semitism initiated by government officials and surrounding peasants, shtetl life was precarious. Yet a rich, highly developed culture flourished in these encapsulated settlements, based on a shared sacred religious history, common customs and beliefs, and two languages—Hebrew for prayer and Yiddish for daily life. A folk culture, *Yiddishkeit,* reached its fluorescence there, and though it continues in various places in the world today, by comparison these are dim and fading expressions of it. When times worsened, it often seemed that Eastern Europe social life intensified proportionately. Internal ties deepened, and the people drew sustenance and courage from each other, their religion, and their community. For many, life became unbearable under the increasingly reactionary regime of Czar Alexander II. The pogroms of 1881–1882, accompanied by severe economic and legal restrictions, drove out the more desperate and daring of the Jews. Soon they were leaving the shtetls and the cities in droves. The exodus of Jews from Eastern Europe swelled rapidly until by the turn of the century, hundreds of thousands were emigrating, the majority to seek freedom and opportunity in the New World.

Basha dresses simply but with care. The purchase of each item of clothing is a major decision. It must last, should be modest and appropriate to her age, but gay and up-to-date. And, of course, it can't be too costly. Basha is not quite five feet tall. She is a sturdy boat of a woman—wide, strong of frame, and heavily corseted. She navigates her great monobosom before her, supported by broad hips and thin, severely bowed legs, their shape the heritage of her malnourished childhood. Like most of the people who belong to the Aliyah Center, her early life in Eastern Europe was characterized by relentless poverty.

Basha dresses for the cold, even though she is now living

in Southern California, wearing a babushka under a red sun hat, a sweater under her heavy coat. She moves down the boardwalk steadily, paying attention to the placement of her feet. A fall is common and dangerous for the elderly. A fractured hip can mean permanent disability, loss of autonomy, and removal from the community to a convalescent or old age home. Basha seats herself on a bench in front of the Center and waits for friends. Her feet are spread apart, well-planted, as if growing up from the cement. Even sitting quite still, there is an air of determination about her. She will withstand attacks by anti-Semites, Cossacks, Nazis, historical enemies whom she conquers by outliving. She defies time and weather (though it is not cold here). So she might have sat a century ago, before a small pyramid of potatoes or herring in the marketplace of the Polish town where she was born. Patient, resolute, she is a survivor.

Not all the Center women are steady boats like Basha. Some, like Faegl, are leaves, so delicate, dry, and vulnerable that it seems at any moment they might be whisked away by a strong gust. And one day, a sudden wind did knock Faegl to the ground. Others, like Gita, are birds, small and sharp-tongued. Quick, witty, vain, flirtatious, they are very fond of singing and dancing. They once were and will always be pretty girls. This is one of their survival strategies. Boats, leaves, or birds, at first their faces look alike. Individual features are blurred by dentures, heavy bifocals, and webs of wrinkles. The men are not so easy to categorize. As a group, they are quieter, more uniform, less immediately outstanding except for the few who are distinctive individuals, clearly distinguishable as leaders.

As the morning wears on, the benches fill. Benches are attached back to back, one side facing the ocean, one side the boardwalk. The people on the ocean side swivel around to face their friends, the boardwalk, and the Center.

Bench behavior is highly stylized. The half-dozen or so benches immediately to the north and south of the Center are the territory of the members, segregated by sex and conversation topic. The men's benches are devoted to abstract, ideological concerns—philosophical debate, politics, religion, and economics. The women's benches are given more to talk about immediate, personal matters—children, food, health, neighbors, love affairs, scandals, and "managing." Men and women talk about Israel and its welfare, about being a Jew and about Center politics. On the benches, reputations are made and broken, controversies explored, leaders selected, factions formed and dissolved. Here is the outdoor dimension of Center life, like a village plaza, a focus of protracted, intense sociability.

The surrounding scene rarely penetrates the invisible, pulsing membrane of the Center community. The old people are too absorbed in their own talk to attend the setting. Surfers, sunbathers, children, dogs, bicyclists, winos, hippies, voyeurs, photographers, panhandlers, artists, junkies, roller skaters, peddlers, and police are omnipresent all year round. Every social class, age, race, and sexual preference is represented. Jesus cults, Hare Krishna parades, sidewalk preachers jostle steel bands and itinerant musicians. As colorful and flamboyant as the scene is by day, it is as dangerous by night. Muggings, theft, rape, harassment, and occasional murders make it a perilous neighborhood for the old people after dark.

Farther up the boardwalk other elderly Jews stake out their territory on benches and picnic tables used for chess, pinochle, poker, and Mah-Jongg. The Center members do not regard them as "serious" or "cultured" people, while they, in turn, consider the Center elderly too political or religious, too inclined to be "joiners," for their taste. Still other old Jews periodically appear on the boardwalk selling Marxist periodicals, Socialist tracts, collecting money for Mexican laborers, circulating petitions to abolish capital punishment. For them, the Center people are too politically conservative. All the elderly Jews in the neighborhood are Eastern European in origin. All are multilingual. Hebrew is brought out for punctuating debates with definitive learned points, usually by the men. Russian or Polish are more used for songs, stories, poems, and reminiscences. But Yiddish binds these diverse people together, the beloved *mama-loshen** of their childhood. It is Yiddish that is used for the most emotional discussions. Despite their ideological differences, most of these people know each other well, having lived here at the beach for two and three decades.

Signs of what was once a much larger, more complete Yiddish ghetto remain along the boardwalk. Two storefront synagogues are left, where only a few years ago there were a dozen. There is a delicatessen and a Jewish bakery. Before there were many kosher butcher stores and little markets. Only three

* Mother tongue.

Jewish board-and-care homes and four large hotels are left to house the elderly. The four thousand or so elderly Jews in the neighborhood must find accommodations in small, rented rooms and apartments within walking distance of the Center. A belt, roughly five miles long and a mile wide, constitutes the limits of the effective community of these Eastern European immigrants, nearly all of whom are now in their middle eighties and up. Several special organizations in the area meet some of their present needs—a secular senior citizen club operated by the city, an outreach city- and state-funded social service center, a women's private political-cultural club, a hot-meals-for-the-elderly service held at a local school. At the edge of the community, still within walking distance of the Center, are several expensive apartments and board-and-care homes (known as "residential facilities"); these accommodate the handful of members who are relatively well-off.

A decade ago, census figures suggest that as many as ten thousand elderly Eastern European Jews lived in the neighborhood. Then Yiddish culture flourished. Groups such as the Workmen's Circle, Emma Lazarus Club, women's philanthropic and religious organizations, various Zionist and Socialist groups were plentiful. Poetry and discussion groups often met in people's homes. There was a dance hall and a choral society. Then, it was said that the community had "the *schonste** Yiddishkeit outside of New York." Around thirty years ago, Jews from all over the country began to immigrate to the beach community, particularly those with health problems and newly retired. Seeking a benign climate, fellow Jews, and moderately priced housing, they brought their savings and small pensions and came to live near the ocean. Collective life was and still is especially intense in this community because there is no automobile traffic on the boardwalk. Here is a place where people may meet, gather, talk, and stroll, simple but basic and precious activities that the elderly in particular can enjoy here all year round.

In the late 1950s, an urban development program resulted in the displacement of between four and six thousand of these senior citizens in a very short period. It was a devastating blow to the culture. "A second Holocaust," Basha called it. "It de-

* Most beautiful.

stroyed our shtetl life all over again.* Soon after the urban development project began, a marina was constructed at the southern end of the boardwalk. Property values soared. Older people could not pay taxes and many lost their homes. Rents quadrupled. Old hotels and apartments were torn down, and housing became the single most serious problem for the elderly who desperately wanted to remain in the area. While several thousand have managed to hang on, no new members are moving into the area because of the housing problem. Their Yiddish world, built up over a thirty-year period, is dying and complete extinction is imminent. Perhaps it will last another five or at the most ten years. Whenever a Center member leaves, everyone is acutely aware that there will be no replacements. The sense of cultural doom coincides with awareness of approaching individual death. "When I go out of here, it will be in a box or to the old folks' home. I couldn't say which is worse," Basha said. "We've only got a few more years here, all of us. It would be good if we could stay till the end. We had a protest march the other day, when they took down the old Miramar Hotel. I made up a sign. It said, 'Let my people stay.' "

Yet the community is not a dreary place and the Center members not a depressed group. The sense of doom, by some miraculous process, functions to heighten and animate their life. Every moment matters. There is no time for deception, trivia, or decorum. Life at the Center is passionate, almost melodramatic. Inside, ordinary concerns and mundane interchanges are strangely intense, quickly heating to outburst. The emotional urgency often seems to have little to do with content. This caldronlike quality is perhaps due to the elders' proximity to death and the realization that their remaining days are few. They want to be seen and heard from, before it is too late. Fiercely, they compete with each other for limited supplies of time and attention. Perhaps it is due to the members' extreme dependence on each other; though strongly attached, they are ambivalent about living so closely with others brought into contact with them more by circumstance than choice. Perhaps it is because these elderly people enjoy the strong flood of energy

* The word *Holocaust*, referring in this setting to Hitler's destruction of six million Jews, mostly Eastern European, was not used casually by these people.

and adrenaline released in intense interactions, assuring them that they are still alive and active.

In spite of its isolation, the beach community is well-known in the city, primarily because of its ethnic distinctiveness and longevity. It is small, stable, cohesive, delimited, and homogeneous in terms of the people's cultural and historical background, an urban ghetto—closed, encapsulated, and self-contained. Relations between the older beach citizens and the broader urban and Jewish worlds are attenuated and episodic. Periodically, various charitable organizations and synagogues offer the Center services and aid, for it is well-known that the majority of old people are isolated and living on small, fixed incomes, below national poverty levels. But Center folk are not easy people to help. Pride and autonomy among them are passions. They see themselves as givers, not takers, and devote enormous effort toward supporting others more needy than they, particularly in Israel. These elders, with few exceptions, are cut off from their family and children. From time to time, relatives visit them or take them back to their homes for holidays or to spend the night, but on a day-to-day basis, the old people effectively are on their own. They miss their family but cherish their independence.

As the numbers of such people shrink and the neighborhood changes, the Aliyah Center becomes more and more important to its members. Sponsored by a city-wide philanthropic Jewish organization, it is maintained as a day center that emphasizes "secular Judaism." Officially, about three hundred members pay dues of six dollars a year, but these figures do not reflect the actual importance of the Center to the community. Many more use it than join, and they use it all day, every day. The Center is more halfway house than voluntary association, making it possible for hundreds of people to continue living alone in the open community, despite their physical and economic difficulties. Daily hot meals are provided there, and continuous diverse programs are offered—cultural events, discussions, classes of all kinds, along with social affairs, religious ceremonies, celebrations of life crises, anniversaries, birthdays, memorials, and occasional weddings. The gamut of political and social processes found in larger societies are well-developed in Center life. Here is an entire, though miniature, society, a Blakeian "world in a grain of sand," the setting for an intricate and rich culture, made up of bits and pieces of people's common history.

Center culture is in some respects thin and fragile, but its very existence must be seen as a major accomplishment, emerging spontaneously as a result of two conditions that characterize the members: continuities between past and present circumstance, and social isolation. Several marked similarities existed between the circumstances of members' childhood and old age. They had grown up in small, intimate Jewish communities, cohesive, ethnocentric, surrounded by indifferent and often hostile outsiders. Previously, in Eastern Europe, they had been marginal people, even pariahs, as they were now. They had strong early training in resourcefulness and opportunities to develop sound survival strategies. Then, as now, they had been poor, politically impotent, and physically insecure. Then, as now, they turned to each other and their shared Yiddishkeit for sustenance, constituting what Irving Howe has called a "ragged kingdom of the spirit."[2] It was not a great shock for these people to find themselves once more in difficult circumstances, for they had never given up their conviction that life was a struggle, that gains entailed losses, that joy and sorrow were inseparable. They knew how to pinch pennies, how to make do, and how to pay attention to those worse off than they and thereby feel useful and needed. They had come to America seeking another life and found that it, too, provided some fulfillments, some disappointments. And thus, they were now not demoralized or helpless.

Their culture was able to emerge as fully as it did because of the elders' isolation from family and the outside world, ironically, the very condition that causes them much grief. Yet, by this separation, they were freed to find their own way, just as their children had been. Now they could indulge their passion for things of the past, enjoy Yiddishkeit without fear of being stigmatized as "not American." With little concern for public opinion, with only each other for company, they revitalized selected features of their common history to meet their present needs, adding and amending it without concern for consistency, priority, or "authenticity." It had taken three decades for this culture to develop to its present state of complexity, now a truly organic, if occasionally disorderly and illogical amalgam of forms and sentiments, memories and wishes, rotating around a few stable, strong symbols and premises. Claude Lévi-Strauss had used the word *bricolage*[3] to describe the process through which myths are constructed in preliterate societies. Odds and ends, fragments offered up by chance or the environment—almost anything will do—are taken up by a group and incorporated into a tale, used by a people to explain themselves and their world. No intrinsic order or system has dictated the materials employed. In such an inelegant fashion does the *bricoleur* or handyman meet his needs.

Center culture was such a work of bricolage. Robust and impudently eclectic, it shifted and stretched to meet immediate needs—private, collective, secular, and sacred. Thus, when a Center Yiddish History class graduated, a unique ceremony was designed that pasted together the local event with an analogous, historical counterpart, thereby enlarging and authenticating the improvised, contemporary affair. And the traditional Sabbath ceremony was rearranged to allow as many people as possible to participate—making speeches, singing songs, reading poems, taking into account the members' acute need for visibility and attention. Among them, two or even three women instead of one were required to light the Sabbath candles—one singing the blessing in Hebrew, one in Yiddish, one putting the match to the wick. Similarly, Center folk redefined the secular New Year's Eve, holding their dance a full day and a half before the conventional date, since this made it possible for them to get home before dark and to hire their favorite musicians at lower rates. These improvisations were entirely authentic. Somehow midday December 30 became the real New Year's Eve and the later, public celebration seemed unconvincing by comparison. In all this no explicit plan or internal integration could be detected. Cultures are, after all, collective, untidy assemblages, authenticated by belief and agreement, focused only in crisis, systematized after the fact. Like a quilt, Center life was made up of many small pieces sewn together by necessity, intended to be serviceable and to last. It was sufficient for the people's remaining years.

The vitality and flexibility of the Center culture was especially impressive in view of the organization's meager budget. Enough money was available only to pay for a few programs and the salary of the director, Abe, who had devoted himself to these elderly people for fourteen years. Sometimes he was a surrogate son, sometimes a worrying, scolding, protecting parent to them. Thirty years younger than most members, Abe was a second-generation American, from the same background as they. A social worker by training, he watched over the elders' health, listened to their complaints, mediated their quarrels, teased and dominated them when they lost heart, and defended them against external threats, insisting to them and the outside world that they survive. Without his dedication, it was unlikely that they would have been able to continue for so long and so well, living alone into advanced old age in an open, inhospitable setting.

I sat on the benches outside the Center and thought about how strange it was to be back in the neighborhood where sixteen years before I had lived and for a time had been a social worker with elderly citizens on public relief. Then the area was known as "Oshini Beach." The word *shini* still made me cringe. As a child I had been taunted with it. Like many second-generation Americans, I wasn't sure what being a Jew meant. When I was a child our family had avoided the words *Jew* and *Yid*. We were confused and embarrassed about our background. In public we lowered our voices when referring to "our people" or "one of us." My grandparents had also emigrated from an Eastern European shtetl as young people. Like so many of the Center folk, they, too, wanted their children to be Americans above all and were ashamed of being "greenhorns." They spoke to my parents in Yiddish and were answered in English. None of the children or grandchildren in the family received any religious education, yet they carried a strong if ambivalent identity as Jews. This identity took the form of fierce pride and defensiveness during the Holocaust, but even then did not result in any of us developing a clear conception of how to live in terms of our ethnic membership.

I had made no conscious decision to explore my roots or clarify the meaning of my origins. I was one of several anthropologists at the University of Southern California engaged in an examination of Ethnicity and Aging. At first I planned to study elderly Chicanos, since I had previously done fieldwork in Mexico. But in the early 1970s in urban America, ethnic groups were not welcoming curious outsiders, and people I approached kept asking me, "Why work with us? Why don't you study your own kind?" This was a new idea to me. I had not been trained for such a project. Anthropologists conventionally investigate exotic, remote, preliterate societies. But such groups are increasingly unavailable and often inhospitable. As a result, more and more anthropologists are finding themselves working at home these days. Inevitably, this creates problems with objectivity and identification, and I anticipated that I, too, would have my share of them if I studied the Center folk. But perhaps there would be advantages. There was no way that I could have anticipated the great impact of the study on my life, nor its duration. I intended to spend a year with them. In fact, I was with them continuously for two years (1973–1974, 1975–1976) and periodically for two more. In the beginning, I spent a great deal of time agonizing about how to label what I was doing—was it anthropology or a personal quest? I never fully resolved the question. I used many conventional anthropological methods and asked many typical questions, but when I had finished, I found my descriptions did not resemble most anthropological writings. Still, the results of the study would certainly have been different had I not been an anthropologist by training.

Sitting in the sun and contemplating the passing parade on the boardwalk that morning in 1973, I wondered how I should begin this study. At eleven-thirty the benches began to empty as old people entered the Center for a "Hot Kosher Meal—Nutritious—65¢," then a new program provided by state and private funds. Inside there was barely enough room to accommodate between 100 and 150 people who regularly ate there. The Center was only a simple, shabby hall, the size of a small school auditorium, empty except for a tiny stage at one end with a kitchen behind it, and a little area partitioned off at the other end, used for a library and office. The front window was entirely covered by hand-lettered signs in Yiddish and English announcing current events:

> TODAY AT 2:00
> Jewish History Class.—Teacher, Clara Shapiro
> *Very educational.*
>
> SUNDAY AT 1:00
> Special Event: Films on Israel
> *Refreshments. Come. Enjoy.*

MONDAY AT 3:00
Gerontology Class.—Teacher, Sy Greenberg.
Informative. Bring your questions.

TUESDAY AT 10:00
Rabbi Cohen talks on Succoth.
Beautiful and enlightening.

Over the front door hung another handmade sign, written and painted by one of the members: "To the extent that here at the Center we are able to be ourselves and to that extent Self feels good to us." The walls were adorned with pictures of assorted Yiddish writers, scholars, and Zionists. Two large colored photographs of the Western Wall in Jerusalem and of Golda Meir hung above a bust of Moshe Dayan. Seniors' arts and crafts were displayed in a glass case. Their paintings and drawings hung along one wall, depicting shtetl scenes and household activities associated with sacred rituals—the lighting of the Sabbath candles, the housewife baking the Sabbath loaf, a father teaching his children their religious lessons, and the like. Portraits of rabbis, tailors, scholars hung there, too, along with symbols of Jewish festivals and holidays—a papier-mâché *dreidel*, and cardboard *menorah*, a *shofar*.* A large, wooden Star of David illuminated by a string of Christmas tree lights was prominently displayed. Framed certificates of commendation and thanks from Israeli recipients of the elders' donations hung alongside photographs of kibbutzim children to whom the Center elders had contributed support. The wall opposite bore a collective self-portrait in the form of a room-length mural, designed and painted by the members, portraying their common journey from the past to the present in several colorful, strong, and simple scenes: a picture of a boatload of immigrants arriving at Ellis Island, a shtetl marketplace, a New York street scene, a shtetl street scene, and a group of picketers bearing signs, "Better Conditions First," "We Shall Fight for Our Rights," "Power and Justice for the People," and one that simply said, "Protest Treatment." The last sequence rendered the elders at present, seated on benches along the boardwalk and celebrating the Sabbath inside the Center.

* A dreidel is a top used for a Chanukah game; a menorah is the branched candelabra also used for Chanukah; a shofar is the Ram's Horn blown on the Jewish New Year.

Over the small stage, the line from the Old Testament was lettered, "Behold How Good It Is for Brethren to Dwell Together in Unity," and opposite, a prominent placard that read, "Cast Me Not Out in My Old Age But Let Me Live Each Day as a New Life." More than decoration, these visual displays were the people's icons, constituting a symbolic depiction—the group's commentary on itself—by reference to its sources of identity, in particular, its common history. This use of symbols pointed to a community that was highly conscious of itself and its own distinctive ideology.

I followed the crowd inside and sat at the back of the warm, noisy room redolent with odors of fish and chicken soup, wondering how to introduce myself. It was decided for me. A woman sat down next to me who I soon learned was Basha. In a leisurely fashion, she appraised me. Uncomfortable, I smiled and said hello.

"You are not hungry?" she asked.

"No, thank you, I'm not," I answered.

"So, what brings you here?"

"I'm from the University of Southern California. I'm looking for a place to study how older Jews live in the city."

At the word *university*, she moved closer and nodded approvingly. "Are you Jewish?" she asked.

"Yes, I am."

"Are you married?" she persisted.

"Yes."

"You got children?"

"Yes, two boys, four and eight," I answered.

"Are you teaching them to be Jews?"

"I'm trying."

"So what do you want with us here?" asked Basha.

"Well, I want to understand your life, find out what it's like to be older and Jewish, what makes Jews different from other older people, if anything. I'm an anthropologist and we usually study people's cultures and societies. I think I would like to learn about this culture."

"And what will you do for us?" she asked me.

"I could teach a class in something people here are interested in—how older people live in other places, perhaps."

"Are you qualified to do this?" Basha shot me a suspicious glance.

"I have a Ph.D. and have taught in the university for a number of years, so I suppose I am qualified."

"You are a professor then? A little bit of a thing like you?" To my relief, she chuckled amiably. Perhaps I had passed my first rite of entrance into the group.

"Faegl, Faegl, come here!" Basha shouted to a friend across the room. Faegl picked her way neatly over to where we were sitting. She was wiry and slight as Basha was heavy and grand. "Faegl, sit down. Faegl, this here is—— What did you say your name was? Barbara? This is Barbara. She is a professor and wants to study us. What do you think of that?"

"Why not? I wouldn't object. She could learn a lot. Are you Jewish?" Faegl leaned past Basha and carefully peered at me over her bifocals.

Basha accurately recited my qualifications and family characteristics. Faegl wasted no time. She moved over to sit next to me and began her interrogation.

"So you are an anthropologist. Then you study people's origins, yes? Tell me, is it true that human beings began in Africa once upon a time?"

"Many scholars think so," I answered.

"Ha! And once upon a time this country belonged to the Indians. That's right?" she went on.

"Yes, certainly," I answered.

"Now a lot of people don't think it's right that we took away from them the country just because we were stronger, yes?"

"Yes." I was growing wary, sensing an entrapment.

Faegl continued systematically. "So this business about putting all the Arabs out of Israel because we said we had our origins there, maybe that's not right either? It is not so simple, is it?"

"No, no. Certainly it is not simple," I answered.

"So Bashaleh, what do you say now?" Faegl asked her. "She's a professor and she says maybe it's not right. Like I told you, even from the Arabs we can't take away the land."

Basha looked at me closely while Faegl waited.

"You don't believe in *Eretz Yisroel?*"* she asked me. "You are some kind of anti-Semite?"

* The land of Israel; the Promised Land.

Faegl rescued me. "Basha! You think everyone who isn't a Zionist is an anti-Semite? Shame on you. You used to be an internationalist. You used to have beliefs."

Their argument had grown loud enough to attract attention. Abe, the director, came over to see what was going on. Again, Basha introduced me. I asked him about the possibility of doing my study here. He was noncommittal but friendly and after the lunch, we walked along the boardwalk together. He was exceptionally well-informed about the changes in the neighborhood during the last decade and a half. He seemed to know everyone on the streets, not only the elderly. But when he spoke of them, his voice was thick with affection, and anger at their being neglected. He evidently knew all the members, where they lived, how much money they had, where their families were, their state of mind and health, on an hour-by-hour basis. Abe was a naturally gifted sociologist and he had a remarkable memory. Because of these qualities, and his lengthy association with the area and its people, he proved to be an invaluable source of insight and information throughout the work I did there. In the course of our walk and talk, he filled me in on the background characteristics of most Center members.

Nearly all came from poor families, he explained. Their fathers were craftsmen, traders, peddlers, and middlemen, and their mothers worked, too, despite numerous children. The shtetl of their childhood was still very much a presence among them. They remembered it with intense affection and nostalgia in spite of its terrible hardships. Self-regulating, highly stratified, valuing religious education and study even above wealth and family connections, the shtetl Jews had held themselves apart from the surrounding illiterate peasantry; but by the end of the nineteenth century, these communities were being rent apart by internal as well as external forces. The new movements sweeping that part of the world—communism, Zionism, the international trade union movement—the secularization and concern with worldly matters known as the Haskala* began to pull young people away from shtetl customs. Youth were growing impatient with their parents' strict religious orthodoxy, conservatism, and fatalism. Immigration to the New World swelled until around the turn of the century nearly everyone had a relative in America, someone who could help one start a new life.

* The "Enlightenment" or "Awakening."

Most Center folk had come to America as children or young adults, settling first in the urban industrial centers of the East Coast. They worked there as petty merchants, retailers, wage workers, and artisans and went to night school to learn English. They married people like themselves and dedicated the next twenty years of their lives to their children's education. It generally took American immigrant groups three generations or so to accomplish what these people achieved in one; as a result, they were dubbed, "The one-generation proletariat." Professors, scientists, musicians, industrialists were the children of peddlers, craftsmen, and laborers. But the cost of such a rapid ascent was the development of strong social and cultural barriers between the Old World parents and New World children. They had jettisoned much of their Yiddish practices and beliefs, for it seemed to them that, as one writer puts it, "a clean break with religion . . . was the best and surest way of becoming an American."[4]

"You know, these people may seem unique to you, but there are others like them all over the country—Pittsburgh, New York, Florida," Abe explained to me. "They're a proud bunch. No wonder. Look what they've lived through. You gotta be strong to survive what they have. Something in them, something about their background must have given them tremendous courage and independence. We don't know what that 'something' really is. It would be good if you could find out. You don't have long, because they'll be gone soon. And when they go, there's nobody else. The sixty- and even seventy-year-olds who were born here, they're nothing like that. So if you really want to do this study, you had better get going."

For the next four years I was to be involved with these people, as an anthropologist, doing fieldwork, as a friend, and sometimes as a family member. When Josele Masada decided that I looked like his mother and told everyone I was his long-missing granddaughter, Barbarinka, no one was certain what to make of this, for boundaries between his memories, dreams, and the present were often blurred. Did he "really" think there was a biological bond between us, was this a wish, a metaphor, a great compliment? Since no one was certain of Masada's notion, our relationship could neither be affirmed nor denied, and it remained a puzzle to everyone, including me. I was right in expecting that my closeness to the subject would be both troublesome and advantageous, but there was no way I could have anticipated what the specific struggles and compensations would be.

The anthropologist engages in peculiar work. He or she tries to understand a different culture to the point of finding it to be intelligible, regardless of how strange it seems in comparison with one's own background. This is accomplished by attempting to experience the new culture from within, living in it for a time as a member, all the while maintaining sufficient detachment to observe and analyze it with some objectivity. This peculiar posture—being inside and outside at the same time—is called participant-observation. It is a fruitful paradox, one that has allowed anthropologists to find sense and purpose within a society's seemingly illogical and arbitrary customs and beliefs.[5] This assumption of the natives' viewpoint, so to speak, is a means of knowing others through oneself, a professional technique that can be mastered fairly easily in the study of very different peoples. Working with one's own society, and more specifically, those of one's own ethnic and familial heritage, is perilous, and much more difficult. Yet it has a certain validity and value not available in other circumstances. Identifying with the "Other"—Indians, Chicanos, if one is Anglo, blacks if one is white, males if one is female—is an act of imagination, a means for discovering what one is not and will never be. Identifying with what one is now and will be someday is quite a different process.

In working among the elderly—also, I suspect, among the very young—an exceptionally important part of one's information is derived from nonverbal communication and identification, this because the bodily state is such a large determinant of well-being for the growing and declining organism. At various times, I consciously tried to heighten my awareness of the physical feeling state of the elderly by wearing stiff garden gloves to perform ordinary tasks, taking off my glasses and plugging my ears, slowing down my movements and sometimes by wearing the heaviest shoes I could find to the Center. Walking a few blocks to the day-old bakery in this condition became an unimaginably exhilarating achievement. Once by accident I stumbled slightly. The flash of actual terror I experienced was shocking. From the close watching of the elderly it seems I had acquired their assiduous need to avoid falling, though of course, to one my age in good health such a minor accident presents no real danger. This recognition occurred after I had been watching two very old women walk down the alley with great concentration, arms tightly linked, navigating impediments in slow-motion movements that were perfectly coordinated and mutually supportive. So great was their concern with balance they might have been walking a high wire.

The work with the very old people at the Center was not the first time I had employed this imaginative identification as a source of information. Years before, in doing fieldwork with the Huichol Indians of Mexico, I had had similar experiences.[6] However much I learned from that was limited by the fact that I would never really be a Huichol Indian. But I would be a little old Jewish lady one day; thus, it was essential for me to learn what that condition was like, in all its particulars. As a society, we are increasingly cut off from the elderly. We do not have them in the midst of our daily lives, and consequently have no regular access to models of successful old age. How can we then do anything but dread the coming of age? I consider myself very fortunate in having had, through this work, an opportunity to anticipate, rehearse, and contemplate my own future. This has given a temporal integration to my life that seems to me an essential ingredient in the work of maturing.

I *see* old people now in a new way, as part of me, not "they." Most normal, relatively sensitive people identify naturally with children. They remember what it was like to have been a child themselves and as a result *see* children—are aware of them as a part of life, appreciative of their specific needs, rights, and characteristics. But in our culture today, we do not have this same natural attentiveness to and empathy with the elderly, in part because they are not among us, and no doubt they are not among us because we don't want to recognize the inevitability of our own future decline and dependence. An insidious circularity has developed—ignorance, based in part on denial of our future, leading to fear and rejection of the elderly, engendering guilt that is often expressed as neglect or mistreatment, then more guilt, avoidance, and ignorance; agism is characterized by the same self-fulfilling processes that operate and racism. Our anxiety about the future is guaranteed by our own behavior, assuring that our worst unspoken, unspeakable fear will be realized: Our children will treat us as we treat our parents.

As usual, Basha had a *myseh** on the subject, told to her by her grandmother. Paraphrased, it went as follows:

> Once there was a rich man who decided he would give all his money to his son as soon as the boy was grown instead of following the custom of making the boy wait till the father's death to inherit. He did this, but soon the son began to neglect his elderly father, and one day the son put him out of the house. The old man left and came back many years later. He saw his little grandson playing outside the house and told the child who he was. "Fetch me a cloak, child," he said, "because I am cold and poor." The little boy rummaged in the attic for an old cloak and was cutting it in half when his father came in. "What are you doing, child?" he asked. "Father, I am going to give half of the cloak to my grandfather and keep the other half for you, for the time when I am grown up and you have grown old."

What the Center people taught me went beyond knowledge about old age. In addition they provided a model of an alternative life-style, built on values in many ways antithetical to those commonly esteemed by contemporary Americans. The usual markers of success were anathema to them—wealth, power, physical beauty, youth, mobility, securtiy, social status—all were out of the question. Lacking hope for change, improvement, without a future, they had devised a counterworld, inventing their own version of what made "the good life." It was built on their veneration for their religious and cultural membership and it was full of meaning, intensity, and consciousness. This they had managed on their own, creating a nearly invisible, run-down, tiny world, containing a major lesson for any who would attend it. It was not the first time that an anthropologist had found in obscure, unworldly folk a message of wide applicability for the larger outside society.

It was especially their passion for meaning that appealed to me so deeply, this the Center folk valued above happiness or comfort. Their history and religion provided them with ample raw material for enacting their celebratory attitude toward their lives. "It's good to be a Jew. It's hard to be a Jew. What else is new?" laughed Basha when contemplating the pros and cons of her contemporary situation and past history. The word *Jew* in this context served as a metaphor for being human. She used it

* A little story or folk tale.

the same way other people might have said, "That's what life is like." Basha shared with others in the Center an acute sense of dignity, irony, and stoicism, and these were enormously helpful to her in meeting the challenges of her present life, and so, too, the recognition maintained since her early shtetl experience—that a sense of humor is redeeming and ultimately one must face being alone.

Among the Center people life was highly ritualized, and their penchant for ceremony and symbol was aided by Judaism's particular richness in these domains. Drawing on their cultural background, Center people were able to elevate mundane affairs, bringing to each moment a heightened consciousness that rendered suffering and scarcity explicable, and because explicable, bearable. Most of these people had developed some conceptual framework in terms of which their afflictions become comprehensible. This was particularly evident late one Friday afternoon not long ago, when following the Center's celebration to welcome the Sabbath, I lingered to walk along the ocean front with Josele and Nathan. I left them talking on a bench in front of the Center, somewhat uneasily, because I had noticed a young woman familiar in the neighborhood, pacing back and forth, evidently hallucinating, ranting wildly to herself. Just as I was about to pull away, I glanced at the rearview mirror of my car and was shocked to see her attacking the two old men. She had thrown over a huge garbage can next to the bench where they sat. Josele had shouted at her and waved his cane to try to shoo her away. She had seized the cane and thrown him to the ground. He rolled about helplessly, trying to cover his face as she beat him about the head with his cane. As I ran toward them, I heard her yell, "Dirty Jew, fuck you, I'm going to kill you, dirty Jew!" I couldn't wrest the deadly flailing cane from her, but shouting for help, I managed to draw her away from Josele by enticing her to chase me down the boardwalk. Bystanders seized and held her before she got to me. Someone had helped Josele onto the bench. He was bleeding from the mouth and nose and there was a purple lump over one eye the size of a tennis ball. I insisted that Josele wait for the police and paramedics. He didn't want to. "I got no use for police," he said. "What could they do with this poor crazy girl? Nothing. Could they make my poor head stop hurting? Police don't know from these things.

"Today is not the first time I got beat up. When I was only

a boy I was already a revolutionary, working for justice, that's all I cared about. Then the Cossacks threw me to the ground and beat me up with clubs yelling all the time like this girl, 'Dirty Jew.' So what has changed? As long as these things happen, I know my work is not finished. Now I go home. I don't keep the Sabbath with prayers. I got my own ways." He chuckled, heaved himself up from the bench, and picked up his cane. "On Fridays the cats on my street get extra rations. Since we got no more beggars in America, we got to do the best we can with what we have." He limped off down the alley.

Being so rooted in their Judaism helped the old people in their struggles and celebrations. They were sufficiently comfortable with it to improvise upon it and adapt it freely as needed, for small requirements and large. Basha exemplified this when she described her dinner preparations. She ate alone in her tiny room. Over an electric hot plate, she cooked her chicken foot stew (chicken feet were free at the supermarket). Before eating, she spread a white linen handkerchief over the oilcloth covering the table, saying:

> This my mother taught me to do. No matter how poor, we would eat off clean white linen, and say the prayers before touching anything to the mouth. And so I do it still. Whenever I sit down, I eat with God, my mother, and all the Jews who are doing these same things even if I can't see them.

Such a meal is a feast, superior to fine fare hastily eaten, without ceremony, attention, or significance. I wondered if Basha's daughter knew how to dine so splendidly. Because of such things, I came to see the Center elderly as in possession of the philosophers' stone—that universally sought, ever-elusive treasure, harboring the secret that would teach us how to transmute base metals into pure gold. The stone, like the bluebird's feather of happiness, is said to be overlooked precisely because it is so close to us, hidden in the dust at our feet.

Alongside death and the ocean, a third invisible protagonist was present among Center members—guilt. These people were a distinctive breed, survivors all. A group selected to endure many times over, living considerably beyond the norm, they were biologically elite. And they were also psychologically and socially special. Unlike most of their siblings, cousins, and parents, they had found the courage and vision to break with family, home, and community to better their own and their unborn children's lot. Because of their decision to leave Eastern Europe, they had escaped extinction; virtually all who remained behind perished in the Holocaust. Subsequent courageous choices and sacrifices had allowed them to realize their most cherished ambitions—providing education and freedom for their children. In the course of their history, these people had demonstrated their capacity for survival many times over; they were determined, and resourceful beyond the norm.

But one's own survival, when loved ones are being destroyed, is not experienced as a simple triumph or stroke of good luck, as the literature coming out of Hiroshima and Hitler's Europe demonstrates so clearly. It is an extremely problematic condition, often arousing the most severe, even crippling anguish, "survivor's gulit."[7] The Center people were survivors twice over, once due to their escape by emigration from the unnatural ravages of the Holocaust, and again later by living into extreme old age, surviving their peers, family, and often children. That the more recent losses were the natural, inevitable results of the mere passage of time did not necessarily make them more bearable. These elderly men and women, like all those who cry out in moments of extreme pain, asked, "Why me, O Lord," requesting explanation, not for their affliction but for their escape. Thus do victims and survivors alike petition the gods to know the sense behind their destiny. "How do I deserve this? In what ways am I better or worse than those who perished?" There is evidence that suggests it may be universal for survivors of mass destruction to believe that the best die, that by merely being alive, one is guilty, that somehow others died in one's stead. It must be said even when it is self-evident, that survivor's guilt is often irrational, an expression of humanity's metaphysical passion for morality and order. Survivor's guilt, as well as a reality, is a metaphor, referring to that sense of intermingled destinies that denies impotence, solitariness, and the irrelevance of each of us for the others. These elderly Jews were not, strictly speaking, survivors of the Holocaust, for by emigrating they had escaped. Still, they participated in the Holocaust with intensity and depth, and most spoke of it as though it had been their own experience as well as that of the families and peers they left behind. Although they had not actually been through it, they were much more than spectators, and they asked themselves many of the same questions and manifested many of the same characteristics noted among actual survivors. They searched their consciences often and with severity, and held themselves responsible for the fates of those who had not survived. This guilt was not "realistic," for as nearly as I could determine every person I met had strained him or herself utterly, exhausting all the human and material resources they could mobilize to bring their families to safety in America, as soon as possible. Still they wondered what more they might have done. Still, they tormented themselves with questions about why things had turned out as they had. Faegl described her struggle to bring her parents and younger sister to America. For two years she had nearly starved herself to scrape up money for their passage. Her parents came but the sister would not. They did not stay long—they missed the younger daughter too much and returned to Poland. All were killed in Auschwitz. "How can I account for this?" Faegl closed her eyes and wrung her hands when she talked of it. "Were my parents killed because they loved their child so dearly? Was I saved because I didn't love them enough to go back with them?"

The need to reiterate here the irrationality of survivor's guilt comes from the ever-present tendency to blame victims for their fate.[8] To find them in some way responsible for what happened—by their alleged collusion, passivity, weakness, cowardice, selfishness, or denial, as well as more venal attributes—is reassuring. It tells us that people get what they deserve, that they have power over themselves, that the universe is predictable, so that if we are strong and attentive we can avoid the victim's conduct and assure our own safety. "It can't happen to me," comforts onlookers but not survivors themselves. They know by what slender threads their lives are distinguished from those who died; they do not see in themselves soothing virtues or special merits that make their survival inevitable or right. They know how easily it could have happened to them; to these people complacency is forever lost.

Survivor's guilt can be crippling, but among these elderly people it was not. Instead it served as a transformative agent that made it impossible for them to lead the unexamined life. Life for these elderly was many different things: gift, relentless struggle, challenge, a curse, and all the shadings in between. But it was never taken for granted. Above all, it contributed to their passion for meaning.[9] It is common for survivors to attempt to re-create an orderly universe, one that can be found somehow to be sensible; despite the brutality of the concentration camps, inmates during internment and afterward pursued and seized upon any evidence of sense and justice in the world. Meaningless accidents, chaos, and inexplicability are more insupportable than suffering and cruelty. Survivors have a heightened desire for interpretation, for finding the comprehensible elements in their experiences. Says psychiatrist Robert Jay Lifton, who has documented the psychology of survivors of Hiroshima as well as the Holocaust, ". . . Any experience of survival—whether of large disaster or intimate personal loss . . . involves a journey to the edge of the world of the living." What he calls the formulative effort—the search for meaning—is the survivor's means of return from that edge.[10] Then it was not merely these elders' proximity to their own deaths that so enlivened them—rather it was due to their survival of loved ones, the guilt and responsibility this generated, and the subsequent necessity for understanding what had brought about the destruction of their people and their natal world. These were what turned them so strongly toward the symbolic life.

Survivorhood accounted for other, positive features among them. It validated their values. In foiling enemies determined to destroy them, by merely outliving them, they demonstrated that they were indeed Chosen People. And survivorhood also caused them to intensify their dedication to social justice; they not only sought evidence of morality in a shattered, disordered world, but also worked to establish it. Such activity—"collecting justice" Lifton calls it—is common among survivors, and of course these people's traditions had always emphasized it. Their sense of responsibility for the welfare of others was the transformation of survival guilt into conscience, another commonplace among those who live despite others' efforts to destroy them, as historian Terence Des Pres observes.[11] Their philanthropic activities, the construction of a symbolic universe made out of the long past, the quest for meaning, and their concern for human dignity—all were signal traits in Center life, accentuated by the survival experience.

In the beginning phases of my work with the elderly I too suffered severe pangs of guilt. It took many forms and floated about, settling on different issues at different times. At first it focused on questions concerning my competence in the task I was embarking upon. Did I know enough Judaica? Did I know enough Yiddish? Was I too young? Was I too emotionally involved? Should I be working for the old people's welfare instead of studying them? and the like. In the course of a conversation with Shmuel, a very learned man who was to become one of my principal informants, I confessed my fears about not being able to do justice to the materials he was giving me. There was so much I did not understand. As usual, he was severe but not unfair in his response.

> You don't understand. How could you expect to understand? You ask me all these things, but you know nothing. You don't know Yiddish. You don't know Hebrew. You don't know Aramaic. You don't know Russian and not Polish. You have not set your eyes on any part of the place we lived in. How can you expect to understand?

I agreed with him and was terribly discouraged. For a while, I stopped to study Yiddish, then realized that I was taking too much time out of the fieldwork. It was wasteful in view of the Center people's fluency in English. I also spent some time studying Jewish law and history, but the subjects were overwhelmingly complex, needing lifetimes of devotion to achieve more than a superficial understanding. I decided to try to follow the old people's leads in deciding what to study, learning as much as I could from them. I would enter these fields of knowledge in an *ad hoc* fashion, letting the elders point out what I needed to know as the work progressed rather than plowing into it systematically or for its own sake.

Resolving the question of my right to do the work did not free me from the inner and outer taunts. Many of the Center people continued to "make" me feel guilty. After greeting me warmly, Basha would often ask, "Never mind these other things you all the time ask about. Tell me, who's with your children?" Men and women alike would admire a new skirt or dress I wore, then turn over my hem for inspection. Nathan remarked, "For a lady professor, you don't do so good with a needle." When I stayed away too long, they scolded and snubbed me. When I was not completely fair (and sometimes even when I was) in the distribution of attention, I paid dearly for it. The old people were genuinely proud of me, generous, and affectionate, but at times their resentment spilled over. My presence was a continual reminder of many painful facts: that it should have been their own children there listening to their stories; that I had combined family and a career, opportunities that the women had longed for and never been allowed. And too, that I knew so little of their background suggested to them that they had failed to transmit to future generations any but fragments of their cherished past. I felt guilty about invading their privacy, for however much I explained my publication intentions, I knew our conversations sometimes crossed the invisible line from informed disclosure to inadvertent confidence. Diffuse and even irrational guilt plagued me until I had to laugh at myself. I had become a tasteless ethnic joke, paralyzed by Jewish guilt: about my relative youth and strength, about having a future where they did not, about my ability to come and go as I chose while they had to await my visits and my convenience, when I relished food that I knew they could not digest, when I slept soundly through the night warmed by my husband's body, knowing the old people were sleeping alone in cold rooms. (In some African tribes, all the elderly are loaned a child for warmth and companionship at night.)

I considered quitting. It was unbearable to abide the countless ways in which the Center people used guilt, often unconsciously, intending not to hurt but only to make themselves feel potent. But after a time I accepted the fact that one cannot be "made" guilty. One volunteers. The arousal of guilt is what I have called "a strategy of intimacy," one of many used by the Center old people. Useless among strangers, it is based on interdependence and connectedness. The bright side of guilt is that it is an expression of a sense of responsibility for another's well-being. When I realized that, I became resigned and even grateful about my responses to my subjects.

I had been with these people for almost two years when I hit on what seemed the most significant component of my complex feelings about them. I chanced to read a comment by Isaac Bashevis Singer in one of his novels about survivors. A single statement of his suddenly clarified matters for me. In reference to his own difficulties in writing about victims he remarked, "Although I did not have the privilege of going through the Hitler holocaust . . . ."[12] Yes, it was that feeling that they were set apart from the rest of us and hallowed by their suffering.

Paradoxically they were the privileged ones for having lived on our behalf through what was in one sense our common fate. How, then, could anyone look at them dispassionately? How could I feel anything but awe and appreciation for their mere presence? In view of their proximity to mass destruction, it was indecent to ask more of them than that they be alive and in good spirits. But they were more than their sufferings; too great an appreciation on my part was a disservice and falsification, ultimately disrespectful. I wanted my people to be loved and admired as a result of my study, for in addition to being survivors, they were presently poor and maltreated. I wanted to protect them, even from my responses. But finally I accepted the necessity for sacrificing that desire. A reverential, protective attitude would allow the reader to distance him- or herself from them. The elders' accomplishments were important precisely because they were not heroes or saints, indeed this was one reason why they and the life they created were so colorful and appealing. Their flamboyance, humor, tendency to self-parody and self-criticism, their reaches for dignity and integrity, their occasional failures and lapses into foolishness, selfishness, and unkindness were part of what contributed to their success as survivors. My work would have to be a full-length portrait, light and darkness with more shading than sharp lines. Since neutrality was impossible and idealization undesirable, I settled on striving for balance. If these people emerged as real in their entire human range and variety, arousing admiration and disappointment, laughter and tears, hope and despair, I would be satisfied. My admiration for and gratitude to them must be evident. In the end, the only acceptable answer I could find to the question "Am I qualified to write this book?" was that my membership and my affection were my qualifications. When I judge these people, I judge myself.

The amount and variety of information accumulated in a field study is overwhelming. There is no definite or correct solution to the problem of what to include, how to cut up the pie of social reality, when precisely to leave or stop. Often there is little clarity as to whom to include as "members," what to talk about with those who are. The deliberate avoidance of preconceptions is likely to result in the best fieldwork, allowing the group or subject to dictate the form the description ultimately takes. But always there is a high degree of arbitrariness involved. Choices must be made and they are extremely difficult, primarily because of what and who must be omitted. In this case, these methodological dilemmas were especially troublesome. Nearly everyone at the Center wanted to be included, feeling so strongly as they did the wish to be recorded and remembered.

In this work I decided to concentrate on the Center, its internal affairs, and its most active members as much as possible. This eliminated the nonjoiners, the marginal individuals, the majority of people living in the neighborhood and, accordingly, limited the generalizations that I could make in the end. I decided not to compare Center elders with others. I felt the Center people and their generation were sufficiently unique to warrant most of my time. The choice favored depth over breadth, tight focus rather than representativeness. My interpretation, therefore, must be read as pertaining to these particular people at a given period of time—how much they have in common with others must be determined by someone else.

Of the three hundred Center members, I met and talked with about half, though I observed all at one time or another during the years of the study. Of these, I knew eighty personally, and interviewed and spent most of my time with thirty-six. I tape recorded extensive interviews with these, ranging from two to sixteen hours, visited nearly all in their homes, took trips with them from time to time outside the neighborhood—to doctors, social workers, shopping, funerals, visiting their friends in old age homes and hospitals, and often following my subjects to convalescent homes and hospitals; I went to many funerals and memorial services. Apart from these excursions and my interviews with outsiders who knew Center people well—teachers, rabbis, local politicians, volunteers—I concentrated on the Center and its external extensions, the benches, boardwalk, and hotel and apartment lobbies where they congregated.

As often happens, I established a particularly strong and gratifying attachment to one individual, and also as often happens, in addition to being particularly knowledgeable and articulate about the community, this person was also an outsider. "Shmuel the Filosofe," he was called, and in a very significant way he was my teacher, critic, and guide. To him alone, a complete chapter (chapter two) is devoted, and his voice is heard throughout the book. I have included my own voice in his chapter, for it proved impossible to expunge. His statements and retorts did not make sense without that, for he was directing his commentary to me. That is not the only place I have included my words and reactions. For a long time I resisted this. I wanted to focus on the Center, not myself, but it became clear that what was being written was from my eyes, with my personality, biases, history, and sensibility, and it seemed dishonest to exclude that, thereby giving an impression of greater objectivity and authority than I believed in.

As often as possible I have included verbatim materials, heavily edited and selected, inevitably, but sufficient to allow the reader some degree of direct participation. I have tried to allow many individuals to emerge in their fullness and distinctiveness rather than presenting a completely generalized picture of group life without reference to the living breathing people who comprise it, and who are in the end the only reality. In the interest of economy and privacy, I have combined several of the minor characters who appear on these pages, though most would have preferred to have been identified. Wherever possible I have altered identifying biographical features that seemed insignificant. All verbatim statements are presented as they were given, usually taken from tape recordings. Major figures are disguised as much as possible but uncombined. Events reported are actual occurrences, subjectively witnessed and interpreted by me.

The always complex problem of assuring privacy to one's subjects was made more difficult in this study because of the production of a documentary film on which I collaborated with Lynne Littman toward the end of research. Also called *Number Our Days*, it was based on my fieldwork at the Center.[13] We were not at all sure that the film would cross the ethnic barrier, and were surprised when it was widely viewed and enthusiastically received. To our great satisfaction, it brought the elderly concrete benefits in many forms—unsolicited funds, attention and favors from strangers and friends, and above all, visibility, which they so long for. But it made effective disguise of the Center and its director impossible. Nevertheless, privacy for individuals could be preserved, and so I have changed all names of people and groups mentioned here, this to allow myself freedom to record some of the unflattering things I saw there, as much as possible to prevent the elderly from recognizing themselves and each other, to save them and their children any embarrassment that might accrue. Certainly, I did not want to cause the old people pain that could be avoided, nor did I wish to jeopardize my welcome among them.

Several conscious decisions distinguished the film from the book. The film, Lynne Littman and I agreed, should focus on people's survival strategies, their resourcefulness and courage, emotional vitality, their bold and often joyous use of religion in their response to aging and adversity. Deliberately we glossed the troubles and antagonisms within the organization and among people. The film could do what the book should not do—serve to repay them for some of what they had given me.

The format of this book is designed to meet several purposes. In addition to wanting to speak within it as a participant, and wishing to preserve particular individuals, I wanted to render the elders' speech. Many verbatim statements are included; the most extensive of these are called "*bobbe-myseh,*" or grandmothers' tales, speeches and exchanges between people that occurred in a "Living History" class, which I will describe shortly. The bobbe-myseh were drawn from miles of tape, intended to convey the texture of the speech, people's characteristic thought, and interaction style. It was Shmuel, the critic and philosopher, who dubbed these stories and exchanges "bobbe-myseh." He found them inelegant and rambling. Sometimes they build to a significant point about Center people's beliefs and experiences, but even so, these are much embedded in "trivia." Seldom grand, occasionally self-serving, always vital and original, it was inconceivable to leave them out.

The middle section of the book (chapters three through six) is given to four situationally specific episodes, social or sociocultural dramas as anthropologist Victor Turner has called such events.[14] These are public occasions wherein a significant crisis emerges and is resolved. Usually an orderly sequence of stages occurs: The drama begins when a threat to collective life is perceived. Often this happens when someone in the group violates an important rule or custom. The mechanisms that operate to contain or dispel conflict fail and the difficulty spreads, drawing in more and more members until it constitutes a genuine crisis. Some mending, some action that restores order and redresses the violation is called for, and this occurs in the third stage. The last part, the conclusion, achieves an equilibrium and often is accompanied by a realignment of social relationships where dissident factions or individuals are reintegrated into the group. The final stage of the sequence is often accomplished through symbolic displays of unity or ritual performances that affirm members' widest or most basic beliefs. This model perfectly suits the developments in two of the chapters (four and five). The other two episodes (chapters three and six) revolve around crises more of belief than social relations. They follow the same sequences as those set forth by Turner, but there is a significant difference in the redressive work they accomplish. No social rearrangements are accomplished, rather redress consists solely of the performance of the group's shared and unquestionable truths, made unquestionable by being performed. As such, these dramas are religion-in-the-making, for in them the Center people are agreeing upon and making authoritative the essential ideas that define them. In these dramas they develop their collective identity, their interpretation of their world, themselves, and their values. As well as being social dramas, the events are definitional-ceremonies, performances of identity, sanctified to the level of myth.

It was not an accident that the performance of definitional-ceremonies often occurred among Center people. Always, self and society are known—to the subjects themselves and to the witnessing audience—through enactments. Rituals and ceremonies are cultural mirrors, opportunities for presenting collective knowledge.[15] Like all mirrors, these reflections are not always accurate. They may also alter images, sometimes distorting, sometimes disguising various features, and for various reasons. More like myths than photographs, nevertheless they were the means the Center people employed to "see" themselves. Because their invisibility was so exceedingly painful to them, and they struggled to find opportunities to appear in the world, thus assuring themselves that indeed they existed. No natural audience in the form of progeny or a younger generation was recording their existence. No one would remain after they died to "bear witness" for them. They had to serve as their own witness and audience in these dramas. Enacted beliefs have a capacity for arousing belief that mere statements do not. "Doing is believing," hence ritual and ceremony generate conviction when reason and thought may fail.[16] And Judaism is particularly highly developed in the area of ritual. Center folk had tradition and ample source materials to work with here.

The character of Center social life was distinctively tumultuous and dramatic. In part this was due to the tensions arising from contradictions within their ideology, most conspicuously, between their Zionism and internationalism, their agnosticism and Judaism, their identification with modern American society and the Eastern European past. All cultures are ridden with internal inconsistencies but they do not generally produce the kind of social disorganization so evident at the Center. More troublesome than the inconsistencies in their beliefs were certain paradoxes or structural conflicts that disrupted solidarity and prevented their society from developing the stability it otherwise might have. Three paradoxes were particularly evident: First was people's need for passionate experiences, in opposition to their desire for dignity and harmony. Second, people had extreme need for each other socially and psychologically, with no corresponding material, economic need; this resulted in a peculiar imbalance that generated much strain and confusion. Finally, Center elders required witnesses to their past and present life and turned to each other for this, though it is a role properly filled by the succeeding generation. Lacking suitable heirs to their traditions and stories, they were forced to use peers who, they realized, would perish along with them, and thus could not assure the preservation of what they had witnessed. Center people were tightly bound to each other, but in a web of relations that never fully coalesced into the firm, clear shapes typical of many social organizations.

Let me return now to a discussion of the Living History classes, for in these a private process was unfolded, parallel to the public processes revealed in the socio-cultural dramas. Center people, like so many of the elderly, were very fond of reminiscing and storytelling, eager to be heard from, eager to relate parts of their life history. More afraid of oblivion than pain or death, they always sought opportunities to become visible. Narrative activity among them was intense and relentless. Age and proximity to death augmented the Jewish predilection for verbal expression. In their stories, as in their cultural dramas, they witnessed themselves, and thus knew who they were, serving as subject and object at once. They narrated themselves perpetually, in the form of keeping notes, journals, writing poems and reflections spontaneously, and also telling their stories to whoever would listen. Their histories were not devoted to marking their successes or unusual merits. Rather they were efforts at ordering, sorting, explaining—rendering coherent their long life, finding integrating ideas and characteristics that helped them know themselves as the same person over time, despite great ruptures and shifts. No doubt their emigrant experience and the loss of their original culture made them even more prone to seek continuity and coherence. Survivors, it is often noted, are strongly impelled to serve as witnesses to what has been lost. Often these materials were idealized and sentimentalized.[17] Despite its poverty and oppression, shtetl life was often described as a golden age in comparison with much of the present, which was found lacking. But in recounting the past, they kept that early life alive, weaving it into their present. Freud suggests that completion of the mourning process requires the survivor to develop a new reality that no longer includes what has been lost.[18] Judging from experience of the Center elderly, full recovery from mourning may do the very opposite—preserving what has been lost, restoring it to life by incorporation into the present; Center culture was built around just such a revitalization of the past.

I was eager to respond to Center people's desires to tell me their stories and puzzled as to how to find the means and the time to listen to as many as possible. Abe was helpful here, too. He suggested that I offer a class in the Center where people could assemble for recounting their life history. We pondered the subject together and decided it should be called "Living History." Such a class would provide a forum in which a stable group of people could reminisce and sort out their individual and collective memories, for themselves, each other, and for a written record of some sort. People would have an opportunity to bring in their writings, poems, and the like, and read them to the group, an activity they enjoyed greatly and found few opportunities for in the Center's crowded schedule. They might bring in photographs, letters, and any materials they wished to have included. The class was to be the creation of another arena of visibility and performance, an unstructured and unpressured opportunity for the elders to receive attention. The class would also provide a suitable means for me to gain entrée into the community. Abe would help me get started, he said. He thought it would work, especially if I brought refreshments. But, he warned me, I would have to be careful not to let the sessions take on the appearance of group therapy. If people thought they were expected to publicly discuss their problems and share very private, painful materials, they would be reluctant. I agreed with that. But, I wondered, would people be willing to tell me, a stranger, their life history, and would they be inhibited if I tried to tape record the sessions?

Abe and I sat on a bench talking about the class in the early days of my work. Basha came out of the Center and Abe called to her, "Basha, how would you like to have the professor make a book from your life?" Basha did not hesitate. "You got a pencil? You want to get it down right. I begin with my childhood in Poland. Tell me if I go too fast. Naturally, it's a long story."

The following month, classes began. I was prepared with cookies, tea, coffee, tape recorder, and two-dozen notebooks and pencils for people who would be willing to use them at home. Abe had made a sign for the window: "New Center Class: Living History. Come and tell your story. Help teach our Professor Barbara about the beautiful life of the elderly. Tuesdays at 10." For five months we met in the little room over the Center that had recently been converted into a library, then we met again after the summer for another four months. It was light and pleasant upstairs, and quiet. But the stairs were too hard for many people and eventually the classes had to be moved to the noisy hall below. That was just as well because the upstairs room still carried the taint of therapy, having been used for that by a social worker previously. Those seen walking up were in danger of being labeled "crazies." It was used, too, for political discussions by the left-wing intellectuals, the "linkies,"* and others were wary of being associated with them. But we overcame these associations and met happily for two hours each week. I asked people to speak in English, or if they used Yiddish to keep it short and provide a translation, to ease the problems in transcribing the tapes. I promised everyone an opportunity to speak each week, however briefly, and insisted everyone listen to each other with a minimum of interrupting. This was very difficult for the old people and only after many weeks of meeting were they certain enough that they would have a chance to talk to manage to hold back their offerings. They—and I—used the tape recorder to good purpose. Pleading that the typist could never work with

* Left-winger.

tapes in which everyone spoke at once, I turned the machine off when they tried to shout each other down. As gently as I could, I took the microphone away from anyone who went on too long. When I told them that in transcribing the notes, their names would be changed, they were disappointed. Everyone wanted to leave a personal statement, wanted to be identified with an enduring record, some indication of what had happened to them, what they believed, that they had been here.

At first a half-dozen people came, but after the word spread that there were no political fights and no insistence on public disclosure of personal matters, more attended. Soon a core of about twenty people had formed and they came faithfully. Cynics and onlookers wandered in and out from time to time. Those who would not or could not listen to the others were naturally discouraged and in time the discussions were fairly orderly. In this setting, people heard and saw one another in a new way—as they had not previously. Neighbors and *landsmen** who had known each other for decades learned things never before revealed. Listening was not these people's custom. They yearned desperately for an audience, but for many reasons it was very difficult to allow others center stage. Coherence in the discussions suffered when people were required to speak strictly in turn. But only this format gave them enough trust to wait. I spoke as little as possible, occasionally focusing the topic or asking questions. Generally a common theme emerged and clustered loosely around a set of broad topics: memories of the Old World, the meaning of Being a Jew, being old, and life in America today. The people referred to me as "the teacher" and they liked the concept and model of a class and learning, but it was soon clear that they were the teachers and I, surrogate grandchild, was the student. I was deeply moved and saddened when people blessed me for merely listening.

The longer the classes lasted, the more people had to say. They stimulated one another's memories. And they validated certain images, values, accomplishments, subtle and grand, that made their histories subject to comprehension and approval. Suffering, failure, and disappointments came into the discussion, too, and were woven, incorporated, into their accounts. The work they were doing was not a cosmetic operation; it was the search for pattern and continuity amid the accidental features of their

* Fellow countrymen.

life. Always in these stories, they sought evidence that they were still the same people now that they had once been, however transformed. The sense of constancy and recognizability, the integrity of the person over time was their essential quest. In the process they created personal myths, saying not that it had all been worthwhile, neither that it had not.[19] Truth and completeness of accounts were never at issue in this work, and no one questioned private or shared pasts. As people brought in more of the deep memories, they also brought in dreams, wishes, and questions about ultimate concerns, often profanely interlarded with daily, trivial matters, woven into the always pungent, swift, funny, cutting interchanges among them.

I loved these classes and the style of the exchanges and stories. Shmuel was right to call them grandmothers' tales, for they were the kind of rambling, bubbling, unfocused, running comments that a bobbe might tell her grandchildren without putting down her dough or her sewing. Too busy to stop and shape a tale with grace and art, but too alive to imagination and verbal expression to be silent, so she might weave a kitchen tale that despite its crude surface, came from and went to a deep place. This was "Domestic Religion," as Rachel once called it, and its roots were in the heart and bones and genes.

Hitting on a format that allowed for storytelling was a fortunate accident. When we began the sessions, there was no way I could have anticipated the significance of these exchanges. In time it became clear that storytelling was a passion among these people, absolutely central to their culture. Even Shmuel, who disdained the Living History classes, had great respect and affection for the art of narration. Once when we were taping part of his life story, he stopped to explain why it was so important that we record his history correctly, in terms of events and with just the right attitude. He first acquired his taste and regard for stories from the "wonder rebbes," Hasidic rabbis who visited his shtetl from time to time.[20]

"Oh, the stories they would tell us, full of wisdom, full of humor. It was immense. These rebbes could speak to you in such a way that it stays with you all your life. They understood the simple people who lived in these little towns. They learned from somewhere, I don't know from where, how to put into the Bible and the Talmud a life you could never imagine. They could put you directly in touch with Abraham, Jacob, Isaac, and the God of Jacob. The rebbes knew how to put things in terms of spirits and demons, and into the most ordinary events they would bring out mysterious and wondrous things. All of us, little boys by the dozen, would follow them when they came into the town. You could always tell them by the chalk on their caftans, this they carried to mark around them a circle of chalk that would keep out the spirits. My father did not approve of me listening to them, but I would sneak out whenever I could, because what they brought you was absolutely magic. This experience was developing in me a great respect for telling stories. This is why it is important to get just the right attitude and just the right words for a story. You should get everything just right because no matter how pleasant, it is a serious thing you are doing."

The Center people who came to the Living History classes were increasingly pleased with the storytelling sessions. Here is Rachel's comment on the class toward the end of our meetings:

> All these speeches we are making reminded me of a picture I have from many years ago, when we were still in Russia. My brother had been gone already two years in America. I can see my mother like it is before me, engraved in my head. A small house she goes out of, in wintertime, going every morning in the snow to the post office, wrapped up in a shawl. Every morning there was nothing. Finally, she found a letter. In that letter was written, "Mamaleh, I didn't write to you before because I didn't have nothing to write about." "So," she says, "why didn't you write and tell me?"
>
> You know this group of ours reminds me of that letter. When I first heard about this group, I thought to myself, "What can I learn? What can I hear that I don't know, about life in the Old Country, of the struggles, the life in the poor towns, in the bigger towns, of the rich people and the poor people? What is there to learn, I'm eighty-eight, that I haven't seen myself?" Then I think, "What can I give to anybody else? I'm not an educated woman. It's a waste of time."
>
> That was my impression. But then I came here and heard all those stories. I knew them, but you know it was laid down deep, deep in your mind, with all those troubles mixed. You know it's there but you don't think of it, because sometimes you don't want to live in your past. Who needs all these foolish stories?

But finally, this group brought out such beautiful memories, not always so beautiful, but still, all the pictures came up. It touched the layers of the kind that it was on those dead people already. It was laying on them like layers, separate layers of earth, and all of a sudden in this class I feel it coming up like lava. It just melted away the earth from all those people. It melted away, and they became alive. And then to me it looked like they were never dead.

Then I felt like the time my mother got that letter. "Why don't you come and tell me?" "Well, I have nothing to say," I think. But I start to say it and I find something. The memories come up in me like lava. So I felt I enriched myself. And I am hoping maybe I enriched somebody else. All this, it's not only for us. It's for the generations.

CHAPTER TWO

Needle and thread: the life and death of a tailor

Abe pointed out Shmuel Goldman as one of the most educated and interesting people in the community. I was looking for someone to study Yiddish with and Shmuel seemed ideal, if he would agree. We attempted a few Yiddish lessons together, but he was too impatient with my ignorance for us to continue. Still, we both enjoyed our time together. Shmuel loved recalling his childhood and eventually I decided I would like to record his life history at length. He was doubtful at first, but finally agreed and for the next two months we met at least once a week for formal, prearranged recording sessions, nearly all of which were taped. These were long and often taxing for both of us. In between, we met casually in and around the Center and Shmuel provided a running commentary on the people and events there. Abe was right. Shmuel was a philosopher, and an outsider, though he had lived in the neighborhood for thirty-two years. His psychology and principles made him intolerant of formal organizations, and ideologically he was at odds with nearly everyone in the Center. But he was too sensible, too learned, and too deeply rooted in their common traditions to be ignored by them. He and the Center people could not leave each other alone, but neither could they find peace together.

My friendship with Shmuel troubled many of the Center people. They were fearful lest I adopt his often judgmental, stern attitude toward them. Paradoxically, I usually ended up defending them and Center life to him. I, the newcomer, was more participant and enthusiast, and he the critic and observer. He was my foil and teacher, goading and challenging my interpretations at every point. In time, our differences became sharper and clearer and more often than not a source of mutual amusement. We knew each other for eighteen months. At the end of this time I could see things from both our perspectives at once. I have often wondered if this was his chief purpose in agreeing to work with me. Certainly it was one of his most valuable lessons.

What follows are extracts from our recordings and conversations. I have preserved the chronology and whenever possible, Shmuel's exact words. Those conversations that were not taped, I reconstructed from the notes I made either during or immediately after they took place. This constitutes what I regard as Shmuel's intentional lessons. Their application to Center life appears later, in the context of the events they referred to, save the last episode (chapter six), which occurred after Shmuel's death. But by then, I think I could anticipate what he would have said about it.

> I have a friend. A woman I know already many years. One day she is mad at me. From nowhere it comes. I have insulted her, she tells me. How? I don't know. Why don't I know? Because I don't *know* her. She surprised me. That's good. That is how it should be. You cannot tell someone, "I know you." People jump around. They are like a ball. Rubbery, they bounce. A ball cannot be long in one place. Rubbery, it must jump.
>
> So what do you do to keep a person from jumping? The same as with a ball. You take a pin and stick it in, make a little hole. It goes flat. When you tell someone, "I know you," you put a little pin in.
>
> So what should you do? Leave them be. Don't try to make them stand still for your convenience. You don't ever know them. Let people surprise you. This likewise you could do concerning yourself. All this, I didn't read in any book. It is my own invention.

Invented, I was afraid, specifically to warn me. Shmuel delivered this speech as we trotted down the boardwalk on the way to his house, our arms linked tightly, less for closeness than to regulate our gait. He set a fierce pace. He didn't believe in strolling. I didn't mind. It gave me courage to walk with him in this way, regardless of his reasons.

Shmuel had agreed to let me record his life history. But clearly he was full of doubts about revealing himself to me and about my ability to understand him. I shared his fears but was prepared to put doubts aside and try. The differences between us seemed less formidable as I contemplated our long shadows running before us in the clear afternoon light. Many people believe taking their picture captures their soul, and taking a life story is even more threatening. Inevitably, in trying to know him, I would be putting pins in him. Our shadows were exactly the same size—small, compact, heads enlarged by wiry curls. Despite the forty years that set us apart, despite our differences in sex, history, knowledge, belief, and experience, we resembled each other. Same big nose, dark eyes, sharp vaulted cheekbones. It could be seen that we were of the same racial stock. Shmuel had a way of reckoning all differences between us in his favor, mocking but without cruelty, yet in a way that always made me feel somewhat apologetic. I was grateful for all our similarities and read them as signs of hope in the validity of my attempt to comprehend him. It didn't help that I was a professor with a Ph.D., for both of us were aware that his self-directed education was much broader than mine, not to mention his greater experience.

I had explained to him what anthropology was, how it was a way of attempting to penetrate someone else's world from within, to enter another person's culture imaginatively and experience it as he did. I talked to him about the methods of participant-observation, where by sharing a segment of his life —and Center life—I would try to know it firsthand to some degree, while at the same time preserving my separateness and a measure of objectivity. I explained what a "key informant" was and said that I had selected him to be a teacher about his culture, if he would agree.

"So you want me to be your 'native.' No, that's flattering but not good," he said. "I'm not typical. Get some of the others at the Center. I'm not like them. I don't join clubs. I'm not a Zionist. I don't believe in God. Find someone else."

Eventually I convinced him that I was drawn to him for his learning and philosophical approach, not for his typicality. He had thought more about his experiences than most, had struggled to make sense of them. He yielded to this argument. I added that this work had personal meaning for me as well. I had not had the opportunity to learn about the world of my grandparents directly. I wanted to hear a firsthand account of

Yiddishkeit and the shtetl. My grandparents had not taught me this, and now they were dead.

"Your grandparents did not speak Jewish to you, or to their children?"*

"It was the usual story, Shmuel. They talked Yiddish to their children and the children answered in English. What there was to learn they ran away from as fast as they could, to become American."

"So now that you are big enough to choose for yourself, go talk to them."

"Too late, Shmuel. They're all dead. I can only get it in this roundabout fashion. When I hear Yiddish and Hebrew, often I don't know what the words mean, but I know that they are part of me all the same."

"What you ask, we will try. But it needs patience and time. How much I have of that, I don't know. Now I begin by telling you to see something you would not notice without me at your side." He pulled me closer and I stuck my ear close to his mouth to catch his quiet words.

"Look at those women sitting there on the benches. Sturdy little grandmothers." I had noticed them. As usual on a sunny day, each bench held a brace of old women. Motionless, they emitted great resolution. Their mere existence, then as now, was a political-social attitude. Their continuing survival mocked their historical enemies, and time itself.

"Look if you will at something important about these women," Shmuel whispered. "Each one is wearing a coat. What's so special about a coat? you could ask. These are poor women here. But still everyone has a coat. A coat is not an ordinary garment. It was our people who brought coats to the world. Before the little Jewish tailors came to America, what poor person could have a coat?"

I never knew if Shmuel's attitude toward his work came from his Socialist beliefs, from some Judaic elements, or were entirely of his own making. Creativity and seriousness belonged to work. It was both religion and play. When he worked, his imagination was freed.

* Shmuel preferred the term *Jewish* to *Yiddish* in referring to his native language, this in order to emphasize its status as a bona fide language and not, as some supposed, a mere dialect.

"The mind must be alive when you sew, if you are in a good shop or a bad. I have been in both, and all those in between. The outside conditions do not apply. You must bring it up from the inside, looking always for a way to express yourself.

"Do you know what this means for me? When I am in a shop, I am told to make a whole coat for a dollar. It must be done. You can't tell the boss he is crazy. You can't quit. In my shop, the other men would say, '*Nu,** I can do it.' They put down the little screw on the machine to make bigger stitches. But such a coat doesn't last the winter. This coat goes to a poor woman, her only garment for warmth. You wouldn't know this but it gives out in the Bible that a pawnbroker cannot keep a poor man's caftan or cloak for deposit or for pawn overnight, because a Jew can't profit from someone else's need. 'You shall not sleep in his pledge. When the sun goes down you restore to him his pledge, that he may sleep in his own cloak.' This comes from Deuteronomy, which no doubt you have not read. No, it is not the way of a Jew to make his work like there was no human being to suffer when it's done badly. A coat is not a piece of cloth only. The tailor is connected to the one who wears it and he should not forget it."

Shmuel's garments had lasted. He had always made clothes for his friends and his wife, Rebekah, saving shop remnants of his finest material for her. Rebekah still wore the long velvet skirts and frilly blouses he had made. Years after his death, she cut a fine figure in his garments.

We arrived at Shmuel's house, a single-story duplex a few doors from the boardwalk. "Do you want some tea? You are tired?" He knew I was and it pleased him that he was not. "Well, come in then, Rebekah will be glad to see you. By now she will be home from all her meetings."

We went into the large, rather bare living room, furnished with the landlord's castoffs. Two golden Naugahyde couches were pushed against the wall, and in between them stood a brave little table bearing heaps of magazines and papers—*Jewish Currents, Yiddishe Kultur Verband, Morgan Freiheit, The Nation, The People's World*. In one corner was a kitchen chair and a child's school desk, the drawers crammed with scraps of paper—Shmuel's poetry and essays in Yiddish, Hebrew, Polish, Russian, French, and English. Rickety bookcases held diction-

* All right; so.

aries, novels in all those languages, plus used college textbooks on political science, history, art, psychology, sociology, economics, and philosophy. In the center of the room, a huge bare-breasted ceramic woman in yellow harem pants held aloft a tiny fluted lampshade.

I fiddled with electric sockets and my tape recorder while Rebekah put up water for tea. Shmuel waited quietly, wearing his quizzical monkey look. He didn't look eighty. Time had sharpened his facial planes, paring off all nonessential flesh. The lips were a thin neutral line, the eyes deep and close together, unclouded by cataracts or glaucoma. His smile was restrained and rare. Only his hair and ears and cheekbones were exuberant. His teeth were jagged and stained, but they were his own. I liked them and realized how depressing I found the false white sameness of the others' dentures. The cables of his neck wired his great, gaunt head onto a springy, tidy frame.

Rebekah came to the couch and sat down next to Shmuel. She too had her own teeth, and like him lacked the equipment that makes so many among the elderly look alike at first glance —the heavy glasses, hearing aids, dentures. Rebekah was also small, energetic, and erect. Even their hands were the same size, the backs blotched with brown spots but the fingers uncrimped by arthritis. Rebekah was seventy four.

Both were healthy, apart from Shmuel's heart condition for which he frequently took nitroglycerin pills. "My doctor tells me not to have emotions," he said. "I should damp down everything. Is this a philosophy? To live longer by not being so much alive? Now, in honor of your tape machine, I take one of his pills.

"So, you are here in our modest home. You see we are not poor. We do not have too much money, not too little either. When this is so, you pay attention. Spend carefully, eat carefully, you think about what you wear, what you eat, chew slowly with pleasure. So you end up paying attention to being alive. This is not such a bad thing. I don't envy the rich. When we were young, in my little town—*that* was poor. That was hunger. But because we didn't know anything else we didn't think of ourselves as poor. Everyone lived the same in the town. One was hungry, all were hungry. Not so hard as here where you see there are very rich and very poor."

"Shmuel, can you tell me more specifically how much you

spend for your life now, and where the money comes from?" I asked.

"For this house, we pay one hundred dollars a month with utilities. From the Social Security we get two hundred seventy-six dollars and from the union pension seventy-five dollars. For food we spend thirty-five dollars a week and our medical bills come under insurance, costing us maybe two hundred dollars a year. Clothing, still I make mostly. I have my sewing machine. What else is there? Entertainment—I have books and papers. Sometimes we go to a concert, we have a radio. This house is the best we ever lived in. Our son does not give us money. We send money to him for the grandchildren's presents. This is how it should be. In Jewish we have a saying, 'When the father gives to the son, both are happy. When the son gives to the father, both weep.' "

"Shmuel, do you think being a Jew makes the life of a retired person different from others—easier or harder in any way?" I asked. My questions came haltingly. Shmuel was wary, waiting for me to prick him. He was polite, seeming always to defer but guarded. How much of his life must he have lived this way, I wondered. I had seen this stance before, in Indians who hold off the intrusions of powerful outsiders with dignity and persistence, not allowing entry where it would deeply touch them. Would I ever be more than an outsider to Shmuel—presumably one of my own people?

But my question had interested him. When he could draw out a moral he was at ease.

"You can see this is not an observant home," he answered. "So, you would ask, what kind of a Jew is it that lives here? My son is a better Jew than me. But I am not a Jew like my father. He believed blindly. For me, acts more than beliefs make a Jew. Judaism means you know yourself, your traditions, your history, you live them. To be a good human being, in the Jewish way, to believe in life, to believe in humanity, to follow the Ten Commandments, that is enough to be a good Jew.

"Now you will ask me, does this approach make life in retirement easier? How can I answer? It is how I have always lived. I'm doing what I have always done. My thinking hasn't changed, so my attitude hasn't changed. You could say I'm still working. Am I retired now because nobody pays me for this?

The only thing that happened was when I was sixty-five I took off my watch.

"Now if you ask me the right questions I could tell you the man who doesn't like his work is a slave, a slave to boredom. Maybe for him retirement is a different kind of life. But in my life I have never been bored. If you cannot tell a story to yourself when you are sewing, you are lost anyway. The work has no beginning and no end, but the story is told, it goes on in the head. A needle goes in and out. You hold a thread in your fingers. It goes to the garment, to the fingers, to the one who wears the garment, all connected. This is what matters, not whether you are paid for what you do."

Rebekah interrupted us. "Shmuel, you are telling her the questions. You should stick to the answers. How can she do her job this way? Come now into the kitchen for tea." The kitchen was messy, fragrant, no signs of the landlord here. The tea was poured into jelly glasses. Shmuel drank his with the spoon in it, sipping it through a sugar cube he held in his teeth. Rebekah put out a plate of almonds, sunflower seeds, and raisins. Here it was easier to ask different kinds of questions.

"Rebekah," I asked, "how did you and Shmuel meet?"

She answered, "You see we had the same background. Shmuel was in the Bund with my brother. One night we were at the same meeting and that same night we walked out hand in hand. That's how we walked."

Shmuel nodded. "Since then, that was fifty-four years ago, we've been holding hands together. That's why I could never make a lot of money. I wanted to hold her hand always."

"Do you have any family members nearby?" I asked them.

"There isn't anybody left of our family except my sister," Rebekah answered. "She lives downtown and sometimes comes to visit us when she can get a ride."

"Do you see your son often?"

"He lives in Philadelphia," she said. "Like you he is a Ph.D., with a degree in sociology. He loves his work, has four fine boys. During the war he was a pacifist, a radical. He used to scold us for not teaching him Yiddish and Hebrew, so he studied these himself when he went to college. Now he keeps a kosher house and all the boys made Bar Mitzva. When the children were younger they came here a lot. Now we go there, maybe once a year. We have a good life here. Thirty-two years ago we moved to the beach. Shmuel worked on costumes for the movie people and got a good pension when he retired. For thirty years I have been active in the Emma Lazarus Club, this was one of the first progressive political organizations for women. We belonged to the Freiheit Chorus and all kinds of reading and discussion groups. A few years ago we stopped many of these things because the clubs meet downtown and it's too hard to take buses after dark. Our friends are getting on and don't drive so much to the beach. Still, I wouldn't complain about our life, if only I didn't miss those grandchildren so much. It's like the heart is cut out of me."

"Why don't you live back there with them?" I asked.

"This is not so easy. There, we can't go out in winter. No exercise, no work to do. Here is our life, our friends, our home, and the ocean. Except for those little boys, this would be all I want."

"No, Rebekah," interrupted Shmuel. "It's not worth talking about. He is our son and we are proud of him, but that's his own life, and this is ours. It is a fact of life to be hurt by your children. It doesn't matter how good they are. That must be accepted, so if you have only your children in life, you will have only pain. And after the children—it's still no-man's-land on the other side. I know that. But still I sing every morning in the shower."

"It's true, he does," Rebekah agreed. "For all our life together, every morning I wake up to the sound of Shmuel singing. He's still a *chazzen** and this house is our own shul. Look at our home. It is nothing fancy but filled with books, filled with ideas and love."

"It's not a disgrace to have a life like this," added Shmuel. "My son a Ph.D., from me, a tailor, son of a tinsmith. It could be worse. All this we have arranged and none of us have ever crossed a picket line."

The following week I passed the Center on the way to Shmuel's house for our appointment, and Hannah walked along with me for a while. "I saw you talking with that linkie, Shmuel," she said. "He's no good. He's a Jew-hater, you shouldn't hang around with him. I know, I know he's a very

* The one who sings passages of the liturgy in temple services.

smart man. A filosofe. He knows a lot of things, but what does it do for him if he hates himself?" She gave me a warning poke as we parted, and beneath her question was the veiled threat of exclusion from her and her friends' confidence if I persisted in my friendship with Shmuel. It made me very angry that I couldn't afford to take the threat lightly.

Shmuel opened the door for me with exaggerated courtesy. "Oy vay, the lady professor is here for more questions. Rebekah, warm the tea, she looks cold and she's covered all over with machines." I bumped past him feeling ridiculous, encumbered with camera, notebook, tape recorder, purse, and a box of cookies. Rebekah was about to leave for her Spanish class. She studied Spanish, she explained, because of her work with Mexican migrant laborers. After the class she would be passing out petitions supporting their strike.

"Do you enjoy that work?" I asked as I was setting up my equipment.

"Who could enjoy standing in a parking lot on a cold day, arguing with ignorant strangers? You don't do these things to enjoy. It has to be done, that's all." It never occurred to her, evidently, that her age might excuse her from political responsibility.

"Shmuel, a disturbing thing happened on the way over here," I began. I told him what Hannah had said.

"Yes, I warned you what they think of me. I am persona non grata over there. I will tell you what happened. I have always had mixed feelings about Israel. I told you I'm not a Zionist.

"Here is what I believe. Only life itself is sacred, not a nation. A nation is no different from any other—not America, not Israel, not Russia. 'Behold, the nations are like a drop from a bucket. All are counted as the dust on the scales.' This comes to us from Isaiah. If those ignoramuses would know the Bible, they would understand things better. They think I should fall on the ground of America, of Israel. I kiss no country's ground. According to them, this makes me an anti-Semite.

"Those people at the Center forget their own past. Most of them were at one time Bundists, internationalists, at least Marxists. We all got along all right with our differences until the Six Day War in Israel. Then they went crazy with Zionism. There was one of them, Weidman, a real peasant he is. He shows me a picture from a newspaper. There I see an Arab soldier. Dead. An Israeli soldier, smiling with his foot on the Arab's chest. By me, this is an ugly sight. This Weidman says, 'You see, how we have crushed the enemy!' 'Shame on you,' I tell him. 'Are you proud of that? Do you think that's not a man lying there? Are we less brutes than them? In the Talmud it warns us not to treat even our enemies this way.' To him I quoted this: '. . . You have turned justice into poison, the fruit of righteousness into wormwood.' From Jeremiah, the prophet."

"I suppose they didn't thank you for your opinion," I remarked.

"How could they understand? They haven't got the view, so uneducated. The weight of Jewish history, Jewish thought, is too heavy for those people. They are too small to bear the Covenant." Shmuel sighed heavily and reached into his pocket, where he kept the nitroglycerin pills.

Rebekah added, "What do you think they said to him about this? They spat at him. They throw curses at him. This he wouldn't tell you. He protects them. Disgusting are those people, *am ha-aretz** all. Shmuel, I don't know why you go in there."

"What could I expect them to say? Should they thank me? My presence pierces them like a polished arrow. This happened also to our prophets, especially to Jeremiah. With him I felt a great kinship always. 'They hate him who reproves at the gate. They abhor him who speaks the truth.' At least, I have the satisfaction of knowing I am in good company."

"I can't stand around here talking about such people when there's serious work to do." Rebekah left.

"Shmuel, I wonder too. Why do you go back when they treat you that way?"

"That's not so easy to explain. You see in the old days, this neighborhood had plenty of room for everybody's opinions. We had our discussion circles, poetry circles, Yiddish organizations, union groups, all those things. Now the urban renewal pushed most of them away. Our neighbors die or go to Homes.† Every day, our world shrivels. It frightens people. And now those that are left are all thrown together at the Center. Many of them have nothing in common, but they have to stay together. They remind each other of what they are reduced to.

* Ignoramus.
† Homes for the elderly.

social clubs for old people where they don't hear Jewish words or see a Jewish face. So why do I go there? I too need to hear Jewish sometimes. And, maybe, it's because they need me. You know, I am like the fly that pricks a sleeping mule. Now we work."

Shmuel held up a batch of papers covered with Yiddish. He had prepared for today's session by writing out some of his recollections from childhood. He put on his reading glasses and signaled that he was ready to begin.

"Oh, how often in our dreams, like a bird, we fly back to the place of our birth, to that little Polish town on the Vistula, which would be to you a small speck on the map, maybe even too insignificant for a map. A few thousand people huddled together, hidden in the hills, but with a view in sight of the beautiful river. In this place, the population was nearly equal Poles and Jews. All were poor. There were the poor and the poorer still.

"If you walked through the Jewish quarter, you would see small houses, higgledy-piggledy, leaning all over each other. Some had straw roofs, if shingles, some broken. No cobbles on the streets, and you might not even want to call them streets, so narrow and deep rutted from wagons. Everywhere, children, cats, geese, chickens, sometimes a goat, altogether making very strong smells and noises. Always, the children were dirty and barefoot, always the dogs were skinny and mean, not Jewish dogs. They came over from Gentile quarters looking for garbage and cats. You would go along this way until you crossed the wooden bridge into the main platz. Here were the women on market day, sitting in the open, or in little wooden stalls if they were well-off. Around the platz, a few Jewish stores, a stable, the pump with a roof and a bench.

"Most important, you would see here two buildings, facing each other on opposite sides of the platz, without smiling. There was on one side the Catholic church, enormous, two big towers of bells, and across from it, the synagogue, small but dignified, topped by pagodalike roofs covered with sheet metal.
other all the day. Thc church was built with splendor inside and
Under the sun, it was shining like silver, like a sparkle in God's eye. Otherwise it was all wood. The church stands there sternly, the synagogue's historical enemy—those two looked at each other all the day. The church was built with splendor inside and

out. Its glittering beauty displayed itself when the great portals opened. The Jewish children were afraid even to look inside."

Shmuel warmed to his subject and broke off reading. "You see, that church was the biggest thing we ever saw. From everywhere in the town you could see the towers. You could never forget about it. It was such a beautiful building, but when the great bells tolled it meant trouble for us Jews. When we heard that, we children would run home as fast as we could, back into the Jewish streets. On Sundays and Easter, those were the worst times. The processions came out from the church. The peasants were drinking all the day and night, staggering down the road behind those pictures of the saints they carry. Then, if they came across a Jewish child or woman, it could be murder. The hatred would pour out.

"You see, matters were never simple there. The pogroms were all around us. Then the soldiers on horseback would tear through the town and leave dead Jews behind. One time, we heard the big bell ring out and there was no reason for it. We were so scared we hid in the synagogue. That was probably the worst place to go, but we were small boys. All night we stayed huddling together there and heard terrible noises outside—horses, screams, shouts. We were afraid to light the lamps or stove. In the morning some men came to get us. Someone, it must have been a Pole, had warned the Jews with the bells that the soldiers were coming through. Everyone got away very quickly, hiding in the forest and in neighbors' homes. Who knows what would have happened without the warning? As it is, the soldiers tore up the Jewish streets, broke windows, threw the furniture out. We came out into the sparkling sunshine and the streets were white like in winter. Everywhere were feathers from where those Cossacks cut up our featherbeds. Dead animals also on our streets. From all this you can imagine our emotions when we walked past the great doors of the church. We would hardly throw a glance inside, even though the beauty would draw us like moths.

"Now, by comparison the synagogue you might not think was a beautiful place. It would be misleading to say it had any architecture. But do you think I noticed that? This synagogue was my first introduction to Judaism. The first time I went there I was with my beloved father, who up to the present moment I feel is with me, so that when I think of the synagogue, I can still feel his hand in mine as he introduced me to the world it held.

"I will tell you a little bit what it looks like. You walked up ten broad steps to the door. Why ten? I don't know, but probably it had some meaning. Then to enter, you walked down again, ten steps more. Why? The reason I think is symbolical. Because from the depths of your heart, you seek God, and you should feel that brings you up. But right away, you realize you are in the presence of God. Your body vibrates with how high He is, and how you are very small. Of this you are reminded by the steps down. That is how I thought of it.

"But like most things symbolical, there is also a practical side. You see, the Poles had a law that the church must be the highest building in the town. So the Jews, to make their buildings high, built it up from the inside, very quietly. You could not see from the outside what was happening. This was typical of the way the Jews lived with the Poles at that time. Everything done inside so as not to attract notice. Oppression made us very cunning. In this here case, the floor of the synagogue was lowered. They dug down into the ground, so from the inside only it was a very tall building.

"Inside the synagogue, no saints, no gold. There is no big beauty. It is an empty room. Benches, a *bima*,* the ark, not very bright. Now here is another thing. In the top by the ceiling, there were murals. Animals, Hebrew characters, flowers, birds of all kinds, and signs of the zodiac. There was also an elephant. Who had ever seen an elephant in Poland? Actually, he looked more like a deer with tusks. I raised my small head and looked up at that elephant until I thought my neck would crack. Some painter, some obscure fellow who never saw an elephant, he was the one who brought me all of a sudden to a thing I had never known before. You see, it was not a Jewish custom to decorate our homes. No pictures in our books. No carvings on the furniture. You know Jews forbid making religious pictures, and everything in those days was for religion. Why the synagogue was decorated at all, this I cannot answer. But in our little town, the only beauty which we could look at was the murals in the synagogue and the ones in the church, which you were too frightened to have a good look at.

* Platform from which the Torah is read.

"Now, if you have enough tape, I will give you the best part. I will describe my favorite picture in that mural. OK. This one was covered with musicians and angels playing horns and flutes. In the middle was a picture of Abraham in his devotion to God. He took his only son and got ready to sacrifice him for the sake of God, until the Angel took ahold of his knife and saved Isaac. "It seems strange, but there have always been people who are ready to make sacrifices on an altar without reservation. So the Bible in this story is showing us that people have always been ready to sacrifice the younger generation. We still send the innocent out to be slaughtered.

"Now you see, these pictures formed me. I never forgot that. There is no such thing as a small place. Some people would call that little town a small shtetl, or say it was a small synagogue. But people are formed by their passions, in the same ways, no matter how small or big is the place they live. They become who they are, with all the troubles, all the passions, with all the things which are bound to come up and face them, from these childhood pictures. That picture of Abraham is such for me. So that to this day, when I see children being sent out for slaughter, with those bugles playing and drums beating, while the angels are flapping their wings so you shouldn't hear the cries of the children being killed and shouldn't smell the blood, it stinks in my nostrils. But that is mankind. You cannot cut it out."

"Tell me, Shmuel," I asked, "didn't it confuse you, to love Judaism as you did, but see it condoning the sacrifice of an innocent victim for God's wishes?"

"Do you think that Judaism saves us from being men? Even as a boy, I saw Abraham's fault and knew it was his responsibility, not God's, to decide what was right.

"Like I said, sometimes things happen that make you realize how helpless you are. Not only were we children. We were Jews and the outside would come up against us. This was like being a child twice over, you felt very small, very weak. To give you an example, sometimes the Polish nation would step into our hidden little world in the synagogue. This was when the governor, appointed by the czar, would visit our little town once a year on the czar's birthday. When we knew he was coming, we cleaned everything, the best way we could. The women would come in and scrape all the candle wax and ashes off the benches and floors, oil the wood, make the books line up on the shelves. All the children would wear their best clothes, borrow shoes if they had to.

"The leadership of the synagogue was so afraid, they wanted not to displease the governor. Everything was done to impress him. A rug was put down, from somewhere we got it. And a big chair put in the middle where the bima should be sitting. We, the boys, the cantor, the rabbi, would stand up there, straight and stiff, full of palpitations to receive him, as he entered the door, dressed in a beautiful jacket, gray, with red lapels and gold trim, with a huge cross hanging from his neck.

"As he entered we turned and faced him. He never smiled. We never smiled. He had little glasses that glittered. Very straight and big. He was much bigger than any of us, maybe six feet tall.

"The rabbi would make him a receptional speech. This rabbi was very short and bent over, a frail old man, nearsighted and scared to death. He held that paper right up to his nose, trembling all over from the ordeal. He delivered it in Russian, careful with all the words, to make it to the satisfaction of the government. It filled my heart with pity to see that kind old man so frightened, like a small, unloved boy.

"After the speech, we children began to sing the Russian hymn, a hymn on the dull side. But we sang with gusto. This hymn was also a delicate business, because it was introduced after Poland was partitioned by Russia. And we were Jews—not accustomed to placing any man superior to any other, except God himself. But this was the way we were required to pay homage. I will never forget this hymn. All mixed up with it was the fear if we make a mistake, something terrible will happen. I can hear still our beautiful clear voices, and see that tall man's fine uniform, with the synagogue so sparkling clean, and always I come back to the old rabbi's terror. I get it all back together with the hymn."

Shmuel abruptly pushed back from the table. He tore his glasses off his nose and pulled himself up to his full five feet two inches. Voice trembling, but sweet and grand, he gave forth the Russian hymn. I applauded when he finished and shouted bravo. For a few moments his tears and laughter spilled out freely. I had never seen him so unguarded. Neither of us heard Rebekah come in. Shmuel quickly reached for another pill.

"What am I hearing? Is it possible? Why do you sing that terrible song, Shmuel?" Rebekah asked sharply. "Those things only meant unhappiness for us. You shouldn't let him talk about those times," she reprimanded me. "It makes me shudder."

"Rebekah, Rebekah, it was there," Shmuel protested. "You won't make it any different if you say it wasn't there. The hymn, the czar, the fear, the beauty, it was all there. It must be kept all together. To take out one part and lose the rest, to try to keep the good parts is to make every day the Sabbath. So far, the Messiah has not come. When every day is beautiful, we will be in Paradise."

"Shmuel has no understanding in some things." Rebekah turned to me. "He thinks because he has these ideas about things the world is changed. He will try to tell you living with the Poles was not so bad. He maybe hasn't told you what happened to him? Did he show you his scar? He met a boy, a *shaygets,** and it was wintertime, after Christmas. Shmuel wore a heavy sweater and scarf. This boy took out a knife and stabbed him in the neck."

"No, he hasn't told me. What happened, Shmuel?"

"I must have been about eleven years old. I was coming home from another village. I didn't see anyone. It was just growing dark and I was hurrying and took a shortcut through the woods. All of a sudden, something was on me with a knife, from the back. I felt a terrible pain in my neck and fell to the ground. He left me for dead. But it's not so easy to kill me. You know, they say that Jews are a stiff-necked people. He picked the wrong place to stab me. You could say my scarf saved me, or you could say maybe it was the characteristic of our people." Shmuel made his mischievous monkey face, eyes wide and round, eyebrows jumping up, mouth pulling down, nostrils flying open.

"Well, this happened. It is true. I carry the scar to remind me till now. I never saw this fellow's face, but I knew who it was from the voice, one of our neighbors. Not a bad boy, but

* Non-Jewish boy.

an ignorant peasant. But this is not characteristic. I cannot depict this here like it was a regular part of life in our little town."

"Did you see him again?"

"Of course, every day."

"Did you talk about it ever? Why do you think he did it?"

"No, we never spoke about it. After that, he was a little afraid of me. I think he thought I was some kind of a ghost. For why he did it, I can't say. He was a bully and a small Jewish boy was like a fly to him. But it must be remembered that there were Jewish bullies also. Who knows what they would do if they wouldn't be caught and punished? Without the law to govern them, do they find it in their hearts always to behave? Because they were the Chosen People? Not even the Messiah would expect that. Without consequences, do you think men ever find it in their hearts to do what is right? If that was so, why would we need the Torah?"

"Why are you undoing your tape machine? Are you getting ready to go? I just got back." Rebekah was very disappointed. She had wanted to make a tape recording of a poem she had translated. I was already late for dinner, but I knew if I left now, Rebekah would be annoyed with me for weeks.

Shmuel sensed my conflict and intervened. "Leave her alone, Rebekah," he said. "She'll come another day. She's a busy lady and I'm a hungry man. Come, I'll walk you to your car. This is a dangerous neighborhood and my neck is stiffer than yours." He winked, gathered up my packages, and held open the door.

When we met again, Shmuel wanted to continue discussing his early life and how it had shaped him. This time he spoke spontaneously, no longer feeling it necessary to write out what he planned to tell me.

"Perhaps the deepest impressions of life are where the roots are set," he began, "but at the time we were not aware of it. Late it comes up to you, what that was. I was a happy boy, but did I know it? I was too busy. My middle name is Simcha, that means joy, and it seems that this name influenced me greatly. Until the present day, I would rather see life in a way that is full of color, also full of shade, because without the shade we don't have the color. On this Rebekah and I do not have the same views. She keeps track of the shade too much. But my view is more from Jewish wisdom. God is not all good, not all bad, like everything. This matches also common sense.

"My roots, you could not separate from what I was reading, from the very beginning of my life till now, that always made a big impression on me. Naturally, because of where I grew up, the only reading was religious until I was nearly grown.

"You can imagine that it didn't take me long to learn to read. Soon I was introduced to the Torah, the big history of our people. I was absolutely enchanted by it, even though it was really premature for me, since then I was only five years old when I began on it. I was brought by it to that Ancient People—very thrilling, different nations, tragedies, greatness, drama. It all came forward and took me into it, thousands of years among the Jewish people. I liked it immensely. The text itself gripped me and held me. I felt the greatness of it. Not till later did I understand what that was. Still, from the start, I was taken with its . . . how to say it, with the great unity and endurance of our people.

"Like all the small boys in our town, I started *cheder** when I was only three years old. "When I think about it, we had there a very strange way to learn. It was so noisy in that room you couldn't hear yourself think. For one thing, we were many small boys. The teacher had to do many things with us to keep our attention, games, riddles, jokes, tricks, because we couldn't sit still too long. So we made all the letters into different stories and songs. A *hey* was a man with a broken leg, so we would limp around the room. The *beth* was an open mouth, ready to take in learning. Some had morals like *gimel-daleth*, to be kind to the poor. We would say the *gimel* looks at the *daleth* to remember we should look after the poor. But the *daleth* turns away his face, so no one should see his shame at taking charity. The older boys would also use the pages in the books for guessing games, for gambling. So everyone used sacred books not only for wisdom but for enjoyment. We didn't stop learning when we left school, not like in this country. No, it went all through our time.

"We cheder boys were always together whenever we weren't helping our parents. We were raised on four cultures. We knew Jewish at home. We knew Polish, naturally. After the

* Religious primary school for Jewish boys.

czar took over, we had to learn Russian. And there was Hebrew, of course. Hebrew was our spiritual culture. The March of the Kings held us in that tongue. The people were so real for us, the melancholy King Saul, the brilliant singer Solomon, the angry poetic suffering of Jeremiah—he was my favorite. We could always find heroes for us in there. We played our games in Jewish, but from Hebrew came the ideas. Whenever we were free from school, we would play out certain games. We always fell back to the Bible itself and played it out.

"When you play like that you have to have a deep understanding of the characters, their psychology. It's not only like reading about something. These people in the Bible grew enlarged for us, how they behaved, what they did when we gave them situations and troubles to handle, that was our game. Until the present day, I can feel the greatness of those stories working in me, giving color, giving itself into my own way of thinking. Sometimes I'm really astonished to which extent it reached out into me, and this was completely without any other studies. So I would have to say it was the simple beauty of the Bible itself that became part of my makeup. Even now, when I come across certain words, certain phrases that I know, I can branch out on them and relate to other things I learned since. Many people went to school and studied many things, but it seems their attention was not riveted to what stories they came across as mine was.

"Going out from school, we would look for the right place to play. Where the earth was soft, somewhere outside the little town, and where we wouldn't bump into any Poles. Youngsters need such food for their imaginations. For example, we would talk about Jacob, what went wrong with him? We would compare him to our own fathers. You see, children, when you let them be like this, together, warm with those beautiful stories, the lessons of them ring out, very sturdy, very sweet. Those Bible stories taught us how to live.

"Now we also played the character of Isaac. He had troubles because he had no child for so long. With no children, what happens? There are standing in each and every corner of a room people praying to a different God. Why? Because they have no common blood. As soon as a child is born, they are united by it. They have then one understanding and one God. You read such things as a child yourself, and you have no understanding. But gradually it comes out, when you take these parts into yourself. There's a hidden thought that comes, but you can't yet put it into words. So later, you are grown and you find, from somewhere, you have ideas about how to raise children. It is these Patriarchs who have taught you that. So the Jewish ways get into you from the earliest times and you are raising children in a special way. It happens to be the Jewish way. I don't mean it is the best way, but it happens to be our way. That's all. It is planted in our gardens. Does that mean that other gardens should be destroyed?

"Now I will tell you about culture. Culture is that garden. This is not a thing of nations. It is not about Goethe and *yeshivas.** It is children playing. Culture is the simple grass through which the wind blows sweetly and each grass blade bends softly to the caress of the wind. It is like a mother who would pick up her child and kiss it, with her tenderness that she gave birth to it. We don't see this anymore. In the present time we see nations. They are not natural outgrowings. Their roots are too harsh. They grew up too fast. They have not got that natural sweetness."

"It sounds like most of your memories about your childhood in the little town are sweet," I said.

"It was a sweetness in the middle of fear and oppression. That is how the Jew lived and how the Jewish language was born. In the long journey from one nation to another, from one country to another, here and there, the Jew picked up a language. From the Arabs, the Germans, the Poles, the Russians. The Jews were like a flock of sheep. They would go into a place and against every tree they would leave some wool and pick up some moss. The Jew exactly. But it was in Germany that they were pushed to the point that they had to have a language all their own. Here they got their voice. Hebrew was all right to speak to God, but when you had to speak man to man, to your own wife with love, or to your naughty child, when you had to curse your mule, Hebrew was no good for you. Too mighty. So little by little the Jew assembled his language.

"Now there are some people, even scholars and teachers, who you will hear say, Jewish is not a real language. For them, it was inferior. It came out of exile, or the language of exile, for the marketplace. It was for women to talk to children. Not good

* School of advanced Jewish studies.

for big subjects. For these you need Hebrew or Russian or Polish or English. This is nonsense. Jewish we call the mama-loshen. That means more than mother tongue. It is the *mother's* tongue because this was the language the mother talked, sweet or bitter. It was your own. It is a language of the heart. This the Jewish writers knew, and they used it with love.

"It had another aspect. It was not only that Jews from everywhere could talk with this language. Also, it had words in it that could be used differently for the inside sweet world and the hard world outside. Now this mama-loshen kept apart the Jewish and Polish worlds. My father, for example, used to say, 'I took the shortcut, past the church, *l'havdil,** to get to synagogue sooner.' That 'l'havdil' kept the church from being in the same breath with the synagogue. For cursing and blessing of all kinds, the Jewish language was the best. And it was a language that very few Poles understood. For us it was itself l'havdil, keeping us apart from the ones who hated us.

"So Jewish gave us unity. We passed by, we rubbed off, we gathered what we needed here and there. In the shtetl Hebrew was not the link, except for a few scholars. Whenever you went to the Judenstrasse in a new town, Jewish you spoke. Even in the schools, Jewish is standing by, patiently waiting to assist Hebrew. Always we traveled along in these two tracks, side by side, Hebrew and Jewish. Then another thing. In Hebrew you couldn't sing songs except for those Psalms, which is not a song by itself. You couldn't amuse yourself in Hebrew. We could sing the personal, lyrical songs in Jewish. Lullabies, love songs. A boy likes a girl. He couldn't go up to her and say, 'I like you.' This would not be permitted. So how could he approach her and catch her attention? He would make up a song, and sing it as if to himself, naturally in Jewish, but so she could hear it. This is the sweet grass from which the language grew. Young boys singing songs. The language was our republic."

A few days after this session, unexpectedly I encountered Shmuel at the Center. He was sitting on the side, consciously enacting his outsiderhood, observing as the Gerontology class discussed upcoming local elections. Several controversial propositions would appear on the ballot and the people were dutifully informing themselves on the issues. Voting days were

* Hebrew: "to separate."

patriotic ceremonies among them, whether they cast a ballot for an officer in their own Center or for national candidates. They came to the polls early, the men wearing dark suits, the women gloves. They felt the weight and wonder of their full American citizenship at such times. Shmuel thought the whole business was nonsense: "The stuff of nations, not culture." Shmuel, as usual, was nattily dressed except for the disorderly newspapers and magazines and scraps of notes poking out of his pockets. He regularly offered pungent comments, quoting Spinoza, the Talmud, Voltaire, Goethe, Marx. He soon found a tasty opportunity to deliver short discourse on the history of Yiddish. The speech was liked well enough until he concluded by extolling its virtues over Hebrew, a point that received loud objections. He was having a splendid time and was in excellent form as the discussion came to a proposition concerning nudity on the beaches just outside.

"It's disgusting to see how some people come around here," complained Manya. "The men wear a little G-string, not much better than nothing. Feh! You can see everything." "Manya, who told you to look?" rebuked Sofie. "Sofie, I'm only human, like you are."

Shmuel leaped in with delight. "If nakedness is sinful, why did God send us into the world without any clothing? If nakedness is not in tune with God, why do you think He did not prohibit it Himself? Why didn't He put trousers on the animals? In this life, there are many good men, but none of them are me. Who should judge when I will wear clothes and when I will not, but me? Now, I will tell you a piece of important wisdom from the commentaries, very wise, little known." He stood up and whipped through a Hebrew paragraph. "So here is what I conclude from the wisdom of our great sages. Even the greatest among us, underneath his clothes, he is naked!" The group complained and jeered, and Shmuel looked exceptionally pleased with himself.

Next they took up a proposition dealing with capital punishment. On this subject people were very much in conflict; some felt it might impede violence against older people, and so favored it. Now Shmuel was irate in earnest.

"No, this is wrong. It is not Jewish. This is not what our people do when they are afraid. Do you think killing someone you don't know will make you safe? Are you so weak that you need to feel strong in this way? Two thousand years ago, in Israel, in order to convict a man for the death penalty, seventy-one rabbis had to agree. Do you think seventy-one rabbis could agree on anything, much less taking a life? What's more, it gives us from the *Mishnah** that the court is too severe if it comes out with a death penalty more than once in seventy years. If you would know Jewish Law, you would understand that we do not believe in an eye for an eye. That is the idea of justice, *mishpat*. For Jews, more important than justice is *tsedakah*, which you could call righteousness. This means even when the Law would tell us one thing, to be just, we may overlook it, in order to show compassion. What happens when Cain murders his brother? Is he himself murdered? That would be just. But no, God does not avenge Himself. He pardons. Instead of saying, 'You have broken the Law, now I am going to break you,' God says, 'Look what you have done. The voice of your brother's blood is crying out to Me from the ground.' I give this to you to show you how barbaric you are. In the name of your heritage, you should be ashamed to talk about capital punishment. You cannot do this and call yourselves Jews."

"Listen to him. I wouldn't believe my ears if I didn't hear it. *That* one calls us not Jews?" Manya shouted out above the commotion that arose when Shmuel finished his tirade.

Weidman was outraged. "Don't listen to that dirty Communist! What kind of a man is that? He keeps himself apart and only comes around to make fun on us. Him, the anti-Semite, sticking with the Arabs against the Jews. A curse on your house!" He spat in Shmuel's direction. With dignity and disdain, Shmuel left the hall as the discussion continued within, Manya scolding Weidman for his crudeness.

I caught up with Shmuel outside. He ducked his head when I took his arm without asking permission. I could see tears on his cheeks. "Those people are so narrow, so uneducated," he said softly. "All this way they treat me is coming out from how I feel about Israel. This is our tragedy. Now that Israel exists, we have a handicap between us and our real Jewish culture. We can't jump across the subject of Israel, so we are divided from our Jewishness by that."

"Why do you go there if they treat you so badly, Shmuel?"

"Why do I go? In the Jewish language it is not possible

* Jewish oral traditions given to Moses at Sinai.

to curse your mother. The words are not there. Even if you want to, you couldn't say it. Whatever she did, she's still your mother. Here, too, whatever happens, these are still my people."

"There are others. Rebekah finds others. She won't even go in the Center."

"Am I Rebekah? You know we have a saying, 'Az ikh vel zayn vi er, ver vet zayn vi ikh?' Translated that means, 'If I should be someone else, who would be me?' But not just for myself I go there. They need me. I shake them up a little bit. If you have your tape machine today we could talk some more about my little town. Rebekah says I tell you too much about the sweetness there. I have no hatred. Why should I? But she is right. It has to be said that terrible things happened there, like anywhere. Not only things the Poles did to the Jews. We make our own tragedies also, without their help. So come into my house now. Have some tea because these stories will make your heart cold. You see, much there was that was beautiful. But not only this. Many tragedies also in that town.

"When I was very young, a beautiful, educated young man hung himself on the eve of the Sabbath in the synagogue. This was a desecration and a disgrace for the whole town, because he was driven to it. He got himself caught up in the rivalry between the Hasids and the rabbis and he made an end to it in this way. What could have been worse? For me, something happened that was worse. Now this story tells a bad part about me in it, but I am telling you truthfully because that is part of it. We children would escape from the grown-ups on Saturday afternoons. Then my father and mother went to bed for a nap and we never knew what to do with ourselves. We would go any little place we could find outside of the town. We took off our shoes, our clothes, we came to play in that beautiful little lake.

"This is a very sad story. We were a few youngsters and we went over to the shallow part of the lake. Then some Polish youngsters came along and we hid. There were more of them than us, and it was Saturday so we did not want a fight. The boys of the village on Saturdays learned catechisms. I don't know what they learned there, but it was always better for the Jews to stay out of their way after those lessons.

"One of the boys stayed behind to swim after the others went away. He plunged into the water and began to shout. I was afraid, but I went in the water anyway. But I was too small. I couldn't reach him. And then I saw coming a Polish man on the road. He was under the impression that it was a Jewish youngster there in the water. He looked at the boy, then walked on into the town. He didn't want to save a Jewish boy. We ran back to the town to tell someone. I remember I rushed so fast into town, I put my shirt on the wrong side.

"All the Jewish parents who didn't see their children there were afraid when that man told them the news. All those people rushed to the lake. By then someone had pulled the boy out. That was how people behaved. We knew the Polish man had passed him by, but we were afraid to tell on him. My teacher called us together when he heard about it. He took the boys out of school to the lake and said, 'Come be a witness as to how not to behave.' You see, people still make sacrifices of each other even though we no longer do it on altars.

"All right. Now here comes the bad part I am telling about me. I tried to save the boy myself, that's true. I could not manage it. But when I saw the man, that big Polish peasant on the road, why didn't I catch him to come down to the boy? I ran up to the road and there I stopped, frozen into speechlessness. We looked at each other a second, and then I ran away. In that silence, I helped kill a boy, out of my fear. This happened many years before that other one came at me with a knife. If the peasant later told anybody this happened, I doubt, because he was my accomplice. Did the knife come at me many years later in punishment, this I cannot doubt. Sooner or later, our actions come back to us with justice. This is my incurable wound with me all my life since then. I was like Jeremiah who also bore a terrible disgrace from his youth. Like Jeremiah I also was instructed by it. From this moment on, I cannot condemn my fellow man. Fear, that I condemn as our enemy, and this is not only for the Poles."

"Shmuel, did you ever tell anyone about it?"

"No, not my beloved father, not Rebekah, even. All these years I carried it alone."

"You know we have it recorded here on the tape."

"You think I'm so old I can't see the machine is turning?"

"Do you want me to erase it?"

"No, it belongs to the record, maybe the most important thing of all. Without knowing this, you don't know me. I told you this work would stick me with a pin, who knows how many sticks before we finish."

"You don't have to tell me things that are so painful if you don't want to. Only you can decide what is necessary to include."

"Is this serious work we do here or only bobbe-myseh? If you take my time, you take my life, at least you could make it right. Does it matter so much what you think of me, a tailor? No, what counts is what you learn from me. So much you don't know, I can hardly dent your ignorance.

"All of this makes no sense to me. Here you sit, all afternoon listening to the life of an obscure tailor. Better I should make you a coat to express myself. I could do more with a needle and thread than with words. No one will get anything from this work."

"I disagree. Let me give you an example, Shmuel. That story you told me about your attitude when you sew, about how it should feel to do the work, with attention, care, and imagination. I think that has universal value."

"Bah! You are exaggerating again. Be careful."

"OK, maybe I sometimes exaggerate, but I'm not now. It's my considered opinion that your description of the attitude you bring to your work will have meaning for many people. It's a valuable lesson for anyone. No matter what one's task, it can be done as you describe, so that finally peeling potatoes, any routine job, instead of being monotonous, becomes full of possibilities. I really believe your life is infinitely richer than so many people's, for many reasons. This is just one example of what people can learn from you."

"There you go. 'Infinitely,' such a big word. Too big for what you mean."

"OK, you don't like 'infinite.' I like it. It's the way I talk. I'm sorry if it annoys you."

"Will you put this in the record also or will you wipe it out when I scold you?"

"I suppose I'll have to leave it in, won't I? To be fair to both of us. So we'll both be deflated, Shmuel."

"Maybe I'm too hard on you. You can't help your great ignorance. But you should watch out for exaggeration. When you exaggerate, it puts you outside of something. You are not treating it with care. I tell you this because of what I have just given over into your hands. If I'm hard on you, it's because I make this sacrifice of letting you deflate me. A teacher holds nothing back from his students. You should accept all this with the right approach. Now, we take our tea. Soon Rebekah will be home. If she catches me with this heavy heart she will be angry at both of us."

We moved into the kitchen together and Shmuel poured the tea.

"So now you are drinking tea with the spoon in the glass? Maybe you'll become a Jew yet. Do you know why we drink it so?"

"I suppose so that glass doesn't break when you pour the boiling water in?" I answered.

"That is the practical explanation. We always made other explanations in my little town. Everything was made into something Jewish, the most ordinary things had a Jewish nature. Also we were growing boys, very interested in sex. Now you know that on Friday night when a married woman and man united with each other it is said to bring together the Lord and His People. Things happening on earth are not just for themselves. They are connected with what goes on above. I suppose that was a Hasidic idea. We boys also would make a similar equation with drinking tea. The spoon, that is the man, the glass the woman. We bring them together. It's a union, so with the Lord and Israel. What do you think your Dr. Freud would say about such things? We did these things because we could turn everything around and give it extra life. When you live in such a small place, like I said, everything takes on importance. Not a lot happens and you have to find ways to entertain yourself.

"There was always something going on. Not big things always, but things of our own invention. Still, I carry that practice along with me. When I drink my tea with the spoon in it, all those things from my childhood come along with me. I carry with me all the life of that little town to this day. Maybe for this reason, I have so many stories in my head, that I am never bored.

"Now there is something further I didn't yet give expression to. People are under the impression that things stagnate in such a little town, so nothing ever happens. No. It's only covered over. It's very small when you look at it from above, standing up on those hills. But when you walk down into it, you see it becomes life-size, larger than life even. Passion is there. Desire is there, but all the more strong because it is limited to the extent that you cannot be free to do what you want to do. You can't get away from those people. You can't leave, because you are leaving behind everything you know and love. This is like our Center, small and bubbling inside because nobody can get away. There are tragedies here like anyplace else. But they are bigger to you because you feel engaged in them.

"You see, in a big town the things don't strike you so deeply. But when you are a little street of Jews, surrounded on all sides by Gentiles, you only have each other, then such things follow you around everywhere. The individuals have value for each other. In a big town, nobody knows him. He doesn't exist at all. He is a cipher to his neighbors. But in a little town, not so. But there are dangers to this. From my stories, you see them. In a little town, people can treat each other so that they kill themselves and go insane. Of these things there are too many stories for me to try to tell."

Shmuel lapsed into silence. Outside the window a moth tapped lightly on the glass. The kitchen was dark and still. I could no longer see Shmuel's face. At last he began again slowly.

"What do we learn from all this? This little town I loved so much, with all its faults, I have to say we belonged there in such a way that we could never belong in America. Why? Because it was ours. Simple. Not so good or bad. But altogether Jewish. Now this is strange that I say we belonged there. Look how we lived. Hidden in a foreign land that we loved and hated. Even the beautiful river, the forests, none of these are ours. What did we have but fear and hunger and more hunger? So small, cramped, mostly very dirty. A life made up entirely from the imagination. We say our prayers for rains to come, not for us here in Poland, but for the Holy Land. We pass our lives to study the services of the Temple. What Temple? Long ago finished. It doesn't exist anymore. Where do our priests make the offerings? Only in our minds. We feel the seasons of Jerusalem more than the cold of Poland. Outside we are ragged, poor, nothing to look at, no possibilities for change. But every little child there is rubbing elbows with the glorious kings and priests of the Holy Land. The prophets are in our daydreams, so we cannot forget their fight for freedom and justice. In this we find our home. We march and mingle in the teeming streets of Jerusalem and our visions rise. Ideas clash inside us like warriors. A spark of life comes into us.

"Would you say this is insanity? Your Dr. Freud, would he call us schizophrenics? It could be. If we lived more in Poland and not so much in the Holy Land, would all these people be buried now in pits along the river? Do you think if we had had less to console us it would have made a different finish? These things I ask myself. Around and around it goes inside my head, making even the stories stop. When this happens, I lose myself. I think it may be dangerous for me to tell you these things. You should pay attention to the weather in America." Shmuel's voice had grown soft and dark. He shifted his body heavily in his chair and let out a sigh that was almost a groan. I couldn't see his face. "Go home now, madam Professor. I have nothing more for you today."

I stayed away from Shmuel for nearly two weeks after this session, saying that I wasn't feeling well. I wanted to give him time to mend and regain his composure. I felt he was angry at me for witnessing his grief and I didn't know how to limit his growing inclination to probe his wounds. It was necessary to him more than me that he not hold back and it had become clear that he, not I, would regulate and direct the flow of talk. I was afraid to stay away too long lest he think my feelings for him were altered by his revelations. It was quite a surprise when he accosted me cheerily on the boardwalk, scolding me gaily for wasting so much time.

"I have prepared some writings for you. Come to my house and I will read to you some happy things about my life. Also I have some poems you would like to make in your record."

It was a lovely day. Shmuel had set out flowers and arranged his poetry in piles on the table. "I start with this one. It is about sewing, which you seem to think is so important. Here I will try to translate this for you. In English it doesn't rhyme, but you get the idea.

God's greatest invention,
A little needle,
Humble, bright and quick.
A gift to Eve

To make us clothes,
She sews, and takes us
From animals to people.
In Paradise what are we?
Pure nature, without inventions.
Not yet born,
Until a needle
Makes us into men.

"These are a tailor's words. The poem, you see, I wrote in Jewish. That is because Jewish is the right language for the sweatshop. Not Hebrew—too elevated. Not French—too refined. Not Polish—too robust. Only Jewish could express a tailor's thoughts in America, working with his needle.

"Now here I have some poems about my family, my beloved father and brother. These men when I write about them, it is a love story. We think of matters of the heart as something only between the sexes. But no, there are many kinds of love. That is what these poems tell you."

Shmuel read several of his poems, ending with a long lyrical piece about his brother and his talent in visual art. The brother had become a stonecutter, which caused great pain to their father who regarded it as image-making.

"What became of your brother?" I asked.

"I will show you the poem I wrote about that," he replied.

This one, Menachem,
A bright, gay man
Whose eyes could find
The beauty in a stone.
Like many of them, gone.
Swept away and buried
In raging storms of hate.
Where are his dancing eyes?
Where are his gentle bones?
Where is his glowing hair?
A little heap of rubbish
Somewhere.

"And your parents, Shmuel, what happened to them after your brother left?"

"From then on it was the beginning of all of us going out of that little town. After that brother left home, my mother was restless. The hand of enticement was on us, and already everyone is beginning to talk of America, America. Everyone grew nervous. Things were breaking up. Yeshiva boys were reading Karl Marx. Jewish boys carving images, young people beyond the reach of parents and rabbis, going away from those poor, dear silent ones left behind. When they left they knew very well in their deepest convictions that they would never come back.

"Now my mother begins to nag my father to go out also, to follow the children. He doesn't want to leave. One Sabbath, she left the house and gave out all kinds of sweet cakes she had prepared to the children in the street. 'What is this you're doing?' my father asks her. 'I'm getting myself a new set of grandchildren, since I'll never see the others.'

"Now at this time my father is full with work but barely makes a living. 'I have first to finish my work,' he tells her. It happens that there was a rabbi passing through, that kind I told you about, a wonder rabbi. She dressed up and went out to him, palpitating, in her Sabbath clothes. 'Rabbi, what do you say? Should we move from this little town?'

" 'Yes, go,' he tells her.

" 'Will it go better with us?' She gives him then some money.

" 'Yes, when you change your place, you change your luck,' he tells her.

"With this she comes back to my father. The cheeks of my mother were always red, but on this occasion, even more so. Looking very beautiful in her fine dress, she says to my father, 'Now things are settled. We must move. The rabbi said so.' How could he resist this? "But this was a great tragedy for my father. He liked that little place immensely.

"The day comes to go. A summer day, beautiful. My father goes down to the cemetery and I with him. I couldn't stand to go too close to him. I loved him, but the pain that was coming out from him kept me away. Like flames, going out in waves. First he walked up and down. Finally, he gave the rabbi there some money to say prayers and keep up the graves. Then he walked over to the grave of his father. He cried, tears coming down and down his face. His hair was black and gray. Old as he was, there was a youthfulness about him, very remarkable. At this time, I saw that youthfullness go out from him forever, like the departure of a spirit. I could not take this sight in and hid my eyes. Still, when I looked up, he stood there like a small boy crying. He walked over to the others' graves, his mother, his sisters and brothers, then back again to his father. He started up a conversation there, telling his father why he was leaving, asking him for forgiveness and a blessing. All the while his tears are running through his beard until his shirt front is altogether drenched.

"You understand, it had never occurred to him that he would leave that place. His father lived there and his father before him, and so all the way back. My father had the custom of going often to his father's grave. Not just to keep it up, but to talk to him. When he had a trouble he couldn't solve, a fight with his brothers, or when there was a simcha. It was frequent among Jews to go to the graves in this way and invite the dead person to come to weddings and celebrations. So to leave all this behind meant something of the highest seriousness to him.

"Finally he had cried his heart full and he remembered me. He smiled and took up my small hand and kissed it. Both of us walked out of there without talking. I remember all our wealth was packed in two huge bundles placed on two skinny horses tied up outside. That's how we walked out of the little town, behind the skinny horses. A girl I know was standing there when we passed her by. She said to me, 'Is this all? Is this your worldly fortune, all you gathered up in all the time you were living here?' I said, 'No. There's another big bundle coming along with us, but you can't see it.' So we walked along the road out from there forever."

Shmuel leaned back heavily and rested briefly.

"In all this talking we do, I am finding myself carried back and back to my town. Out of my vision have come these pictures, these stories, colored and lively as if they are still there. I would sit down and write about it myself, but I wouldn't want to make an end of it. An end, you see, it has its own, without me finishing it off a second time. Besides this, if I talk about it for one hundred twenty years, it wouldn't be finished. How can I hope to tell you about what life used to be? So much we have talked, so much there is still left out. If I made the full story I would have to tell you how it was in Poland going back to my father's father, how they all lived.

"All this I give you was broken up, torn out, and thrown into the ovens. What words are there to lament this sufficiently? Even if Jeremiah himself would come back and cry out, 'Let my eyes run down with tears night and day, and let them not cease. For my dearly beloved people is smitten with a great wound. With a very grievous blow.' Even this would not be strong enough. When Jeremiah ran through the streets of Jerusalem, his eyes running like fountains, still it would not be enough crying. No lamentation could be strong enough to depict this tragedy. It was not only what befell the Jews. The ones who did it, they were no better off than the Jews. They lost their humanity; we lost only our people and our way of life. Although Hitler committed suicide, it was actually mankind who committed suicide, and this can never be undone.

"I cannot say good-bye to all that. As long as my eyes are still open, I'll see those beloved people, the young, the old, the crazy ones, the fools, the wise, and the good ones. I'll see the little crooked streets, the hills and animals, the Vistula like a silver snake winding in its beauty, and then I fall into a dream. It's a dream you can feel, but you cannot touch it. You see it still, you feel it, you become a part of it. Spring with its promises passes out, then very peacefully winter enters, gradually becoming more forceful until it is a fury all around you. Then the elderly men bend over in the streets and the children run with smoke coming out of their mouths, their poor feet blistering in the cold through the skimpy shoes. Maybe from wisdom, maybe from cold, the old men walk slower, bent over with age until their beards fall over their hands held for warmth against the breast. The walk has a heavier tread. The black caftans shine with frost. All this is natural. It has no moral, no consequence.

"In that little town there were no walls. But we were curled up together inside it, like small cubs, keeping each other warm, growing from within, never showing the outside what is happening, until our backs make up a stout wall. It is not the worst thing that can happen for a man to grow old and die. But here is the hard part. When my mind goes back there now, there are no roads going in or out. No way back remains because nothing is there, no continuation. Then life itself, what is its worth to us? Why have we bothered to live? All this is at an end. For myself, growing old would be altogether a different thing if that little town was there still. All is ended. So in my life, I carry with me everything—all those people, all those places, I carry them around until my shoulders bend. I can see the old rabbi, the workers pulling their wagons, the man carrying his baby tied to his back, walking up from the Vistula, no money, no house, nothing to feed his child. His greatest dream is to have a horse of his own, and in this he will never succeed. So I carry him. If he didn't have a horse, he should have at least the chance to be remaining in the place he lived. Even with all that poverty and suffering, it would be enough if the place remained, even old men like me, ending their days, would find it enough. But when I come back from these stories and remember the way they lived is gone forever, wiped out like you would erase a line of writing, then it means another thing altogether for me to accept leaving this life. If my life goes now, it means nothing. But if my life goes, with my memories, and all that is lost, that is something else to bear.

"We talked a lot here about God. Do I believe in God, you asked me? What does any of this have to do with God? This I cannot say. Some people are afraid to be alone and face life without God. Hemingway killed himself because he was searching for something and couldn't find it. The wise man searches, but not to find. He searches because even though there is nothing to find, it is necessary to search. About God, I would say I am an agnostic. If there is a God, he is playing marbles with us."

"On this note about God, we finish now," he said. "You have all I can give you. Take it and do something with it. What it is I don't know. You have to take it in your own way. How you will do this with all your ignorance, I cannot think, but maybe something comes together and makes sense for you.

"We'll see. Now, *maidele,** go home with all this package of stories. I'm tired." Shmuel had never used an affectionate term to me before. I was touched by it, but remembering his discomfort with my "exaggeration," I refrained from telling him how much all this meant to me. I wanted to hug him but man-

* Little girl.

aged to hold off and only shook his hand. For the only time since I had been visiting his house, he did not walk me to the door, but remained sitting quietly as I let myself out.

Three days later Rebekah called me to tell me that Shmuel had died peacefully in his sleep two nights before. He had not been ill or in any discomfort. He told her that we had finished our work together and had done as much as we could in the time we had. He was sad but not despondent. He had told her to get the tapes from me when I finished transcribing them, to give to their son. I would copy them for her as soon as I could, I promised her.

Shmuel's *shloshim,* the thirty-day memorial after a death, was held at the Center three weeks later. It was very crowded, and there were many people there whom I had never seen before. These were Shmuel's old friends, people who regularly avoided the Center because they found the prevailing political and philosophical climate unacceptable. Women from Rebekah's clubs were there, and so was her sister. Conspicuously absent were some of the core Center members and the ladies from the Zionist clubs. Abe, the director, and Shmuel's friend Abe Beidleman, had planned the simple program.

At the front of the hall, on an oilcloth-covered table were two candles and a bouquet. Rebekah sat composed and dry-eyed near the table. Fighting tears, Abe began the eulogy, describing Shmuel as a religious man, a man whose religion was the brotherhood of all people.

"Whenever I would see Shmuel on the boardwalk, my heart would rise. He would walk along there, reading his papers. So absorbed was he, I was always afraid he would stumble or fall, but no, he never misses a step. He was my intellectual ballplayer. He gave me a good workout every time. He never told anybody what to do, but he gave us direction anyhow. He never raised his voice, he never wasted words, he had more dignity and strength than you could find anywhere. He was a man searching, always searching in everything that went on for what life is about. He was a model for us in getting old. It is not necessary for us to be lonely and feel sorry for ourselves. We must stay involved to the last minute. Shmuel and I met the day before he died. As usual, we had a good battle. We can learn how to live and how to die from him, calmly but vigorously, members of life to the very last minute."

Josele played a Yiddish folk song on his concertina. Then Beidleman delivered his speech. "Shmuel would want to be remembered as a humanist and a worker. You know he was proud of the fact that he never crossed a picket line. He walked in plenty of strikes himself and one time he nearly lost an eye, such a bad fight was that. But he didn't think anything of this. No big deal, for him that was what you did for justice.

"He was a writer also. And he wrote about his work in his poems. Now these poems he loved as much as tailoring. It would be wrong to say he was an artist. Nothing like major people would notice. But he did what he did with an artist's attitude, very carefully, full of respect. He believed very much in the right attitude, not just what you had when you finished with something. He made anything that was ordinary into something special in this way. The sweatshops killed a lot of people, but not Shmuel. He never gave in to monotony. In his head he was always writing and singing. Make the work good, make it right, even if it is piecework. It would be a zipper or buttonholes only, it didn't matter. His poems were not necessarily happy. No, he wasn't a fool for happiness. But he had a way of putting everything together, so it was finally all in one piece, bound up together—his love for Rebekah, for Yiddish, for his work, all his own mix. He believed this way and he lived this way. In my opinion, this is something better than happiness.

"Shmuel you could not put easily into a category. I wouldn't say he was a humble man, because he had more knowledge than most people and he knew it. You couldn't say he was simple, because he had complex thoughts. He didn't have illusions about how important he was or what he would accomplish. With all his union work, he knew human nature would be the same as before, but that didn't stop him from putting his life into it. Shmuel was like a fine cloak, everything well-stitched together, good strong seams, cloth not fine but not cheap, long-lasting. Himself, he was also like a needle—sharp, practical, quick, jabbing people sometimes because that was necessary. He was a little man with a big history behind him."

Then Abe asked me to speak, responding to a sign from Rebekah. I don't remember exactly what I said, something about our work together, his recording stories and memories, his esteem for the Yiddish life whose loss he lamented so keenly. He had wanted to preserve those memories to pass on to his grandchildren, and I would try to help do that. Then it was over and Rebekah and I hugged each other. We said we would meet again when she returned from a long visit to her son. I walked her home and then returned to the benches outside the Center. A fierce argument was going on, and everyone was talking about Shmuel's death and memorial. Manya and Weidman were angry that a service had been held, and reiterated the story about Shmuel's reaction to the photograph of the Israeli soldier triumphing over the dead Arab.

"This is a disgrace, to honor a Jew-hater in our Center." Abe was too raw with grief to pass over the remark with his usual tolerance. "How dare you speak that way about him! He was a precious human being, a philosopher, a good Jew."

"He was also a linkie," Manya added.

As always, Sofie was temperate and sensible. "He was a linkie, but he is dead and can't answer us now. Most of all he was a member, so he has a right to be honored here."

"He was a Jew, and a Jew is a Jew. With or without Israel. Even in Israel they would say this. In Israel there are two legal Communist parties. Since when can't you be a linkie and a Jew at the same time? Who stands here now that wasn't at one time also a Socialist, a Communist?" Beidleman was red and sweating with anger.

"None of you are bringing out the important thing," said Hannah. "Today was a Jewish holiday. A temple wanted to come here for a service. Everybody would have a lot of pleasure from that, but Abe had to interfere and make this a memorial. So now, everyone stays away."

"Not all," interfered Sofie again, even and resolute. "Some of us are here. Do we care if Shmuel was a red or a green or a blue? He belonged to us. America is a free land. He could believe what he wants without us putting him out."

Beidleman took it up again.

"That's right. Remember why we came to America. This way you are talking is how Hitler got started. Stalin the same thing."

A great hubbub ensued. "You are comparing us to Hitler? You are comparing us to Communists? And what has Hitler got to do with Stalin?"

"They're all Jew-haters, so it amounts to the same thing," Weidman shouted.

The fight was not going to end for a long time. I indulged myself by leaving, telling myself that even though I was supposed to be an objective observer, I didn't have to stay to hear Shmuel attacked on the day of his memorial. I didn't want to defend him publicly. I had alienated too many people already by my friendship with him. Now, without him, I would have to try to be impartial on my own. He would be pleased with my conduct, I thought, glad that I held my tongue. Later, I would work on my attitude.

CHAPTER THREE

"We don't wrap herring in a printed page"

BOBBE-MYSEH

The following excerpt was taken from the tape recording made of the sixth Living History class. Twenty people were present, and all spoke eventually, but the discussion was dominated by the five men and seven women who proved to be the nucleus of all the classes. These were Max, Moshe, Nathan, Jake, Heschel, Hannah, Sadie, Sofie, Olga, Sonya, Basha, and Rachel. Most of the morning had been spent discussing the meaning of being a Jew in America. Just before this excerpt begins, Rachel had announced that her granddaughter was marrying a boy who wasn't Jewish but was going to become a convert.

NATHAN: *I would have to say to your granddaughter that even of her husband converts that won't make him a Jew. You could say a broche* over a chicken, that won't make him a fish.*

OLGA: *We are living now in America. This is not a Jewish country. We got to adjust. We got to accept intermarriage as a fact of life. Myself, when I was a little girl, I was very religious. But when I came to America I saw the writing on the wall. I had to write on the Sabbath, take care of money. So if I could do this, I could do everything else, except stealing. Little by little we got loose from the things of our childhood. I love America. But eventually I learned that I got to take care of religion myself, from the inside now. Nothing works outside to help me. When it comes from the inside this way, it doesn't matter where you live. I would have to say I'm Jewish all over,*

* Blessing.

even if it don't show. We can't live here the way we did in the Old Country.

MAX: *We always knew what it is to be a Jew. It don't matter if you go to shul to pray. Between being Jewish and being religious is a difference. If you don't put out your hand against injustice, I don't care if you pray all day. You may be religious, but by me this isn't a Jew.*

HANNAH: *Some people would say being a Jew is how you follow the laws. Some people would say, like Olga, it's from inside. I will give you a little myseh on this. In my town was an old lady who was a miser, very big. Nobody was getting a penny from her. She had money all right. She kept strickly kosher and more so when she was getting older. More strict every day. Dishes she had, you couldn't count them. Sinks, pots, spoons, everything she had separate.* One day she went to the rabbi and asked him if when she died God would think she was a pious Jew. "Well," he told her, "I don't know what kind of a Jew He'll think you are, but certainly He will say you got a very pious kitchen."*

MOSHE: *This is something we don't know as children. All we hear is to follow the rules. You see it was that attitude that made us give over everything. When I was fifteen years old I stopped going to synagogue altogether because we revolted against all the ritual. We threw out the good things with the bad, from the same window. It took me a long time to think out that we were wrong. We were throwing out the vital things that sustain life.*

NATHAN: *My big objection is not with the praying. It's because religion doesn't help you. Man is a killer, no matter if he is a Gentile or a Jew. No religion yet has showed him otherwise. If we would change the social system maybe that would help. It has got to be adjusted to give people equal rights. But religion doesn't work on this. I'm in this country all these years, I never saw a rabbi on a picket line. Only when we have communism can we work on human nature.*

RACHEL: *Human nature is human nature. That's why communism is no good. My hope is that one day we would be only people with one God, no Gentiles, no Communists, all one people.*

* Separation of all cooking ingredients and implements for meat and milk products is required by Jewish Law.

MOSHE: *Rachel, you wouldn't have then no more Jews, unless you are expecting everybody to become Jewish.*

SONYA: *Maybe it doesn't have to come to that. We could all be in favor of good deeds but still have Hindus and Catholics and Jews.*

BASHA: *Jews you could get along without, but not God.*

NATHAN: *If we start to talk about God now we'll be here for five thousand years. These questions you could keep for posterity.*

SONYA: *Have you got better to do with your time than sit here and talk?*

MOSHE: *What we decide about God here is not so important. What matters is what we did with our lives. Nobody cares how many dates we eat, if we got two sinks or one, whether we buy Gentile meat. The important thing is what we did for the community, for the United States, for peace in the world.*

SADIE: *These things are important because we all have different lives, so we should tell people what we did. Myself, I have struggled for others without stopping. I still believe in God. When I go to sleep at night I say a prayer because I always think, maybe I won't wake up in the morning. I'm not such a well person. Even the doctors don't know how I survive. I could list for you all my sicknesses.*

NATHAN: *For this we don't have enough time.*

MAX: *It doesn't make any sense for us to take up such big subjects. The sages couldn't answer what makes a Jew. We are not scientists. We are not Einsteins. We are only ordinary people. What do we know from God?*

SONYA: *Ordinary people got a right to talk about God.*

HESCHEL: *I'll ask you this. Where was God when Hitler came around? Is it possible God could keep quiet through such a thing? No, from what I have seen, I would tell you that if there is a God, He has a heart of stone. The things I saw, I couldn't speak about. It takes the heart out of me.*

SONYA: *So if we go the way you do, we help Hitler make a success of his work and we don't have no more Jews.*

HESCHEL: *I want to show you something, I keep it with me always. This is something I never talked about before. [He took a small, dirty piece of yellow cloth out of his wallet and unfolded it. It was a Star of David. There was an instant hush in the room. Everyone recognized it as the symbol of the Holo-*

caust, the stigma Jews were required to wear under Hitler. He handed it to Sonya who held it gingerly and passed it to Moshe. It circulated throughout the room in silence. When Heschel got it back, he folded it once more, replaced it in his wallet, and resumed speaking.]

What this is nobody needs to tell you. I wore it on my shirt in Belgium. My whole family was already taken away—eight children, wife, mother, father, sisters. Remaining with me was one daughter, eight years old. She was hiding out with a Gentile family. We passed on the streets without talking. I would see her and pray she wouldn't give out a sign if our eyes met. This Belgium family saved her life. Before Hitler it was enough for me to be a Jew. Since Hitler, I have to be a mensh.*

HANNAH: I would say it just the other way around. When I was a young girl in this country, I wouldn't wear a Jewish star. I worked for the union to help the common people, Jew or Gentile. It was good enough. Since Hitler, I wear a Jewish star. Everyone should see it.

NATHAN: What we bring into the conversation is history. It gives us new lessons about being a Jew. America gave us a lesson. Hitler gave us a lesson. It becomes active in you in your own way, not how your parents give it to you from their history. All of us have to examine history to find what lessons it has for us. A saying on this goes, "If you study history, you lose an eye. If you don't study history, you lose two eyes."

MOSHE: If a person is studying our history, he has to doubt God, but he doesn't have to throw Him away. There are many problems in this. According to our sages, God is everywhere. But if God was in the concentration camps, that's another question. Rabbi Mandel of Kiev once asked a small boy where God lives. "God is everywhere," the boy answered. "No," said the rabbi. "He is where man lets him in." Man did not let God into the concentration camps. There is a good force in the world and a bad force. If God is the God of the whole world, which I don't doubt, then God has got to be both, good and bad. In the concentration camps was only the bad, and half a God is not God. So God wasn't there. But it is not meaning from that there is no God.

HANNAH: If we look at the history of the Jews how can we

* Literally, a person; a human being, a member of the human community.

doubt there is a God? Could all this suffering come about by accident? No, it's because from all the nations, God picked the Jews to be the Chosen People. So we don't ask if there is a God. We ask how come the Jews had to be so lucky?

OLGA: Vay ist mir.* "Where is God?" *such an old question. The Jews never get tired of it. I also remember a story about a little boy who asked the rabbi a question about God. "Rabbi, rabbi, where is God?" he asked. "Everywhere," answered the rabbi. "There is no place empty of Him, so whatever you do, you couldn't fool Him." "Is God in our cellar?" the boy asked. "Oh, yes,* bubeleh,† *he is certainly in your cellar." "Ha, ha," the little boy said. "I fooled you. We got no cellar."*

MOSHE: *Questions, questions. Always the Jews are asking questions. Sholem Aleichem said, "The real Jewish question is this: From what can a Jew earn a living?" In my own mind the question is this, when will the Jews stop asking themselves questions?*

All week it had been raining without stop. On Sunday, the day of a big celebration at the Center, the skies cleared. The Center folk burst out of their confining little rooms and streamed onto the boardwalk, which was already swollen with people. A sunny day in the middle of the rainy season intensified its carnival flavor. Everyone seemed in motion. The rental bicycle man had added skateboards and roller skates to his trade. Virtuoso children and adults skimmed by, imperiling the elderly. Still, Sam deftly maneuvered his motorized wheelchair around impediments, blind Eddie and deaf Harry pooled their capabilities and helped each other avoid collisions on their way to the Center. A beautifully muscled young man, earring glinting in the sun, played the flute as he rode by no-hands on his bicycle, bowing his head to admirers. An old couple tucked into an electric golf cart chugged along stolidly. Two small boys popped up and down on pogo sticks.

An impromptu steel band had formed in front of the Center. A dozen or so adolescents were banging exultantly on congo and bongo drums, garbage can lids, and wine bottles under a fragrant cloud of marijuana. A smiling girl rode past with a fully

* Woe is me.
† Little doll.

clothed monkey seated in her bicycle basket. Winos, rousted from their benches by the crowds, muttered and shuffled along, avoiding the squad car that cruised by dispersing the band, which regrouped as soon as it had passed. A tall, solemn man played jazz on an upright piano that had been mounted on a wheeled platform, pulled along by his sweating partner.

The old people held their own as they made their way through the commotion to the Center. They were in a jubilant mood, happy to be outside and in company, and excited about the afternoon's celebration. It was the day of the Graduation-Siyum,* a unique ceremony designed by *Reb*† Kominsky, the new teacher of the Yiddish History class. The occasion was the celebration of the class's completion of a five-month course of study. Kominsky had invented a ceremony that combined an American graduation with the traditional, Eastern European Jewish *siyum;* it was, he assured everyone, going to be "absolutely unique."

Eli Kominsky had extensive connections in many quarters of the Jewish population and had assembled a sizable audience for the affair. He was a newcomer to the community. He had suddenly appeared six months before and announced that he was going to revitalize the Center. Some people viewed him with skepticism, as a "*macher,*‡ all blown up with grand notions." Others were delighted and flattered by his attentions. Everyone was dazzled by his energy. Kominsky was a dynamo, nearly fifteen years younger than most Center people, newly retired, and looking for a place to devote his energy and realize his aspirations. His childhood had been much like theirs, but in addition he had traveled widely and had lived in Israel for many years. And unlike most Center people, he was a fervently religious man. Not only was he schooled in Jewish Law, but he had leanings toward Hasidism. His religion was a powerful emotional force in his life, at times ecstatic and even mystical. Part of his vision included redeeming the Center people, bringing them to the attention of the world and their own children, and drawing them into a more intense practice of Judaism. He was indignant that they were so neglected and grieved too that they had jettisoned so much of

* Hebrew: "completion," a ritual acknowledging the fulfillment of a self-directed program of religious study.

† An honorific term for teacher, or man of learning and stature.

‡ Literally, "maker," a big shot.

their heritage in becoming American. Kominsky's relations to the Center people wavered between identifying them as his parents, deserving of respect and devotion, and seeing them as his errant children, needing his scolding and guidance. The Graduation-Siyum was the first public presentation of Kominsky's plan, and he meant it to be dramatic and wonderful.

The class members had been in a state of high excitement about the celebration for weeks; though some were dubious, none were indifferent. Shmuel flatly refused to attend and was impatient with my enthusiasm. As usual, he was critical of the members' improvisations where I was admiring.

On the day of the Graduation-Siyum, inside the Center people were still discussing the pros and cons of Kominsky's program. Shmuel, it became apparent, was not the only one with reservations.

"This Kominsky has taken leave of his senses," Hannah proclaimed to me, as she pulled me to sit down next to her. "Barbarushka, you know you are in here with a bunch of madmen. Look at what he is up to now, this zealot, Kominsky. He is going to make fools of us all."

"Hannahleh, give the man more credit," objected Sofie. "He's got big ideas, maybe not always so practical, but we should help him because he wants the best for us. All right, he's got *chutzpa*.* But he brings life into the Center, he brings in the outside. And he brings up our Jewishness with a new enthusiasm. Would that hurt us? Why shouldn't we go along? Just because this has never happened before, doesn't mean it couldn't happen here." Sofie as always was patient and open-minded.

"I'll add something to this," Nathan leaned over to join our conversation. He had a story with a moral for every occasion. "When I was a little boy, maybe four years old, a carnival came to town. I stood there, watching those people dance up there on a little bit of a wire. I couldn't believe mine eyes. 'Never in my life have I seen such a thing. It couldn't be happening,' I said. My *zayde*† says to me, 'Because a small boy with only four years of living never saw such a thing—does it mean it couldn't happen?' So, from this I ask you, why shouldn't Kominsky also do something here for the first time? Just because it never happened before, couldn't it happen now?"

* Brazen courage, nerve.

† Grandfather.

It was not surprising that the unprecedented nature of the Graduation-Siyum disturbed the Center people. Kominsky had undertaken a bold and hazardous enterprise in inventing and staging a one-of-a-kind ritual. All rituals are paradoxical and dangerous enterprises, the traditional and improvised, the sacred and secular. Paradoxical because rituals are conspicuously artificial and theatrical, yet designed to suggest the inevitability and absolute truth of their messages. Dangerous because when we are not convinced by a ritual we may become aware of ourselves as having made them up, thence on to the paralyzing realization that we have made up all our truths; our ceremonies, our most precious conceptions and convictions—all are mere invention, not inevitable understandings about the world at all but the results of mortals' imaginings.[1]

A ritual such as Kominsky's risks more than that. As well as being unprecedented it was built upon contradictions, denials and fictions, as we shall see. But rituals are capable of making improbable, impossible claims. Because they are dramatic in form, rituals persuade us by our own senses, appealing to us through color, smell, music, dance, food, rhythm, lulling our critical faculties. We perform in rituals, and doing becomes believing. Kominsky's ritual was properly sensual and its persuasive power heightened by that. But mere aesthetic elaboration is not enough to make a ritual work. Rituals must be built upon shared symbols. Kominsky had at his disposal two powerful, sacred, complex symbols on which to base his ritual: Being a Jew and Learning. How their meanings and emotions were activated in the Graduation-Siyum will soon be apparent.

Kominsky had another disadvantage in arranging an effective ritual for the Yiddish History class. Ritual may be likened to a vessel into which anything may be poured: an order-endowing device, it gives shape to its contents. This ordering function is furthered by the morphological characteristics of a ritual—precision, accuracy, predictability, formality, and repetition. Thus the characteristics of ritual as a medium suggest that its contents—whatever they may be—are enduring and orderly. By virtue of these traits, ritual always delivers a message about continuity, in addition to its other symbolic messages. To make a convincing statement about continuity in a one-of-a-kind situation is tricky, to say the least. Kominsky managed to suggest that the Graduation-Siyum was a traditional, authentic, timeless custom by juxtaposing sacred and secular elements so that they comprised a single flowing experience. He accomplished this by skillfully interweaving symbols associated with the traditional, sacred realm of the siyum with the secular, contemporary realm of the graduation, constructing out of the sacred and the secular a single unifying image or metaphor that gave the whole day's events credibility and effectively masked the many contradictions involved.

"We are all as crazy as Kominsky for coming here," Hannah announced loudly until Sofie hushed her. Despite Hannah and Shmuel's doubts, I had seldom seen the Center so crowded. It promised to be a festive afternoon. The audience was comprised of a broad mix, including members who were not in the Yiddish History class, some of their friends and neighbors, and representatives from the City Council and from the Jewish Alliance, the city-wide philanthropic organization that funded and sponsored the Center. An official attended from Temple Beth Shalom, a wealthy synagogue a few miles away, and the director of the City Parks and Recreation Program for Senior Citizens was also present. The director of Adult Education from a nearby community college, and a couple of reporters and photographers from the local papers completed the list of representatives and officials. The most important sector of the audience was essentially absent—the families of the graduates. Kominsky had specifically intended them to be present to witness their parents being honored, as part of his effort to repair their neglect of the elderly. Sonya's daughter, Rachel's granddaughter, and about a dozen representatives from Jacob Koved's family constituted the entire contingent of the graduates' kin. Nevertheless, the crowd was enthusiastic and the missing spectators seemed not to jeopardize the success of the event.

Seated at a table at the front of the room behind bouquets of blue and white flowers sat the various dignitaries, Abe, and Kominsky. The graduates, twenty-six in all, were arranged in rows flanking the head table. They wore their finest clothing beneath blue and white satin ribbons that crossed the breast from shoulder to waist. Most were solemn and flushed with excitement. Young ushers with armbands bearing the Hebrew character for "order," shooed away the itinerant curious outsiders and the neighborhood winos who regularly patronized the Center bathroom. Kominsky had planned the ceremony with exceeding care. Food and flowers had been donated through his efforts. He had worked his networks skillfully, rounding up the young people, decorations, services of all kinds, and refreshments from anyone who could be cajoled or shamed into making an offering.

The ceremony began at 2:00 in the afternoon with the National Anthem and the Pledge of Allegiance, Kominsky's enthusiastic, stridently off-pitch singing sounding clearly over the din. He introduced the students and officials to the audience and then began his prepared speech:

> This is a *mitzva** for all of you and for us, an absolutely unique event. Still we follow our Jewish customs. We started off with the National Anthem and the Pledge of Allegiance because first of all we are Americans, then we are Jews. According to the Talmud, the law of the country precedes even the law of the Jews, except in cases of conversion, idolatry, and homicide, which things do not concern us here. You, our audience and friends, are privileged to be here with us today. I too am privileged. These people you see here are the ones who gave their whole lives for the children. Now, you the children, I am giving a chance to honor them. Myself, I never had a chance to honor my parents. So, I see in these people, the graduates, my own father and mother. These are humble people, not much education. Nobody gave them attention. They worked always for others—for their children and for Israel, struggling with the little bit of education and opportunity they had. How they are now forgotten is a disgrace, so I take it on myself to bring them to light.

Kominsky's eyes blazed bright blue. His abundant white curls were not kept in place by his red velvet, gold trimmed skullcap. His small stocky body fairly shook with the force of his mood.

"I, for one, would appreciate it if he wouldn't make us out to be quite so humble," Hannah whispered to me. "It gets worse already. And tell me please where are all these children who are supposed to be here to see us?" She shook her thick shoulders with disgust. "This madman wanted me to tell him the names of my daughters so he could send them invitations to this siyum. He sent off invitations to everyone's children who would give him names. I told him that my daughters got more important

* A religious obligation and a blessing; a good deed.

things to do with their time than come to watch Mama make herself look stupid. What do you think he answered? He says then to me, 'Hannah, if you wouldn't give me your daughters' names, I wouldn't let you come.' One daughter is a doctor, the other one a teacher. These are busy people. For this business here I should ask them to give up an afternoon?"

Hissing and shushing on several sides quieted Hannah for the rest of Kominsky's speech. He concluded and introduced Sonya, the valedictorian. She was a fine-boned woman with translucent skin and the straightest back I had ever seen, a former actress in the Yiddish theater. At eighty-five she moved with a consciousness of her lasting beauty. When people looked at her, her dainty head snapped up and she drew her stomach in. Her voice was lovely and clear. She read her speech in English, in which she lauded and thanked America, "the land of freedom and democracy, which gave to all of us a new life." Following her, Jacob Koved read a poem he had written in Yiddish, about his mother, "a poor woman who could always find a little water to put in the samovar so that a guest was never sent away without at least a glass of tea. If it was weak, still it was hot and the mother's hospitality gave it taste enough for anyone."

Kominsky then introduced a sixteen-year-old boy to whom he had been giving Hebrew lessons. "This boy, Dovid, like so many of your American young people, never got a Jewish education. From him you may learn it is never too late." Dovid read a passage from a poem by the Hebrew poet Bialik, which he had translated with Kominsky's help. Facing the graduates he read:

> *. . . You are*
> *Silent and humble*
> *Who weave their lives in a hidden way*
> *Modest in thought and deed, unheralded,*
> *Unsparing in speech and rich in beauty*
> *Hidden is your fine spirit . . .*

"Oy vay, more how we are humble," moaned Hannah.

"Humble maybe, but silent, not so much," added Nathan. At once the chorus of hushing started again.

The public officials began their round of speeches, all following a similar pattern: commending the seniors for their accomplishments, initiative, and dedication to the study of their heritage. They were lauded as exemplary elders who knew how to use their "golden years" to good purpose, and were congratulated as ideal senior citizens and Jews. The rabbi's speech was much the same: Scholarship was described as the essence of Judaism, and the luckiest man among Jews was a retired man who had the freedom to study Torah to his fill.

"That's right—the luckiest man," Hannah leaned over me to tell Nathan. "And what about the girls who were never taught Hebrew? He doesn't speak about what old women are supposed to be doing with all this freedom, you notice. Our rabbi, may he rest in peace, told me an educated female was a cinder in God's eye. Fortunately he meant educated in religion. So because I was a girl, me they let go to school to study science. For the boys, they got the *real* education." Her sarcasm was unmistakable. Hannah read and wrote in Russian, English, Polish, and Yiddish, but had never been taught Hebrew. She had received three years of advanced secular schooling, but still regretted deeply not being able to read the Holy Books.

Kominsky began to pass out the diplomas. They were standard commercially printed forms intended for children's temple confirmations and graduations from Hebrew school. They carried messages about, "Hope for the future . . . congratulations to ———, who . . . is carrying on our Jewish heritage, who will thereby improve the world and help create a better tomorrow." At the bottom the year appeared in the Hebrew calendar. In the blank provided, Kominsky had entered each elder's name in Yiddish and English. He used the people's nickname and childhood name, most of which ended in the diminutive form commonly reserved for children. These names were generally known but seldom used, names from the Old World, intimate and affectionate; in many cases the elders had not heard them since they had left their parents decades ago. The graduates stood in place to receive the diplomas as Kominsky handed them out. They had wanted a procession, "In the proper way for graduations," but finally decided it was better not to risk a slow, stately walk to the front of the room. They weren't sure they could carry it out with proper dignity. It would take them a very long time, and everyone was afraid of stumbling.

"This part was my idea," Sofie whispered to me with some pride. "I went to my grandson's graduation lately. The class was so big that they didn't dare make a procession. They stood in their places, like we do here. So it's still a real graduation this way."

After the diplomas had been distributed, the rabbi's twelve-year-old daughter and her friend sang some Israeli folk songs, accompanying themselves on guitar. Finally, Kominsky began what he regarded as the highlight of the ceremony. He read congratulatory messages from Israel. These had been gathered by his friends and family there. They had asked for telegrams and letters to the senior citizens from all the important people they had access to. The most precious message came in the form of a tape recording of the sounds of yeshiva students singing and praying at the Western Wall, the remains of the ancient Temple in Jerusalem. (The Wall is the most sacred place in the Jewish world, the *axis mundi* of all Judaism.) The chanting of the ancient prayers brought a rare hush into the hall. Tears of awe gleamed on some of the most skeptical faces present.

Kominsky made his speech in a ringing voice, the Charge to the Class. He alluded once more to the exemplary nature of the graduates. Despite poor health and bad weather, he said, like good students, they came eagerly to the class, their lessons prepared. Limited means notwithstanding, all had their own small library. Though none had had time for formal study during earlier phases of life, from childhood they had imbibed a proper respect for study, and now in retirement, they were able to fulfill themselves as Jews. He finished by explaining the importance of the Law and learning to all Jews:

"For Jews, study is the most sacred thing. The poorest Jew, the most humble, in the Old Country learned to read. This you couldn't necessarily say even for the richest Gentiles. Among us Jews the highest honor we could give to man was to call him 'rov,' which means teacher. All of us here were raised this way. A Jew is always learning. Above everything we are People of the Book."

Jacob Koved, as president emeritus, was called on next.

"What Kominsky has told you is basically true. All of us were raised this way, even those of us who don't believe in God; we have religion because we have the Law. For us all books are religious. Study is religious. Each page and each letter on the page has its own special character, even the white spaces between the letters are holy. A little boy is honored when he carries his papa's prayer book to synagogue on the Sabbath. In the family, when Papa opened his book, all the house becomes quiet. 'Sha, Papa reads,' the mama says to the children, and all the house respect it when there is study inside. When a book is left open, we put a cover over it, for respect. When it is worn out we give it a burial. It's like a living thing. All writing has something of holiness. Even when it's only a newspaper, it shouldn't be used for anything but study. So it is in the marketplace also. Because we are Jews, we don't wrap herring in a printed page."

"Learning," one of the major sacred symbols in the ceremony, had been touched on throughout the afternoon, overtly and covertly. Most obviously, it had dictated the form and flesh of the ritual itself, designed to honor the elderly for studying. The theme was sounded in the use of the honorific term *rov* for Kominsky, again in reference to themselves as "People of the Book," and it wove in and out of the songs and speeches all through the occasion. The particular inflection of the symbol given in Jacob's speech was important. Like the class song, "Oyfn Pripetchok," which they would soon sing, Jacob stressed the close association of learning and childhood experiences.

For the elders, learning was a part of being a Jew, as important as—and for many more important than—prayer. Learning was one of the first acquired, most deeply embedded values they held, thoroughly intermingled with their love of family and home, belonging to that basic layer of religion that is charged with its context of primary, intimate relationships. As such it was redolent with all the emotions attached to those early experiences.

In the shtetl, learning had worldly as well as religious value, for it benefited the individual, the family, and the community giving a certain source of prestige and social mobility. Thus in addition to being an intrinsic good, learning was a strategy for worldly gain. As symbol and strategy, it was a major unifying concern, joining all the phases of the elders' lives.[2] In their middle years in America, learning was no less important than it had been in their childhood society. By their fierce promotion of learning, the immigrants had taught their children the means for rapid assimilation and advancement in the New World. In America, learning had been devoted more to secular matters, more blatantly instrumental; still it retained its aura of sacredness. When studying for his exams in college, Rebekah told me her grandson always wore his *yarmulke,** "because study is study regardless of the content."

Now, in their later years, the Center members were still dedicated to learning. Here it had become a means for expressing the culmination of life. Jews, they claimed, need never stop learning. Old age gave them leisure for its pursuit, endowing retirement with more possibilities than were available to other groups of elderly. Learning was regarded as "a blessing, defiant of time."

But as symbol and strategy, learning was touched with irony and pain. For one thing, most of the graduates, as women, had never been educated. For another, while learning had been the key to their children's success, it was also the path by means of which their progeny had escaped from them and their traditions.

All children leave their parents behind, but the speed and completeness of the break between the generations here was extreme. Their American-born children were exceptionally well-equipped to make their way up and out of the ghetto, and their parents were genuinely proud of their accomplishments. But at the same time, there was sadness and bitterness as well as pride in the elders' talk about their children.

The ambivalent emotions and consequences associated with the pursuit of learning might have presented a problem in a different kind of ceremony, but this was a ritual, and rituals are exceptionally effective persuasive devices. It is in the nature of ritual to be able to "embrace paradox and celebrate ambiguities."[3] The use of symbols, sensations, and performance gave ritual sufficient rhetorical strength to handle the complexities of meanings involved in the Graduation-Siyum. And Kominsky proved himself to be a master of ritual.

Kominsky called upon Abe next, who turned to address the graduates first: "You are our parents and we honor you today. You have given the world the finest doctors, philosophers, scientists, professors, artists, and musicians, fine businessmen also. For this, your generation is rightly famous. Always your children have given you the *naches*† of their accomplishments. Now it is time for you to give them naches of your accomplishments."

* Skullcap.

† Pride; joy.

He turned to the audience to conclude:

"How proud you must be of your parents and grandparents this day. How you can rejoice over them. All their lives, without thanks, they scrimped to send a dollar here to Israel or there to someone sick, never asking for praise. That was just how they lived. Now you can express your appreciation. You, the children they have produced, are their greatest accomplishment, and you are here to show them you understand what they have done.

"Until now," he continued, "their children have taken them for granted. They come see the mama on Mother's Day. She cooks and cleans for two days. They have dinner with her, bringing her flowers she doesn't need, or candy she shouldn't eat. They kiss and hug her around and tell her she's a wonderful cook, then go away leaving her with the dishes, until the next holiday. Now, all that is changed. Now, we realize what these senior citizens have done for us. They are a model. Their lives have meaning. They show us what Jews are, that study is the highest activity for any phase of life. Learning is what makes us stay young forever, so that a Jew, a real Jew, is ageless."

"This is true," said Sofie. "My grandfather used to tell me, 'If you are ignorant, old age is a famine. If you are learned, it is a harvest.' "

"And what do you think my grandfather said?" asked Nathan in return. "I'll tell you. 'When the brain is green, it does no good, even if the hair is gray.' "

"So because Abe makes an announcement and Kominsky makes a big party, suddenly we are sages," grumbled Hannah. Nevertheless, she held her diploma tightly with both hands. Then it was her turn to give her speech. She began to read her carefully prepared text in English, faltered, then stopped and looked up at the assembly. "I couldn't go on in this way without telling you what is really more important than this here party." Her glasses fogged and impatiently she wiped her eyes and blew her nose before beginning again. She spoke about the recent massacre of the Israeli wrestlers at the Olympic Games in Munich. "Jews have always been scapegoats. All right, this isn't new. But the scapegoat is a sacrifice, and for a sacrifice to do anybody any good you have to give it some attention, to think about what the lesson in it is. In that, here is what I see. In America, we mustn't forget ourselves. We mustn't forget we are Jews because sooner or later someone will come along and remind us. We must hold on to our land, Eretz Yisroel, no matter who tries to drive us into the sea. Even though we sit here today in friendship with the Gentiles, we remember there are those who want to destroy us."

Hannah sat down to an embarrassed silence. This unplanned intrusion of people's most agonized memories was jarring and it ruptured the festive mood. Then Josele, who had taken as a second name "Masada" in remembrance of the martyred zealots of ancient Jerusalem, stood up and pulled his satin banner aside. Dramatically, silently, he pointed to a large rip in his coat lapel, signifying he had fulfilled the traditional Jewish requirement of showing mourning by rending one's garments. That it was his coat, his only coat, showed the depth of his grief, for this was usually required only for the loss of an immediate member of one's family. Everyone knew that Masada was desperately poor, one of the poorest people at the Center, and they knew too how much pride he took in his appearance. His clothes, purchased in rummage sales, were always pressed and clean. The dignitaries and visitors were extremely uncomfortable. Kominsky, though, with perfect poise, walked over to Josele and embraced him. He blessed him in Hebrew and said, "We don't forget, Josele Masada, we don't forget, even when we celebrate."

Hannah's and Josele's unplanned, dramatic references to Israel and Jewish persecution were not genuinely disruptive; in fact, they brought into focus one dimension of the other complex symbol upon which the ceremony—indeed the entire Center culture—rested: the meaning of Being a Jew. The actions of Hannah and Masada were socially embarrassing, it is true, suggesting before non-Jewish guests that all outsiders were potential enemies, but at the same time, these reminders of grief in the midst of celebration were quite traditional. It is a Jewish custom and sometimes an obligation to acknowledge the dualistic nature of life itself—at once a joy and a sorrow—and the simultaneous blessing-burden of Being a Jew.

Being a Jew among Center people was a dense and sacred symbol that referred to at least four related but distinguishable inflections of Judaism: the Great Tradition of formal Jewish Law, study, and shared history that makes Jews One People (in Hebrew encompassed by the term *Klal Yisroel*); the local or Little Tradition[4] of Yiddishkeit; Eretz Yisroel, the in-gathering of all Jews to Israel, the Promised Land; and the Judaism of modern America expressed in nonorthodox temples. Symbols referring to all four dimensions were brought into the ceremony—by design and improvisation—throughout the afternoon.

The formal expression of Jewish learning, as a literate, Great Tradition, manifested itself in the use of Hebrew, in prayer, sacred study, and the awareness of the common history of Jews. This aspect of Judaism gave the old people at the Center—and probably most Jews anywhere—the experience of being One People, despite their geographical dispersion and cultural heterogeneity. Each Sabbath, since the Diaspora Jews all over the world study the same portion of the Torah together and celebrate the same holidays in the same language, acknowledging their common membership with other Jews, and this forges an identity among them, Klal Yisroel, One People.

But not all Jews have equal access to the Great Tradition. In fact, very few of those graduating from the Jewish History class at the Center were learned people. They venerated but did not actually practice the tradition of scholarship. Most of the men had acquired enough Hebrew to read the Psalms, to pray, and recite sayings of the sages; most knew some Jewish history, and all had been to cheder. This was all that the pressures of poverty and immigration had allowed them by way of formal education.

The early, strong emotional experiences of the local or Little Tradition expressed as Yiddishkeit (in the case of many members, flavored by contact with Hasidism as well) was the most influential and immediate source of the old people's identification as Jews. As Shmuel had put it, "Yiddishkeit is our culture," the slowly grown, beloved result of long, intimate relationships, "not a thing of nations," not grand or exalted but associated with family, nurturance, and survival. Yiddishkeit was inflected most powerfully in the mama-loshen. Later, Rachel called this dimension of Judaism, "Domestic Religion." With this layer, all Center people had the most positive and sustained experience. It was the warp and woof of what held them together, the stuff of their common childhood in Eastern Europe, in it they were equals and equally comfortable.

The meaning of Eretz Yisroel was nearly as personal and uniting a dimension of Judaism as Yiddishkeit for the Center people. Ever since the Holocaust, they had come to equate their survival as a people with the survival of Israel. Their identification with Israel preceded that however; like Yiddishkeit, it was lifelong. As children, they had saved pennies toward the support of Israel, had learned songs and prayers about returning to the Jewish Homeland one day. Israel was like the Great Tradition in that it linked Jews everywhere despite their diverse cultural backgrounds, and as such it transcended the very particular, local manifestations of Judaism in the form of Yiddishkeit. But unlike the Great Tradition of scholarship, people's responses to Israel were not filled with awe nor were they at all remote. No one was too uneducated or humble to participate in the support of Israel. Everyone felt responsible for Israel—however old or poor, one could make a meaningful contribution. Philanthropy, a custom and a religious obligation among Jews, was also for the elderly an expression of their potency and utility; as such their attachment to Israel was a major ingredient in their success in dealing with their contemporary marginality and poverty. During their early life and continuing into the present, Israel was regarded as a kind of collective child whose existence was precarious and precious, requiring their protection, indulgence, and attention.

Among the graduates, the most shallow and problematic experience of Being a Jew was associated with its expression in the form of modern American non-Orthodox temple religion. American Temple Judaism offered its own special meanings and conflicts, which had to be incorporated into the ritual. For most of the graduates, since their emigration, Being a Jew had come to mean being old-fashioned and un-American. In this country for the first time Jewish identity became genuinely optional. Judaism in America was a somewhat bewildering condition, embarrassing, and a social impediment, never satisfactorily resolved by most of these people. In America, Judaism lacked the firm roots and social supports of a religious community, and the Great Tradition was little help, for it had never really constituted a compelling, immediate way of life for the elders.

What, then, did it mean Being a Jew in America during their middle years? On this there was great variation. Some individuals had expressed their Judaism by joining Yiddish political or cultural groups. A few joined small Orthodox temples. Most had no time for these activities, and Being a Jew became blurred and uneasy during their middle years. The distinctly American institutions referred to in the Graduation-Siyum were the modern, non-Orthodox temples and schools—institutions the graduates had never participated in directly. The features in the Graduation-Siyum associated with the temple were viewed with some indifference by the graduates, a kind of ritual cargo that they had to include so as not to be rude. Men's clubs, confirmation classes, Sisterhoods, prayer in English led by beardless, bareheaded rabbis were not part of Judaism as they had ever known it, mere forms, lacking any emotional resonance.

Save Yiddishkeit, all these aspects of Being a Jew were touched with ambivalence. Most Center members were Zionists, but most were also troubled about the conflicts between their ideological commitment to internationalism and Israel's status as a nation. And many were troubled by Israel's politics—indeed its conduct of itself as a modern, secular nation, a state of affairs that did not coincide with their picture of it as the Promised Land, untainted by worldly compromise.

The old people's ambivalence about American Temple Judaism and their difficulties with the Great Tradition of scholarship were clear. Even more troublesome was the Klal Yisroel dimension of Being a Jew. It was generally agreed, certainly by Center folk, that the ultimate expression of Being a Jew was not praying but taking responsibility for other Jews. "Among Jews one is never lost," was the often cited saying. But it was no secret that these elders were being sorely neglected, by the wider Jewish community and by their own progeny. This realization was always close to the surface, and a very delicate, painful matter it was. No less painful was the uneasy recognition among them that their solidarity within the Center was strained and fragile. In the end, they were all fellow Jews, to be sure, but not family. Internal discord was more frequent and intense than they would have wished, and on ritual occasions, such as the Graduation-Siyum, the harmonious atmosphere was known to be temporary. Being a Jew made them One People. Their sense of Peoplehood was strong when external threats were grave, but correspondingly weak in times of relative peace.

Following Hannah's and Josele's outbursts, Kominsky took firm hold of the ceremony once more, seizing the microphone to begin the final part of the program. "Now we all sing the class song, 'Oyfn Pripetchok Brent a Fayerl.' " He led the class in a nonmusical but spirited rendition of the popular Yiddish folk song and for the benefit of the audience provided an English translation:

On the oven a little fire is burning,
And it is hot in the house,
And the rebbe's teaching the little children
Their ABC's.

See now, children, remember dear ones,
What you're learning here:
Repeat it over and over again,
*Komets A-lef O.**

Study, children, with great interest,
That is what I tell you;
He who'll know his lessons first
Will get a banner for a prize.

To outsiders he explained, "In this song, we got everything: the Yiddish, the Hebrew alphabet, the kind teacher, the warmth of the fire. In this atmosphere, we understand why the Jewish children learned to love study from their first beginnings."

"What he could also say is that mostly the teacher hated these children and couldn't wait to get back to his own study. Mostly the *melamed*† had his little whip and his curses ready for the student's prize," Nathan added.

It was nearly five o'clock. Kominsky concluded the ceremony by leading the audience in singing "Hatikvah," the national anthem of Israel. Before he could leave the table at the front of the room, Sonya took the microphone and on behalf of the graduates, presented Kominsky with a certificate showing that the class had made a large donation to Israel in their teacher's name, enrolling him in the "Golden Book." "We want to make this honor for our *chaver*‡ and our rov. For him we have planted all these trees in Israel." There was a burst of applause, much embracing and kissing, and then the temple confirmation class, some twenty teen-agers, served cookies and punch.

"This Kominsky has very strict ideas," Sofie said to me as

* Hebrew vowel.
† Teacher of small children.
‡ Comrade.

people began to leave. "I offered to bring my artificial flowers today, but he wouldn't have it. No, he said, only real flowers, and they must be in the colors of Israel. When Basha said she would make the cookies, her he also told no, 'This time the old people wouldn't serve or provide.' It was for the young people to serve us, the other way around from what is usually. We got to just sit here and be honored. Meantime, all this is costing the Center a lot of money. To me it makes more sense to send the money to Israel and not make such a fuss over us."

"All right, so let him make a fuss if he's happy. What I ask is, what is the fuss for? What did we learn here? We're not made into educated people from these few classes we had," said Hannah.

"Never mind what we are learning. You couldn't say it was a siyum except someone brought in the schnapps, finally," said Moshe with a quiet laugh. It was true. On the table at the front stood four open jars of pickled herring, two golden sponge cakes, and two bottles of cognac. The seniors surrounded the table eagerly while everyone asked each other who was responsible for the unplanned treat.

"Look how they stuff themselves. *Fressers** they are," said Sofie. "You would think they never saw a herring before. You show them a free meal and they become beasts. This is a bigger embarrassment than Hannah's speech to our guests. I'm ashamed to be in here today." Masada refused to go to the table. He was fasting in commemoration of the massacred athletes.

For days afterward, everyone talked about the ceremony. Pictures appeared in the local newspapers. Many of the graduates felt they had been truly honored by the event. Nearly all agreed it had been a beautiful day, but whether it could be called a "real" graduation or a "real" siyum was still being debated.

Characteristically, Shmuel was quite outspoken in his doubts about the occasion. And with his usual astuteness he had seen through one of the major fictions in the ritual, its most ingenious but precarious linkage of graduation and siyum. He explained this to me as we walked along the boardwalk toward the bakery that had the day-old bagels he liked, "because they're worth the price and better for a man who wants to keep his own

* Gluttons; one who eats like an animal.

teeth in old age. But," he added, "teeth and memory are false friends, the first to leave when a man gets old."

"Mostly what I am objecting to is how they make everything up, from bits and pieces," he said. "What do they end up with, but a *schmatte,** not a well-made cloak, a rag. Look how they are always deceiving themselves. And for this you expect me to be full of respect.

"Let me tell you what a real siyum was like. I remember very well the days in my childhood when I went with my father to his siyum. I told you already he was a saint, but very poor. He was a humble man but educated, all with his own efforts. Only my father of the poor men sat regularly at the East Wall of the synagogue, with the *shayner leute,*† the rich important men of the town. Now on his siyum, he was called up to read the weekly portion of the Torah, a great honor. He came in there, filled with happiness, and also were coming for this occasion his own father, his brother, and uncles. Some from out of town came for this particular day. After the service, my father announces that he has completed his study, which he has set out for himself, and tells what he is beginning again to study. This is a big part of Jewish study, it never completes itself, because the Torah is your lifelong companion. It has no top and no bottom, no beginning and no end. So when he finished this work, from somewhere he brings out herring and honey cakes and schnapps for all the people. Not abundant. Simple, but even so, where he got the money for this I never understood. Everyone toasts him and enjoys his honor.

"So now why do they call this a siyum at the Center? It's a misunderstanding on their part. Because even though siyum means in Hebrew 'completion,' to be accurate you don't complete anything. Your study doesn't ever finish, it goes around again in a circle, as long as you are living. So these ignorant people here, who never had a siyum in their life, who only saw it a few times maybe, are making one for themselves. No, this doesn't make any sense to me. I couldn't take it seriously."

"They improvise, Shmuel," I answered. "Isn't it better to have a ragged cloak than be cold? I don't see what is the matter

* A rag, scrap of cloth.
† Literally, the beautiful people.

with them giving themselves what they never had before. Why is that dishonest?"

"Then they have to do it the right way," he answered. "If they want a siyum let them go to shul and study Torah. But this they couldn't do if they wanted to. They haven't got the background. They haven't got the understanding. So they make it together with an American graduation and call it a siyum. One thing has nothing to do with the other. In America, you go to school, you study, that's true, but that is not religious study, and when you end it, you are finished. You get your diploma and get a job. So if that's what they want, let them be like Rebekah and go to college. This also they haven't got the patience or understanding for. So they put together two lies and call it a Graduation-Siyum, thinking this makes it even better. It is to me only twice as foolish.

"When they came to America, they couldn't wait to get away from religion. Now when they are too old to do anything worthwhile, they go back into their past. In my opinion they are making this party because they haven't got something else to do with their time."

Shmuel's statement that the Graduation-Siyum was the joining of two lies was harsh, but he was right about the extent of the differences between the two ceremonies. The siyum and graduation were forms borrowed from two quite different realms of experience, linked by a tenuous analogy. As he pointed out, the siyum referred to the study of sacred materials, in Hebrew, undertaken by a man alone but in a synagogue setting. The rite marked a cycle of learning without clear stages, since the student always began another round of study immediately without "progressing" toward an end point. The student selected his own materials for study and set his own pace. His work was accomplished in a setting of peers with whom he continued to have permanent relations after the siyum. And a man's study in this context did not lead directly to worldly success. It benefited the individual and the community, but spiritually, not materially or socially.

In contrast, a graduation ceremony came from the American setting, where it is generally the case that students—of both sexes, but one age group—work on secular materials, in English, in a public school. The purpose of the study is to benefit the individual student in making his or her way in the world. The student does not select or pace the materials studied. This is determined by the institution. He or she does this work in a group of peers of the same age but of mixed sexes. The graduation marks the successful termination of study and the class disperses.

Other important differences existed. The siyum was more closely related to the direct experience of the elders; most of the men had been to one or more, as had the male relatives of the graduating women. And the siyum of course was associated with the Center people's childhood world, in Eastern Europe. The graduation, however, belonged to the world of the elders' children and had never been a direct part of their own life. And it came from the middle years, when they were new immigrants with growing children, whereas the siyum came from their early life. These contradictions were apparent and touched on by Shmuel. He did not point out one of the sad and ironic differences between them: In America, the graduation marks the beginning of mature life, the peak moment of possibilities—biological and social—and usually the moment oriented to a long and promising future. That the old people were given diplomas mentioning "a better tomorrow" was glossed over by everyone who criticized the event. Having no future, there was probably little the elders had to say on the subject.

Shmuel did remark on the other painful truth, that the old people were not really equipped to study. They lacked the educational background, and as their eyes dimmed, their hearing faded, their ability to concentrate, to master new materials, and to attend lengthy classes waned, study was more and more a strain. Far from being a lifelong, time-free activity, as the ritual claimed, it was another of the many losses of advancing age.

But most people were not as discerning as Shmuel, and few questioned the connection between graduation and siyum as closely as he did. Together *graduation* and *siyum* were made into a metaphor, used by Kominsky to design and direct the celebration. This metaphor, as all metaphors, linked disparate domains of meaning, treating them as one. The metaphor was then used in the ritual as the basis for selecting certain features from each domain and overlooking others. If ritual is skillful and built on valid symbols, such operations are unnoticed; the seams do not show.

In this case, the siyum domain was the source of the greatest emotional significance for the graduates. And from this part of the metaphor, Kominsky drew the most intense symbolic materials, the symbols and references associated with Being a Jew and learning; most of the ceremony's songs, all its prayers, the Jewish insignias and decorations, all the Hebrew and Yiddish materials came from the siyum domain of experience. The graduation, more familiar to the largely young, American audience, provided the formal materials Kominsky employed in the ceremony—the Charge to the Class, the selection of a valedictorian, the diplomas, the class song, the Pledge of Allegiance, the National Anthem, and the like.

Even one-of-a-kind rituals must be convincing and appear authentic, and certain standard items must be included for this to occur. Sofie worried that in order to be a "real graduation" there would have to be a procession. She satisfied herself, and others, that standing up to receive the diplomas was appropriate and sufficient as a substitute. Moshe, to really feel he was at a true siyum, required ritual foods, especially the schnapps, and fortunately it appeared mysteriously, making up for Kominsky's oversight in omitting such a critical ingredient.

Even though it had never happened before, the Graduation-Siyum was a convincing, authentic, properly traditional ritual to most people present. Sonya was thrilled. "It was a miracle. We had never before anything like that in here. I can't believe we could manage such a thing. For once everybody was cooperative, so dignified, except for a few people who never know how to behave," she added. Some felt the most important part of the event was the presence of the young people. The confirmation class had demonstrated its respect for the elders, and their presence, along with the rabbi's daughter, was taken by a few people as a sign that even in America, Judaism has a future. Hannah disagreed. "What kind of a rabbi was this to teach his daughter Judaism? No beard, no yarmulke, speaking only English, is this a rabbi?"

No one talked openly about the conspicuous absence of the elders' children. Despite Hannah's disdain, many of the graduates framed and hung their diplomas and displayed them alongside the newspaper pictures of the ceremony in their rooms. A few days later, Moshe brought in a story to read to the Living History class to settle any remaining doubts about the ceremony. "This comes from Martin Buber, the great Hasidic philosopher. I am showing it to the ones who say the Graduation-Siyum was not proper. It tells here about two men who are worried about the holiness of the Sabbath. 'What is it that makes something holy?' they ask. They decide to make a test to see what happens when they have Sabbath on a weekday. So they make the Sabbath in the middle of the week, everything they do right, and it feels the same way as on Saturday. This is alarming, so they take the problem to the rabbi to explain. Here is what the rabbi tells them:

> "If you put on Sabbath clothes and Sabbath caps it is quite right that you had a feeling of Sabbath holiness. Because Sabbath clothes and Sabbath caps have the power of drawing the light of the Sabbath holiness down to the earth. So you need have no fears."

"This I am liking very much," said Moshe, "because it shows how with our traditions we can make things in a Jewish way, and when we do this the Jewish feeling comes into them. So in my opinion we should not worry anymore about if there was ever a Graduation-Siyum before. A Jew has got to adapt above all other things. That's how we survived for thousands of years, and so the way we did things here for ourselves was just as good as the old ways."

The ritual was a totally unique event, blending the sacred and secular, and successfully linking two entirely distinct realms of meaning and experience into a strong, convincing ritual drama. It was an occasion that transcended many contradictions, fused disparate elements, glossed conflicts, and provided a sense of individual and collective continuity in the course of mounting a bold and original fiction. Rituals not only have the capacity to gloss contradictions, they may also make assertions that in other contexts would be unconvincing or unacceptable. Such assertions are claims that often mask painful realities that may be disguised or utterly denied. Most conspicuously, the Graduation-Siyum dramatized the elders' interpretation of the meaning of coming to America. In the drastic decision to leave their natal homes and countries, they were exchanging life in the Old World for a new life. It was a trade-off—America brought them gains and losses. They gained religious freedom but lost their sacred traditions by this move. They gained physical safety and security for themselves and their children but lost their families of origin and communities; they gained access to educational and economic opportunities for their progeny but ultimately this led to severe separation from the following generation, and eventually contributed to their present physical and cultural separation from their children. Sonya summarized matters when she said:

> Life in America—what can I tell you? Of course, it isn't what it was in the Old Country. There we loved our parents. Our grandparents lived with us. Now, look at how we live here. . . . On the other hand, I have to say this is a wonderful country. My daughter is a teacher, my son is an engineer. In Glowno my mother couldn't keep shoes on our feet. You know what that means to a parent? So, if here I'm nobody, I wouldn't complain. Nobody needs an old lady like me. It's enough to know I did all I could, and maybe I didn't do so bad.

Emigration brought some fulfillments to the elders, but at considerable costs. In the Graduation-Siyum, they, and Kominsky, chose to stress the gains over the losses. To do so, it was necessary for them to make a set of assertions, overtly and covertly, which were by implication denials of painful contradictory realities. Some of these we have seen: the claim to be perpetual students, trained to love learning and pursuing it in old age when, in fact, little real studying was possible for them. Similarly, they stressed the oneness of Jews as a people, sharing a common destiny, despite the fact that they were badly neglected by Jews and Jewish organizations. And they asserted that Judaism would continue and that, though America was a secular nation, Jews in this country would not be assimilated and disappear. In actuality, however, the Judaism practiced by younger Americans is so different from that known to the elders, and so diffuse, that it is nearly unrecognizable. The most important dimension of their Judaism, Yiddishkeit, was almost certain to die out with their or the next generation.

Finally, the elders claimed that they had realized their most cherished ideals in life by producing children who were educated, successful, and devoted to them. They realize, they often say, that children must leave their parents, that they left their own families to emigrate when it was necessary, and so they understand the distance between them and their own progeny is inevitable. But the truth is that they counted family ties as the only completely trustworthy relationships, and it was excruciating to them to be so cut off from kinship bonds. Covertly and almost unwillingly, they occasionally reflected on this, asking, "Is this what our parents felt like when we left them? Did they deserve such treatment? Do we deserve this?"

In the ritual, the Center people were able to cope with some of their ambivalence about these problematic matters in their life. Throughout the ritual, in Abe's speech and in Kominsky's, less directly in Hannah's and Sonya's, the elders were able to level a set of veiled accusations against those who were neglecting them. It would have been impossible for them to make an overt complaint to their children and wealthier Jews, stating that they were being treated shabbily. That would embarrass all parties involved and be a humiliating admission of pain and need. But in performing their self-definition as a ceremony, by making their protest indirectly and in ritual form, the old people might arouse guilt in those with whom they were angry without having openly to state the agonies of their condition. Their self-esteem rested on the definition of themselves as autonomous individuals, and as providers for the needy. To have stated that they themselves were needy was unthinkable, but in ritual the "unthinkable" may be presented without being consciously "thought." The message may be effectively delivered and received without full awareness on the part of sender or receiver.

Rituals may disguise realities, portray fictions, save face, and convince all parties that matters are in order and in their control. Rituals allow people to maneuver, fight on their own terms, choose the times, places, conditions, and shape of their claims, to paraphrase literary critic Kenneth Burke on the subject of proverbs.[5] Such maneuvering may result in action, encounter, and change, or may end in poetry, "where," as anthropologist James Fernandez puts it, "instead of being moved anywhere we are accommodated in many subtle ways to our condition in all its contrarieties and complexities."[6] In the Graduation-Siyum, the old Jews presented themselves as people of significance and dignity while shaming those who deserted them. In the ritual, they exercised their basic human prerogative, the right to indicate who they are to the world, to interpret themselves to themselves instead of allowing accident, history, and reality to make that interpretation for them. Here eloquently demonstrated was humankind's undying insistence on stating not only that life has meaning, but also specifying precisely what the meaning is.

It is their very nature for rituals to establish continuity. In the Graduation-Siyum, two distinct but related kinds of continuity were provided: the individual's sense of unity as a single person (individual/biological continuity) and the sense of being "One People" (collective/historical continuity). Personal continuity is something not automatically given by experience. It must be achieved. The sense of being the same person over time, despite great change, and sharp disruption in social and cultural experience does not happen easily or inevitably. For this personal coherence, this sense of psychological integration to take place, the individual must be capable of finding and reliving familiar parts of his/her past history. And often, the most important, charged pieces of personal history come up from the remote past, from the numinous events and experiences of early childhood. The elders' emotional response to the song, "Oyfn Pripetchok," for example, was powerful and instantaneous. The song came from childhood, and its sentimentality and homely quality did not diminish its power in the least. In contrast, the finer poem by Bialik was received by the Center people with relatively little interest; it had come to their attention too late and was unattached to earlier parts of themselves. It could provide aesthetic satisfaction to be sure, but never arouse the flood of nostalgia, the original emotions, the sense of being one with one's memories that the childhood song did.[7]

Personal continuity was an especially important concern for these elderly for several reasons: their extreme age; their proximity to death, for the drive to shape one's life into an orderly story often grows more intense as people prepare for death; and because of the drastic discontinuity caused by emigration. Reviewing one's life and reminiscing, much practiced by the very old, are expressions of their attempt to find themselves to be the same person throughout the life cycle. As elderly and as Jews, their striving for a sense of integration and continuity, unity and oneness, were parallel powerful concerns taken up over and over in the Graduation-Siyum, particularly by its inclusion of the childhood layer of experience.

The Center people were aided in building their culture by a number of important continuities that carried over from childhood to old age, continuities that, like their sacred symbols, linked them to themselves over time and despite many changes. Going all through lives of the elderly, in the Old World and the New, were their continuing passions for Yiddishkeit, learning, and Zionism. For many, during their middle years in America, the most important of these, Yiddishkeit, was somewhat eclipsed by their self-consciousness about their immigrant status, their desire not to look like greenhorns, particularly to their children. But now, in old age, finding themselves alone, they were free to indulge their delight in things from their past, and Yiddishkeit was the foremost among them.

Of the three historical-geographical layers that fed into contemporary Center culture (childhood in Eastern Europe; youth and maturity in various urban American centers; old age in the beach ghetto) most of the strong continuities were between childhood and old age. In both these periods certain features were replicated: In both, people lived in small, cohesive Yiddish-speaking communities that were poor, segregated, marginal, physically dangerous and in turned, against the outside world. In fact the Center people often referred to their present neighborhood as a shtetl; this was clearly a nostalgic rather than factual description, but making it clear that they were quite aware of the similarities between the communities they had known in childhood and old age.[8]

The most important single discontinuity of their life involved the dissolution of the family as they had known it in the Old World. The centrality of a stable family group was essential to a Weltanschauung that held that though all Jews were one, nonfamily Jews were only to be trusted more than Gentiles. The breakdown of the natal community, the segmented social relations in American cities, the rapid social change and social and geographical mobility constituted a profound contrast with the stable rhythms of the past. In one sudden leap, the Center elders went from a steady, coherent, predictable folk world, guided by a tight, consensus of family, rabbi, and community, into an entirely different world.[9] But in the end, it was the continuities between the world of childhood and the world of old age that provided the basis for their creation of an authentic and distinctive way of life, albeit fragmented and contrived, constructed out of desperate need, nevertheless to be counted as a major gain over and against the losses in the history of their life.

A few days after the Graduation-Siyum, with the help of Moshe's story, most of the Center people I talked to were pleased with the Graduation-Siyum and inclined to believe that they had accomplished something worthwhile. For most of them, then, it succeeded. But Shmuel remained unconvinced and was annoyed with the others for being satisfied rather than skeptical.

"This just gives them more encouragement for their foolishness," he said. "What I object to is how they refuse to accept reality. They think they can make it themselves. *Oneg Shabbat** they put in the middle of the day. New Year's Eve, the same, and two days early, because it suits them. It's more bobbe-myseh. They live in a dream world.

"And if that isn't enough, also they exaggerate. There is a saying on that, 'When you add to the truth, you take away from it.' What do they know from truth? They collect a few pennies, some old clothes, and they are saving Israel. They learn some poems, make a book report, and go to a couple of classes, and they are now educated people. They will tell you how much their children love them, how their cupboards are overflowing, and they take a bus miles away to a store so no one will see them using food stamps. 'Well,' you will answer, 'so they are proud, they don't want to complain. They don't want to be pitied.' But no, that's not it. Let them have a bunion on their foot and they send up cries to heaven. 'Lord, why am I stricken? Did I deserve this from You?' "

"All right, Shmuel," I replied, "I agree with you, they make things up. But that's what culture is, a set of agreements on how to see the world, how to live and why. They have courage and imagination. Other people would be crushed by their situation. When I see Hannah going out in all kinds of weather to feed the pigeons because they are waiting for her, 'They need me,' she says, I am moved. Or when Basha picks flowers from the

* A ceremony to celebrate the coming of the Sabbath, properly held at dusk.

neighbors' yards to take to the Center on Friday because she thinks they can't have a proper Sabbath without her fresh flowers—you can look at her exaggeration, her skimpy bouquet, or her resourcefulness. I am not as much interested in exaggeration as how they intensify and give significance to ordinary experience. This is a way of living symbolically where everything has added meaning. The Huichol Indians did this, too. I've seen it in truly religious people who find the gods' designs in everything around them.

"So I will agree with you, Shmuel, that it's all made up. They're all telling themselves stories, but not just any old stories. Some of them are very subtle and complex. Let me tell you a kind of story they told themselves in the Graduation-Siyum, about the meaning of Being a Jew." I presented Shmuel with my interpretation of how this symbol had been dramatized and elaborated during the ceremony.

"This what you are telling me shows me that I was certainly right to stay home from Kominsky's party," he rebutted. "I don't have an appetite for what they call Judaism. In my version, it works very well without God or Zionism. I will tell you a better kind of Judaism in my opinion. 'Seeking after knowledge for its own sake, a passion for social justice, the love of personal independence. For this I am thanking my lucky stars that I was born a Jew.' Albert Einstein said that." Shmuel gave me a satisfied look that suggested nothing more could be said on the subject, then with a mischievous lilt in his voice he continued, "And what else were you learning from Reb Kominsky's production?"

"Moshe told a wonderful story to explain why the ceremony worked even though it wasn't really traditional." I repeated Moshe's tale about 'calling holiness' through a ritual. This seemed to impress and sadden Shmuel. He paused and sighed, then resumed speaking in a softer tone of voice. "I will tell you where Moshe heard that. Do you know his father was for all his life a member of the most famous Hasidic court in Eastern Galicia. Many there were regarded as saints, *zaddikim.** Moshe's father was a disciple of the great Rabbi Israel of Rishin. And they were great storytellers. Everything they studied, they made into a story. You would enjoy how they made things up,

* Hasidic holy men.

since you think this is such a fine thing to do. I will give you a story in this tradition that applies to those sad people that Kominsky treats as scholars, who I see as poor lost souls trying to get back what they saw in others but themselves never really had.

"When the great Hasid, Baal Shem Tov, the Master of the Good Name, had a problem, it was his custom to go to a certain part of the forest. There he would light a fire and say a certain prayer, and find wisdom. A generation later, a son of one of his disciples was in the same position. He went to that same place in the forest and lit the fire, but he could not remember the prayer. But he asked for wisdom and it was sufficient. He found what he needed. A generation after that, his son had a problem like the others. He also went to the forest, but he could not even light the fire. 'Lord of the Universe,' he prayed, 'I could not remember the prayer and I cannot get the fire started. But I am in the forest. That will have to be sufficient.' And it was.

"Now, Rabbi Ben Levi sits in his study in Chicago with his head in his hand. 'Lord of the Universe,' he prays. 'Look at us now. We have forgotten the prayer. The fire is out. We can't find our way back to the place in the forest. We can only remember that there was a fire, a prayer, a place in the forest. So Lord, now that must be sufficient.' "

CHAPTER FOUR

"For an educated man, he could learn a few things"

BOBBE-MYSEH

The following excerpts are from the eighth class meeting. I had suggested that people might use the session to make a record of some of the important accomplishments of their life, past and present.

HANNAH: *Barbara dolly, it may be a good idea, but if you get people around here boasting about themselves you should prepare to sit here for a few thousand years.*
(Laughter)

SADIE: *If you don't mind, I would like to start out because I don't have a lot of time today. I want you to know my name is Sadie Leiberman, with one "n." Does the tape get my voice? I want to say that I have belonged to the Mizrachi* for twenty-five years. Today we are having a luncheon. Yesterday I got up early and went to the store. I got there fifteen pounds of apples and stayed up last night almost till morning making apple strudels for my members. For one of my ladies who is sick I made a tapioca. She couldn't eat strudel. Next month, Mizrachi is going to make me "Mother of the Year." What bigger honor could a person get? I have medals, all kinds, pins, plaques. I'm on the Honor Roll in Israel for giving trees. I always help others, especially when I'm getting older. If I had time, I would tell you about my young life. What I've been through, you wouldn't believe it. But I don't like to complain. Maybe all that suffering I*

* Organization of philanthropic, observant Jews with a Zionist orientation.

went through made me want to do for others. I think that's enough. Thank you very kindly for giving me this time. God bless you all. Now if you excuse me, I gotta go downstairs and put out the gefilte fish. Good-bye, good-bye. (She leaves.)

HANNAH: *How she cooks fish, they would all be better off with tapioca.*

SONYA: *She didn't make the fish, she just puts it out.*

HANNAH: *She puts out the fish, everybody should think she made the whole luncheon.*

GITA: *Please, ladies! We are not here to talk about fish, not good fish, not bad fish. I want to take a turn, please to talk about my husband. He is sitting just now outside. He wouldn't like to talk about his life, but it's very important what he done, so I will tell it for him. His name is Hayim. He is a real philosopher, as many of you know. He was a yeshiva bucher.* * *All his life he studied. He was a poor boy so he had to "eat days." For him this was a torture, waiting for someone to take him in, because he was very shy. He slept on the synagogue floor, and for meals, different people took him home. He outgrew the education he could get in his little town, so the town sent him to Lida, then to the Vilna yeshiva. Everybody knows about that. It was like the Jerusalem of Lithuania. But even that he outgrew and went on to Odessa.*

From there, with all his knowledge, he was called up in the army. Now as you know, none of the Jews wanted to serve the czar. Life was miserable for a Jewish boy. They would stay in the army maybe twenty-five years, going out a young boy, coming back an old man. He ran away to America and then his troubles really began. He had no trade, nothing. He was a rabbi. Who needed a rabbi in America? He had no family, no language. Finally, he got a job afternoons teaching at a Hebrew school and mornings he was working as a peddler, with one of those push-carts, you've seen them. Somehow, he managed until he met me. From then on, I could help him out. He told me all this and I wrote it down the best I could. He can't write now. He's got the Parkinson's. He doesn't like to talk about it. Still he is a student, always with his nose in a book. He says he wants to read everything he can before his eyes give out.

NATHAN: *And what good does all this learning do him?*

* Student of advanced Jewish learning.

Does he understand more or does he just say Hebrew words over and over?

BASHA: *Nathan, you are interrupting. You could wait your turn to talk.*

NATHAN: *Why not? At my age, I can wait all day. What else would I be doing?*

B.M.: *Can we hear from Max now? He doesn't speak up very often.*

MAX: *For a big speech, I would like to give it in Yiddish. Moshe can translate.* (Moshe begins, following Max.) *"He was born in Khelm, Poland. Now he is ninety-eight years old. He wants you to notice he does not wear glasses and has not yet got a hearing aid. He wants me to tell you that he walks five miles every day. He built the bookcases in this room. His mother died when he was born and when he was five years old his father couldn't take care of him no more, so he sent him out to another family. He didn't like it there so he ran away when he was nine. He began his first career when he ran to Vienna, going there on the bottom of trains. He went right off to the Judenstrasse and met there some very nice people. They started him out in life by teaching him to become a thief, but an honest thief. He would steal only what he needed to live. Like many Jewish boys he was a good student and soon learned to pick pockets. Finally, he met a French Jew who took him in to learn carpentry. With that he remained the rest of his life.*

"Pretty soon things began to get bad for the Jews. It was happening all the while that he was learning politics, talking to people. He taught himself to read, and read the papers. Jews were wandering in the streets starving like stray dogs. Nobody had work. Then he met a girl, she was an anarchist. She brought him to Turgenev, Tolstoy, Kropotkin. In a little group, they met and discussed things. Finally, things was so bad he went to America, with that girl, he married. It was January twenty-eight, at four o'clock in the afternoon, they got here. In this country, they started again with the anarchists. His wife was always the leader in their family."

BASHA: *I would like to interrupt this here. I knew his wife. I would be witness to what he says. Oh, she was a beautiful woman, long thick hair. An immaculate housekeeper. Very intelligent. Always working for Israel, for politics, having readings and meetings in her home. She gave him two boys. He was a* wonderful husband. And I would not say you could call him just a carpenter. He's an artist. If you could see his work, you wouldn't believe that with those big hands he could do such things.

B.M.: Where are your sons now, Max?

MAX: One of them, the older, is in New York. He's a scientist. Now he is retired. The other one, the baby, he is seventy-two. He's in Israel, a Communist. I supported them in a good way. I learned to be good with my hands from when I was a pickpocket in Vienna.

SONYA: Barbaruska, I don't want to criticize, but there are other people we could hear from, nobody should get too much time.

SOFIE: If you would like to hear it, I could tell you a little bit about my story. Now basically I never had a real education, but in my life I managed to learn a lot. Starting from when I was still very young, the union was my college. This all began when I started living with the other union girls in New York, in a place called Unity House. It was a settlement house, and we were forty girls. That's where I met Moshe, fifty-seven years ago. He was running after all the girls. He had a lot of success with them, but I wasn't interested.

HANNAH: No wonder he had success, with those blue eyes and that big smile. He's still a good lookin' fella.

SOFIE: If you want to hear about that, you'll interview him. Myself, I considered him a bum. You see we were girls with principles. Money and nice dresses and big houses was not our object. We lived cooperatively, everything shared. We knew how to work together. When we got together in a picket line, you couldn't get us apart.

We were first very young. I was only thirteen when I went there. Most of us didn't have families. We were each other's family. One little girl was only twelve. That was Rivke, a quiet shy little thing. She was working in an electric factory. She was in there sixteen, eighteen hours a day. She never complained but at night she would sit and cry. Her fingers were tied up in rags full with blood. We made her quit that job and she learned sewing from one of the other girls. That same little girl, we didn't save her nothing. Later on she got killed in the Triangle Fire. But we did the best we could.

I got to be something of a leader in my shop. I don't know

where I got the strength, but the idea of justice I always had in me. When I was fourteen, the boss in our shop hit one of our girls. That we couldn't put up with. I started it against him treating us like animals. I threw my sewing machine right out the window, from the second floor. All the other girls saw what I did and they did likewise. We all marched out into the street. Pretty soon, we had a big strike going. About once a week, we got arrested. All this happened, I was only fourteen years old, but I knew we were human beings and we had to fight to be treated the right way.

ABE: Before it is growing too late, I'm wanting to take a turn to introduce myself. My name is Abe Beidleman. I was born in White Russia in what they called a kretchma, that's Jewish for a roadhouse. My grandfather was the owner. By our standards in those days, we weren't poor. My grandfather had twelve children, his oldest daughter, Sarah, she was my mother, may she rest in peace. She was one of the important people in the Russian revolution. She was the first one in our town to carry the Red flag. She was what you call a humanitarian, a most dedicated person. She was always well informed. I wish I would have all the characteristics she possessed. In my life, she had the biggest influence. I am dedicated to the peace movement, to Israel, to Jews everywhere. In plain fact, I do all what I can for humanity, perpetuating the ideas of my mother, so that I want to carry that on for her. I'm not so big, like Abraham, Moses, Christ, and Buddha. But you should know, they too didn't want war. Those people left their footsteps on history, and in my smaller way, I may do that also. I'm not boasting. I just want to bring out a few things.

Now, my job is working for the Center. You'll find all kinds of people here that fill the holes in their life with their doings at the Center. What we got to learn here mostly is to be tolerant. Myself, I like communism because I was brought up that way. But if you believe different, I respect that. I'm one hundred percent American, you shouldn't misunderstand.

OLGA: I don't condemn nobody what is a thinking person. But anybody who is a democrat couldn't believe in what Russia is doing. If we had real communism like they have in the kibbutzim in Israel, that would be different. Communism is the highest ideal, but not the way they do in Russia.

HANNAH: Mr. Beidleman, I seen what you do here for the

Center, and you do a lot of good. But I don't approve of the way you talk. When someone speaks to me about Communists I have to walk away. I couldn't lower myself to sit with them because of what the Russians are doing now to the Jews.

FAEGL: *I don't think we should get lost in arguments. We are all Jews here. We all speak Jewish. But that don't make us all alike. Some Jews got blond hair, some got dark skin. Look at Max, he's dark enough to be a shvartzer.* But he's a Jew. We got to remember that our Jews is like a bouquet of flowers, they come in all different colors. All of them got nice smells. Together they are making a beautiful bouquet.*

MOSHE: *What Faegl says is right. You see, I'm not religious, and especially I am not a reader of Marx. But I saw in the army how the Jews run away from themselves. In the army, I was the first man in my group to put down my Jewish name. The reason we were delivered from Egypt was because even then the Jews wouldn't change their names. Anyhow, you couldn't hide it because if you decide you are not a Jew, a Hitler would come along and remind you. As long as we got Hitlers we got Jews.*

SOFIE: *Excuse if I interrupt, it's nearly time for the luncheon. I bought a ticket. It's for a very good cause, even without eating the gefilte fish, which Sadie never learned to make without too much sugar. So I'll be going.*

HANNAH: *Why does everyone think Sadie made the gefilte fish. I told you already, she made only the strudel. She shouldn't take credit for making the whole meal.*

Summer came and the character of the neighborhood changed. Scantily clad, nubile boys and girls paraded up and down the boardwalk. Outdoor cafés opened. Children capered, dogs multiplied. Street vendors laden with foods and handcrafts jostled tourists good-naturedly. Out-of-town visitors came to spend time with some of the old people. The regular contingent of Center summer members returned to the beach as they did each year. Friendships were renewed and the old people lingered on the boardwalk enjoying the luxury of passing the early evening outside of their rooms. The added hours

* Black person.

of light made after-dinner strolls possible, a great delight to all. And the Oneg Shabbat could be held two hours later, since this still gave the elders time to get back to their rooms before dark. The Sabbath candles were lit, if not at dusk, at least not in midday.

Spirits among the Center people were high, because it was summer, and because of the success of the Graduation-Siyum. No one was more delighted with that event than Eli Kominsky. His always high level of energy and enthusiasm was enhanced by the many tokens of respect and gratitude bestowed upon him by Center members.

Kominsky continually generated new projects and schemes, bustling about, in and out of the Center, carrying his tape recorder, which he might at any moment snap on, sending out gusts of Hebrew songs. His luxuriant curls grew fuller and bleached cloud-white in the sun. His face darkened, forming a dramatic frame for his burning blue and zealous eyes. It was exciting to be in his presence. With his unbending purpose, anything seemed possible. Kominsky brought in new members, some of them strange and not quite the sort Center folk were used to. Others who came were fringe people, drawn to the community but until now peripheral. They wanted to be wooed into fuller belonging and this Kominsky did. To all who would listen, he set out his plans for the Center and its members. It was a vision of redemption.

A great many of the elders were amazed. Perhaps it was possible, perhaps they would come into their own, be recognized, appreciated, and flourish. But their mood of growing optimism was shattered by a sudden, ominous blow. The fund-raising campaign conducted by the Alliance to support the several community centers in the city had gone badly. Israel was in crisis and most philanthropic Jews were sending more of their money there than directing it to local needs. A long-dreaded, much-discussed fear materialized: Abe was withdrawn from the Center for one quarter of his time, his services given to another group. This meant a multitude of small and large hardships fell upon the Center people. Abe's availability and persistent support were diminished and, worse, everyone saw in the move the possibility that the Center would soon be closed altogether. Officials had even proposed a specific date two years hence. Salvation lay in two courses: a substantial increase in Center membership and the mustering of public support for the elderly in the Jewish community at large, generating sufficient pressure to make the Center's dissolution impossible. Few people had hopes for either of these eventualities. Cultural extinction was more than a distant threat. Now it was an immediate likelihood.

The times were ripe for a savior and Kominsky relished the role. His Center classes were well-attended and when Jacob Koved fell ill, Kominsky stepped in to fill the void his absence created. He took over the Oneg Shabbat ceremony and soon it attracted more people. The Center underwent a transformation. Anxiety turned to hope and hope to ambition. Cooperation such as had never before occurred among members was now the norm. Everyone worked enthusiastically with Kominsky and for the next five months, he enjoyed great popularity.

An important feature in the events that followed was Kominsky's clear status as an outsider.[1] He was not a leader generated from within the society, thrown into prominence because of his devotion to indigenous styles and norms. He was a prestigious link to the world outside. At first, his outsiderhood gave him glamour and power but, ultimately, it contributed to his downfall. Many of his points of difference with Center people at first worked to his advantage, and theirs. He was younger, more ambitious, more idealistic, and despite his affiliations with the "modern" world, he was more religious and more righteous. Kominsky was more involved with outside affairs, and well-connected to a wide network of important people. He drove a car, was active in external organizations, lived outside the community, was a member of several religious groups and affiliated with young people. These external ties he used as a set of resources, wheeling and dealing with remarkable persistence and cleverness, bringing Center people visibility and concrete services. No one minded the differences between Kominsky and the Center people because everyone knew he had the Center's interests at heart and was very good at "getting things done." Certainly this was a time for action.

But however urgent the need to "do business," basically Center activities were geared to other concerns. This was well-illustrated by the nominations and elections that culminated in Kominsky's becoming Center president. Emotions surrounding elections ran very high always. For months before people voted for officers and the board of directors, electioneering was intense. Coalitions were formed and reformed. Marginal members were assiduously wooed. Block votes of interest groups were sought. Every assembly of more than two was turned into an opportunity for speechifying.

The nomination procedures followed a form and style all their own, developed out of long usage. It was at the nomination meeting, not the elections, that definitive decisions were made. These meetings were arranged to make it perfectly clear who would be elected *if* voting were open and anonymous. Public humiliation was avoided by allowing a person certain to be defeated to withdraw before the voting. The community, after all, was a small group with many offices to fill and few people eligible to fill them. All those involved were on an intimate footing with one another—they knew each other's qualifications and intentions perfectly, and they needed an election only for the purpose of a ritual reiteration of their de facto leadership and social structure. In such a group, leadership is always by consensus. Elections, anonymous voting, majority support, and representation were concepts designed for the regulation of large groups of strangers. But here, it was as though an assembly of siblings were voting for parents. Nevertheless, voting was a very meaningful action, symbolizing some of their dearest values, a completely American act, what modern people did to express political freedom. As usual, the Center people arranged matters to suit their needs, carefully preserving the labels and forms that would permit them to participate in a "proper" political process, participating thereby in the larger society.

Limitations in filling offices were clear and numerous. The president was always a man (with one exception in Center history); he had to drive a car, have access to some of his own funds, had to have a voice and manner strong enough to command attention at group meetings. He needed to be presentable to outside organizations, acceptable to the Center factions—the Talmudists, the Marxists, the Zionists, the atheists, the Yiddishists, and the philanthropic women. He had to know English and Yiddish, should know Hebrew but could not be Orthodox or too closely tied to any of these factions to alienate the others. There were no such clear requirements for the vice-president, nor was the latter presumed a successor to the presidency. In addition to fluency in Yiddish and English, the secretary had to be able to write and spell in English and rapidly enough to take minutes in meetings. If possible, the secretary should have a graceful literary style as well, for the minutes were considered enduring records of the group life that could shed or detract from the Center's reputation. The treasurer needed the ability to keep financial records, and here continuity of personnel was valued above all since the Center bank account was in the treasurer's name and it was a nuisance to change this every year.

The nomination meeting was called to order and chaired by Abe the director. As individuals were nominated, Abe put the candidate's name on the blackboard, along with the names of all who seconded the nomination and wanted their support to be recorded. When no more names were forthcoming, candidates could let their name stay or ask that it be removed by the formula, "I decline in favor of ———," mentioning the person whom they supported. All these names—candidates and all those seconding them—were left on the board so that it was quite clear who was running, who was supporting whom, and what their competitive chances were. This also gave candidates an opportunity to maneuver on the slate by running against those who gave them the best competitive advantage. Usually, by this means, on voting day only a single name appeared on the ballot for each office, reflecting the predetermined consensus. In this year's election, Kominsky was acclaimed president, uncontested and unanimously.

Voting day, as usual, was a solemn affair. People came early wearing their best clothes, acknowledging the ceremonial nature of the event. "Even to vote for Nixon—such a crook I couldn't believe, but he is for Israel—for him even I wear a suit and tie," said Itzak. Moshe was voted in as vice-president, Gita as secretary, and as expected Itzak would remain treasurer. Everyone looked forward to the installation, it would be a grand celebration.

Safely voted in as president-elect, Kominsky's energy and ambitions redoubled. In the months that followed, he was the Center acting president since Koved was still sick. He made it clear from the first that his leadership style would be different from any that had previously been followed at the Center. At his first meeting as acting president, he announced that he meant to have things proceed in a more orderly fashion than usual. "We got serious business here. We can't *daven** over little things. This Center has its life at stake, so you will excuse me if I rush, because our affairs are urgent." He called for the minutes to be read from the previous meeting. This was the secretary's, Sonya's, opportunity to shine. She had worked especially hard at her minutes, recopying them and checking spelling to please the new president with his modern standards. She stood to read them in a bold, proud voice. Kominsky reprimanded the people for applauding, "Minutes is supposed to be an objective record, not a performance. Sonya, you will learn, you gotta keep out the interpretations, like saying that Sofie wore a new sweater from her daughter in Hawaii at the last meeting. That's not business. No more flowery phrases, please. You'll learn, we'll all help you."

Sonya was angry. "But she did have a new sweater. Everyone here saw that. Why is that not part of the record?"

"It's not about Center affairs," he countered.

"Certainly it is. She wore it to the Center. We all saw it." People nodded.

"Never mind, Sonya," replied Kominsky. "You'll learn to do it, very easy."

"Don't argue with our president, Sonya," shouted Jake. "What he says makes a lot of sense. When you talked about the last meeting, you wrote, 'It's a lovely discussion we had.' It was what I call a fight. You should name it the right way. Do like he tells you. Be objective."

Don't tell me I don't know the difference between a discussion and a fight, Jake," she answered. "It's very simple. Whenever you are around, you make the fight from a discussion."

Rachel came in with her comments. "The minutes didn't mention that Sofie paid for the cake and coffee at the last meeting. It should go in the record, because this was a lovely thing for her to do."

"Please, please!" Kominsky's wonderful smile flashed across his face as he banged the gavel on the table. "Rachel, Sonya, Jacob, sha. This is just what we should not be doing. More order, please. Now we go on with reading the correspondence."

* Literally, pray.

Rachel raised her hand and shyly announced that she had a letter from her grandson in Switzerland. "He writes it very big and dark so that I could read it easily. Isn't that a thoughtful boy? 'Dear Grandma,' " she began.

"Rucheleh," interrupted Kominsky gently, "this here is not what we mean by correspondence."

"I know what is correspondence, Mr. President. This is a letter and I am reading it for the members and so it goes into the minutes. Sofie read a letter last time, nobody objected."

"These are supposed to be letters about the affairs of the Center. Just like I said to Sonya, we don't include everything, only our business. Otherwise we never get anything done. Please, Rucheleh, you read it to me afterward. I would like to hear it."

The meeting bumped along until a motion was proposed and seconded. "I make another second," said Itzak. "I also," said Max. Kominsky pounded the table. "We say 'second' because it means what it says, 'second.' Not three and four times."

"But you don't write down that I am in favor of it, if I don't second," shouted Max.

"We don't have to have everyone's name," Kominsky tried to persuade them. "That's why we have a vote. No names."

The motion was passed with one second and once more everyone clapped. Again Kominsky stopped the proceedings to explain that applause was not appropriate. "You will all learn to do these things a better way than you are used to. You have practiced all these things by yourself. That's fine, but if you want people not to think you are greenhorns, you got to learn to follow the rules that everyone uses when they have a business meeting. Otherwise it is not legal. That was good enough for the old days, but now we take on bigger things."

"Mr. President," answered Basha, "please don't *hok* my *tchynik** on this. I was in the union many years. I was one of the big ones in the Emma Lazarus Club. We were the first woman's libbers in America. A lot of history we made there. Please, I know what a meeting is."

Loyal Olga stood and pleaded with everyone to cooperate with "our learned president, who has much to teach us, if we can find the patience with each other getting started in the new ways he brings here."

* Literally, knock my tea kettle; don't bother me with trivia.

After this the meeting proceeded with unusual smoothness and speed. The old people were outside on the boardwalk much sooner than usual. The ordinary high level of energy that was so characteristic of their gatherings was conspicuously absent.

Among Center people, all talk was an intrinsic good. As people in other cultures come together and express sociability by eating, drinking, dancing, singing, flirting, boasting, or mating, Center people expressed their pleasure at being in company through talk. And a debate was one of the most satisfying forms of talk, an intrinsic good, reminiscent of its Talmudic form, the *pilpul*. Courtesy, parsimony, clarity, and relevance were not appropriate criteria for a good debate in their view. Rather it was the ability to ferret out a hidden angle of a question, unearthing a new perspective that others had overlooked—*that* was prized. In the Center people gained esteem by probing the complexities of already well-explored, seemingly simple issues, laying bare secondary meanings, practical applications, unpacking and displaying their analytical powers as they sought meanings within meanings. Among Center people this kind of discussion was called "talking *tachlis*," referring to the probing of a subject until its very heart had been pierced.

Talking tachlis not only had a Talmudic flavor, it was also valued as an American thing to do, expressive of people's independence and citizenship in a free country. The Center people had a strong appetite for questioning authority of all kinds, in part developed in response to exile, in part issuing from their theology, which encourages each individual to actively scrutinize even the teachings of the Lord of the Universe. It was this kind of talk that Kominsky meant when he spoke of "davening" over the minutes. It was a source of excitement, an opportunity for competition, a chance to display one's learning. But it was not conducive to making decisions and using time efficiently.

Shmuel was with me when we left a meeting Kominsky had chaired. As always, his analysis of Kominsky's behavior was acute. "This one comes in here and understands nothing," he said referring to Kominsky. "Maybe he will get his business done, but in the meantime he will break everyone's heart."

"But, Shmuel," I argued, "a strong leader is what they need right now. Look at all the good things he has already done for the Center."

"You can count on what I'm telling you. He comes in here

like a *meshiach*,* and there is a good reason why the meshiach has not yet come to the Jews. I will tell you. If he would come, we wouldn't notice because we would be too busy discussing. He couldn't get a word in. We have a *midrash*† on this. After the Day of Judgment, all the Jews will be found in Heaven. There they spend eternity studying Torah together, at last arguing with the Lord Himself about the right interpretation of His Law. This is the Jew's idea of Paradise. Do we have angels peacefully riding on clouds with their harps playing, like the Gentiles? No, we have a big debate with God, a pilpul in the sky. People who fight with God won't put up with a dwarf who thinks he is a giant. So you should plan on it, that this Kominsky meshiach will not keep these people in his pocket for very long."

Kominsky's efforts on behalf of the Center were ceaseless. He mobilized his friends and even strangers to do all kinds of services for them. He himself drove people around a great deal of the time, filling in for Abe. A former handyman, he repaired their appliances and furniture. He called their children, helped them write letters, intervened with officials in the Social Security office and with various bureaucrats, or arranged for "people of influence" to do so when he was not successful.

As time went on, it became clear that Kominsky had favorites and that antagonizing him could cost people some cherished opportunities for receiving attention. He exercised tight control over the Oneg Shabbat and repeatedly called on the same women to bless the candles. Similarly, he called on the same men to make the blessing over the wine at the ceremony. He had his favorites, too, among the singers asked to entertain at Center functions. He promoted some of the popular charitable causes and ignored others. And he regularly discouraged the women from serving food, to himself and others. With an impatient shake of his head, he rejected the glasses of water the women proffered to him when he became agitated. At important events, Kominsky insisted on having outsiders bring and dispense food, reiterating as he had at the Graduation-Siyum that it was now the elders' turn to be honored and waited upon. His conduct caused only latent annoyance and grumbling among the people until

* Messiah.
† A philosophical commentary.

he made a series of grave blunders that constituted overt violations of their norms and, ultimately, led to the impending crisis. Three such mistakes stood out:

First, he attempted to have the name of the Center changed to honor a forebear of one of the members. He was wooing the member's prominent, wealthy family, which he wanted in his network. This caused everyone embarrassment by its implied elevation of one of their peers to such prominence. It was perceived as a slight to all the others, who technically—whatever their private feelings—claimed to be of equal worth. And because the member in question was known to be a capitalist, an outspoken enemy of communism, Kominsky's action was regarded as self-serving and destructive of the ideological diversity among them. "If he would have his way, he would make us all alike. This with Jews you cannot do," Basha said to me, after she had led the resistance against Kominsky's plan.

A second violation of Center norms occurred when Kominsky, without consulting anyone, canceled a long-planned Center visit to a liberal temple when he learned that the temple had offered meeting space to a group of young Jewish homosexuals. Homosexuality, Kominsky pointed out, was forbidden in the Bible. The other Center members—regardless of their approval or disapproval of homosexuality—were unwilling to insult fellow Jews by canceling the visit. They then discovered that in his capacity as president, Kominsky had canceled it himself. This outraged everyone. "Because he is president, does that make him me? Who does he think he is to tell people what they will and will not do? Does he think I give up my opinions because I give him a vote?" protested Basha. Quite apart from the substantive issue, the idea of one person representing others was not acceptable to the Center people, and Kominsky was seen as arrogant for having acted on their behalf.

Center people were increasingly uneasy about their president. At the Oneg Shabbat the Friday after the temple incident was discovered, Sadie sang a song she had written about Kominsky.

"It's true that somewhere, sometimes, somehow
things go wrong.
It's hard for us to know just where we do and
where we do not go along.

As far as I can see, the situation here is such:
Maybe our Reb Kominsky is doing now too much.

We all here know he always tries to do his best.
But maybe now it's time he thought about a
little rest.

Kominsky's last and most definitive breach of a Center norm occurred when on the members' behalf he accepted packages of holiday foods donated by a Jewish organization for the next Passover season. Basha brought matters to a head at the following meeting. "We don't take charity here. We give it. For a few pennies, they [the donors] get rid of guilt and expect we should be grateful. Nobody here is so poor they couldn't afford a box of matzo. A lot of people here got plenty of money. If anybody don't believe me, I am going to stand up here and tell just what everyone in this room is worth, because this I know. Then we can write it down and send to the people with the handouts, so they should know too. Tell them this is not the way to do these things. If they got what to give away, let them send it to Israel." People felt Kominsky had humiliated them publicly, depicting them as paupers to the outside world.

After this episode, Schmuel told me that great skill was always required in getting people to accept money or gifts that they might actually need. "You see, one year Abe did a very smart thing. The temple sent around boxes of matzo. Abe just stacked them in a corner, didn't say anything. Someone would come in, look at them, and ask about them. Abe said, 'I'm selling them, I got them cheap. What do you think they're worth? Whatever we get we can send to Israel.' That was smart. People paid what they could. Abe sent the money to Israel in the Center's name. Everyone got Passover foods. You see, all this is laid out by our ancient sages. Jewish tradition is very exact about charity. The one who gives must avoid pride and the one who receives must not be shamed. They arranged this in the old days by having two rooms in the Temple of Jerusalem. In one, the Chamber of Vessels, you put gifts for the Temple. In the other, the Chamber of Secret Gifts, were put gifts that the poor drew out in secret. So no one knows who gives and no one knows who receives.

"Now let me tell you what I think our revered president is doing wrong. Where he does not show an understanding is that every Jew wants above all to be a giver. To give is a mitzva. It comes back to you in Paradise. It is said, 'The one who makes the life of a poor man longer by charity, when his time comes to die, he will have his own life lengthened.' Even if you don't believe in Paradise, doing good deeds does you good in this world. And naturally among Jews it also gets you respect. But always the one who must take, he is ashamed, so he fights it off or tries to find someone himself he can give a little something to.

"Now I'll tell you what the president is up to. He is getting all those mitzvas for himself. He hoards mitzvas. He leaves no room for anybody else. And do they say, 'Thank you'? Are they grateful? No. Every day, they get more mad at him, but they can't say why, because they think he is doing them favors and they should be grateful. He is doing them favors but nobody else does so much. They all look bad next to him. He is making them ashamed. Now, he comes out and insults them by taking the *pesach** packages."

Kominsky realized his popularity was waning. This saddened him but at the same time fed his determination and authoritarian ways. The more unpopular he became, the more rigid and abrasive were his relations with the Center people. It was confusing and painful to all who cared for him, and no one knew how to interfere with the escalation. One day, knowing I was friendly with Kominsky, Moshe drew me aside and asked me if I couldn't speak to him, to "try to help him cool off." Moshe understood my delicate position as an outsider; he had never asked me to involve myself before, but for the welfare of the entire group, he put aside his scruples. After some hesitation, I decided I would at least try to talk with Kominsky, though I wasn't at all sure what I would say. We went for a long walk and I finally broached the topic of his difficulties as president.

"My dear little *shiksa*,"† he began. I winced at the term he used to underscore my ignorance of Jewish Law, though I knew he used it affectionately. "Do you think I am doing all this for myself? No, you know me better than to think that. Some-

* Passover.

† A non-Jewish or non-Orthodox Jewish woman.

times it comes to a man that he has difficult work to do. Myself, I don't have very long. You know what trouble my blood pressure gives me. My doctors tell me if I don't change, I can't expect a long life. What does this do? Does it make me want to change? No, it makes me speed up my work.

"A person sometimes knows he has a special reason for being born. Sometimes he knows this all his life, but it doesn't get clear what that is until it is almost too late. I will explain to you something I have not yet told anyone, but now you should understand to help you get hold of my purposes. It all begins with my mother. She married very young and within a year she gave birth to a girl, my older sister. About fourteen months later, I was born. Then my father went to America with big plans. While he's gone, she gives birth to twins. Right then my sister gets sick and dies. So bereaved is my mother, she cannot take proper care of the twins, so she gives them to a girl friend to watch over, six weeks old they are. And that girl made their formula, I don't know how, but somehow the infants got poisoned and died. So here is a young woman, twenty-two years old, with this kind of tragedy, her husband gone, she loses three children within one week.

"It happens then that I get sick, the same sickness of the kind that killed my older sister. She runs to the doctor and begs him to come. 'Give the boy what medicine you have from the girl, that's all what I could do,' he tells her. He knows she is a poor woman and he couldn't charge her proper, so he didn't want to bother. So she told me, she is going from house to house, crying, asking if anybody could help her.

"As she does this, an old man stops her and asks her for money. His garments are dirty, his hair is long and ragged. She starts looking through her apron pockets, keeping on crying through all of this. She says, 'Here's your penny, now leave me alone.' He says, 'No, I don't want your penny. I want to know why you're crying.' And he is persistent. She cannot shake him off until she says, 'I lost three children three weeks ago and now my only child is sick and the doctor doesn't want to come.' So he says, 'Please take me with you. I want to have a look at your child.' She thought he was out of his mind. But he is persistent. 'Maybe I could help you,' he tells her. 'It couldn't hurt. I'll come and pray for him.'

"My mother is very religious, even what you could call superstitious. So when he starts to talk about praying, she is thinking, 'He's right. It couldn't hurt.' And she takes him home with her.

"Into the house he comes and takes one look at me. He feels my head and then asks my mother to bring a mirror. Now a mirror in the Old Country is not like a mirror here. Because the flies, for some reason or other, they do not lay their eggs on the windows as much as on the mirrors. They would leave there their droppings. Now the old man instructs her to wash the mirror, then he takes that water and gives me to drink."

"Wasn't she frightened to give a sick child dirty water?" I asked.

"Frightened, yes, but she is already under his spell. And she is a desperate woman. At any rate, my fever was so high there was not much to lose. He makes some signs there, having to do with magical powers, I don't know what. These were not Jewish concepts but things the Jews took over from the Gentiles.

"Now before she went out to the doctor, she had sent a messenger to another village to bring my grandfather. And at this time, my grandfather comes running. Though he was an old man, he ran all the way, hearing from the messenger that his grandson was dying. And he comes into the house and looks at that beggar. By then my fever had passed. My grandfather takes my face in his hands and looks at me. Then he turns to my mother and says, 'Why did you scare me? The child is well.' The beggar then kisses me on the head, smiles at my mother, bows to my grandfather, and walks out of the house.

" 'Oh, father,' she said, 'he cured the boy.' 'This was Elijah the prophet. He's always coming around as a pauper, doing miracles,' my grandfather told her. That was a prevalent belief in those days. These ideas had roots in our people. Now, if you ask me, who was that man? I would have to say, I don't know, maybe just a clever man who wanted to make a young woman feel a little better. He was a beggar, but he understood humanity. By appearing in itself, this is a sign of hope.

"This is a story all my life I knew but I never paid much attention to it before. I lived my life in the best way I could. Now my life is close to finished. It comes to me more strongly such a happening is not something to slight. Before this, I tried to live a good life, keeping quietly to myself, what we call a *nistar*. This refers to goodness that is hidden. But when I realize

I don't have all the time in the world, I make the crossover into the world, this we call the *mefursam,* that means 'revealed.'

"This comes to us from a midrash that says there are thirty-six righteous men, the *Lamed-vav,* in the existence of the world. In each generation is coming one of them, and he holds up the world, so great is his justice. He may not even himself know he is such a one. Then there is no problem, but if he knows, he has to choose to remain hidden or come forward for his people. They say the one who remains hidden is the highest, but, myself, I believe the highest is the revealed one because he has to bend away from all kinds of temptations in the world. He is always in danger because of this. He has to be careful with his power. He shouldn't become too proud. But still he doesn't want to stop his work. There are times in our history when the work for our people is more important than the life of a just man. No one is loved for this work. But when justice goes in one direction and love the other, the righteous man goes with justice."

Neither my efforts nor anyone else's succeeded in tempering Kominsky. A great many people were very angry with him by now and this made him terribly unhappy. But still he did not change. Shortly after our talk, a dispute about money arose at one of the Center business meetings. Some funds were unaccounted for.

Kominsky turned on the treasurer, Itzak, and demanded a record of all Center income since Kominsky had been elected. Itzak was bewildered. He had never before been asked for such a thing.

"Don't you keep records?" Kominsky demanded.

"Naturally, I do. I got them right here." Itzak emptied his pockets on the table—bits of torn paper fell out, bearing a few Yiddish characters and numbers.

"These I got from today. The others are at home in a cigar box. I didn't put these ones in yet."

Kominsky was outraged. "Is this what you call a record?" he thundered.

"This is how I always done it. What's wrong? Is something missing?" Itzak was puzzled and hurt. "I could tell you from these just what we got. On Sunday, came in over one hundred fifty dollars for Israel. You want me to tell you who gave what?"

Kominsky pounded the table. "We cannot conduct an organization this way! You got to have a different kind of record. You need a book, with the names and addresses of everyone who gives. And they got to get a receipt for their taxes."

"Who around here got enough money to pay taxes?" asked Sonya incredulously.

"I used to have a little book, but lately my eyes is not so good and it's hard to get all the writing in. I'll show you if you want to see," answered Itzak humbly.

"No, this is no good. On Sunday came in a lot of nickels and dimes. How do we know who gave it, where is it all? No good. I want to appoint a committee. We have to have a better record. A cigar box full of papers is not a report. I don't accept it. Also, I want the records to go back for a year or longer so we don't have any accusations of hanky-panky. No one should say we are *gonifs*."*

There was a great commotion. No one could believe that Kominsky had the nerve to demand records preceding his arrival.

Meekly, Itzak turned to the people around him. "Does he think I line my pockets with this money? Does he calls me a gonif?"

Kominsky had grown very red in the face and shouted people down as they objected. Olga appeared with a glass of water, "Take it easy, Reb Kominsky," she said. "Remember your blood pressure." But it was no use. When resistance continued, Kominsky threatened to go to court to get the records. "People can't get along without records!"

Moshe made his way to the front and took the microphone, attempting to restore calm. "Maybe we should have more specific accounting, but we're not built that way. We're bad accountants, but that has never upset our unity before. From time to time people say, 'Where does all the money go?' We do the best we can to help keep a record. But we follow our ways, and this here is our style of life." After more discussion, it was Moshe who suggested that a committee be appointed to do an investigation, "To make it one hundred percent legal."

"No," Basha replied. "We need trust. We don't have such

* Thieves.

a stream of money coming in that we have to do things that way. This is an insult to our treasurer. He should be treated with dignity. He is one of us, he works hard for us. Now he's got this trouble with his eyes, that don't mean we have to throw him out. We can't put him now in the shadows when we're done with him."

"OK, if you are going to behave this way, you won't need me." Kominsky was so angry he hopped up and down. Olga pleaded with him to take a drink of water, but he was implacable. He gathered his papers and tape recorder, jerked his yarmulke off his head, and left the room. People were momentarily shocked into silence because however much they raged and clamored, such a withdrawal from each other's company almost never occurred. It was an extreme and punitive gesture.

"Is this a mensh?" asked Basha. Sofie said, "He's acting like a *meshuggener.** He gives us a bad name, with such a commotion. All the benches are operating, calling us fools on this. He makes us look crazy in the outside world."

Moshe tried to leaven things. "He's nervous. He's not a well man." Nathan said, "With all his good intentions, he don't know liturgy." Basha persisted, "Either he should make a proper meeting or resign. He tries to tell us the right way to do business. This is not how."

Olga, always Kominsky's supporter, said, "He brought life into our Center. No one will come in here without him. He is dedicated to Judaism. So, he is a little hardheaded, anyhow we got to stay with him." "No," rebutted Basha. "He doesn't understand us. We got a good system, which don't make you corrupt. We don't have enough money to worry. You can cheat with records or without. It's the trust that matters."

"He livened up the Center, that's true," said Sofie. "But he does not have an open mind. He don't like Communists. Everybody here was a Socialist, a Communist, an anarchist twenty years ago. A Jew is a Jew, this is basic. You see what happened. When he came in here he thought he was a *gantzer macher*† and would run the Center. But he was a newcomer. He doesn't understand our democratic process." She moved that a note be

* One who is crazy.
† Very important man; one who gets things done.

sent to Kominsky, offering "to help him become the kind of president we want him to be, telling him we want to go back to the way we used to do things." This was generally well-received and the meeting broke up amid continuing excitement. Hannah when she went by, said to me, "How could he lead a proper meeting? Everyone here has his own meeting."

I spoke with Kominsky briefly outside. He asked me, "Do you think I did the wrong thing?"

"I have to tell you, I don't agree with you. I think that the people's feelings are more important than keeping records and running things according to standards of efficiency."

"No," he thundered at me. "This makes a farce of what we do. It makes us look like greenhorns to the world. This is America. If we do things seriously, we do them in a proper way."

People remained in the Center talking for a long time after Kominsky left. "This one is acting like a *Yekke*,"* said Jake. "The trouble with him is that he is too dedicated," said Olga. Moshe shook his head sadly. "Shalom is healthy. But not to act like this. An organization is sick when there is such conflict between people. Look how much conflict he brings to us."

"We had conflict before he came. We'll have conflict after. For this we don't need him," responded Basha.

"He doesn't show us respect. He brings in outsiders when we ask him on Wednesdays to talk to us himself in the Yiddish History classes. Some outsiders are good, but we shouldn't be so impressed with them that we don't have time for ourselves," commented Sofie.

"Wednesdays here for me are like the Sabbath. It's worth all the heartache he brings us when he teaches us about Yiddish history," said Olga.

"He teaches us about his own life, and that he calls Yiddish history," contradicted Jake.

"This thing with the money is crazy. Does he want us to sit by the door and keep people from coming in if they don't pay? We are a Center, not a policeman. The Center is not a business. I have belonged here fourteen years, and if we get a little money or a lot, it isn't so important as how we behave. We're here to have harmony, first of all," concluded Sofie.

* A German Jew; one who is stuffy and overly formal.

"Most of all, we shouldn't be distracted from working for Israel," said Basha.

Abe offered his interpretation of what was wrong with Kominsky. "What matters here is that people can express themselves. People have to learn to listen to each other. This is more important than what gets done. Kominsky wants to build empires. He's impatient. He is burning with his dream. But the people here don't want to delegate. They want to be important themselves and they want to speak for themselves. He monopolizes too much. All of them, they sit in their little rooms all night and in the morning they come in here like coming back into the world. If nobody talks to them, they could go all day without hearing their own voice. He doesn't want them to talk so much. This is impossible. Nobody here is going to sit still while he pushes them around. They don't care about motions, they don't even hear them. What they remember is the discussion. They chew that over on the benches outside for days. That's what matters, not what actually comes of things."

"Does anybody think the note to him will work?" I asked.

"No, it's a terrible suggestion. He will resign. He can't change." Basha was adamant. "Nobody can think or say he owns the Center. We all got as much right as any president. He'll have to make up his mind to do things in a civilized way." Said Rachel, "What he did to Itzak was not civilized."

"This place is going to the dogs!" shouted Jake as he left.

I went back into the Center to get my coat. The room was empty except for Rachel and Itzak. Quietly, she placed a glass of water in front of him. Itzak's wife had gone home and brought back his box of receipts and money. He was shuffling bits of paper from his pockets into piles on the table, tears sliding steadily from beneath his glasses into his cigar box.

The note was sent soon after and Moshe, Abe, and Jacob Koved had a talk with Kominsky to "try to straighten him out in a civilized way." They came back from it with hopes that Kominsky would stay with them and try to accommodate to "their democratic process."

The Installation of Officers took place a few weeks after Kominsky's outburst at Itzak. It was a grand and expensive affair with flowers, rfereshments, dignitaries, and a couple of surprises that Kominsky had arranged. On his own, he had invited a Hasidic rabbi to make a speech at the installation. The rabbi was a fervent man, extremely Orthodox, and a member of a proselytizing Hasidic sect. Kominsky had recently renewed his acquaintance with the rabbi, seeking consolation and guidance concerning his growing conflicts with the Center people. In the course of their contacts, Kominsky had had a kind of conversion experience, a renewal of his faith; this appeared not to be widely known among members. The rabbi's presence caused a stir. He was a large, stern man with a full, square beard and wild black and white eyebrows that were prominent even under his black wide-brimmed, fur-trimmed hat. His powerful frame was covered from chin to ankle by a black gabardine caftan, traditional Hasidic attire. After the officers had been installed, the rabbi began his speech in Yiddish, telling the people there how fortunate they were to have a man like Kominsky take an interest in them, since without him they would be forgotten and neglected. He likened Kominsky to a tzaddik, a Hasidic holy man, who had come to bring them back to the proper observance of their religion. He continued, saying that Kominsky had recently realized his mission among them. Dramatically he announced that Kominsky would begin this work by establishing a kosher kitchen at the Center.

This news was received in momentary silence. Then people broke into excited side conversations. "Kosher? What for? None of us keep kosher at home. We left this behind when we came to America." And that was true. Unfortunately the rabbi and Kominsky had selected one of the least meaningful religious symbols of Judaism to resurrect people's identification with Judaism. The custom of keeping kosher had been abandoned by many even before they left the Old Country. Only Kominsky was really observant. Center members were willing to overlook this in him, but certainly would not let it be foisted upon them. Despite their surprise and annoyance, the members were loathe to be overtly rude to the rabbi and they allowed him to continue his speech without speaking up. He went on to talk about the plight of Soviet Jews, a subject of widespread and grave concern. "Our hearts and our work must be with those who want to emigrate, those who are the *true* followers of Moses. *They* are the Jews who must be saved," he said.

This was too much for Basha. "Do you suggest that the Jews who are not observant should be left behind? Kominsky, you agree with him in this?"

Kominsky stood up, cleared his throat, but couldn't find words. He seemed unwilling to disagree with the rabbi, but he was obviously distressed by the implications of his remarks.

Basha had no patience with this temporizing. "No, this won't be any good. Which one of us leaving Russia would qualify by such standards? None of us would be here now if only the observant escaped the pogroms. I can't go along. With God, without God, with kosher, without kosher, a Jew is a Jew." It was clear that most people agreed with her, and the din mounted quickly. The rabbi scowled at the group, nodded to Kominsky, and abruptly left. Abe took the microphone and insisted the ceremony be completed.

The next day, the Center officers and the board of directors met and agreed that Kominsky would be asked to resign his office. The installation could have been an occasion for reconciliation. It was a ripe moment, when differences might have been glossed, unaffiliated individuals and disgruntled factions drawn together in a ceremony that emphasized their common goals and destinies and drew attention to the need for solidarity in the face of external threats. Instead, it provided the basis for the members' final repudiation of Kominsky. There was no possibility of reconciliation after the rabbi's blunder, evidently supported—or at least not rejected—by Kominsky. Everyone agreed that Moshe would make a good president.

The resolution of the crisis consisted of Center people going over and over what had occurred and what it had meant; in the course of "talking tachlis," they assured themselves that however painful this experience had been, it was unavoidable and perhaps had been for the best. Kominsky, they agreed, had brought them life, had brought in new members, had recognized in them possibilities not seen by others. But his presence wasn't worth it, after all, they concluded. "Nobody could treat us that way and expect us to be grateful." "He was too grandiose." "He only saw in us what he thought we should be, not what we really are," they said. "So we learned as usual, that we struggle to be ourselves. This is nothing new. We have always done that and it's not the time to quit because you're eighty-nine or ninety," said Sofie. "Fortunately, in this we have good training. At our next meeting, Moshe will knock the gavel and once more we will be ourselves. We are all working for the same objective—not to let our Jewish life be smashed." And Sofie gave the word *our* a special emphasis.

Kominsky reappeared briefly from time to time. One afternoon, we walked together again and he explained to me how tragic he felt his career at the Center was. He spoke about his dashed hopes and disappointments with great sorrow, then again became furious. "What they did to me, putting me out like that, is like the fall of Jerusalem. They have insulted me in public. To insult a man is like murder," he quoted in Hebrew. "But I won't let it go. That wouldn't be my duty. Too many criminal things go on in this country and we don't stop them. I couldn't be quiet about what goes on here." When I asked him what he meant by this, he said that he had initiated plans to take the Center, Moshe, and Abe to court, to force them to reveal all their financial records, making them prove that they were not thieves. What could he possibly hope to accomplish by this except public humiliation for all involved, I asked. He answered, "The great Maimonides said, 'When there is no way to give the truth except to insult ten thousand fools, overlook the anger of fools and save the truth."

This afternoon, Kominsky was not wearing his lower dentures. His once glorious smile was now lopsided and disturbing. Flesh on his face hung loosely, but his eyes blazed as brightly as ever. I was worried about his health but refrained from asking.

Evidently, Kominsky had managed to insult quite a few people on these short visits. Basha reported that he had told her that Itzak, once a butcher, was always known to have a "heavy thumb, before with his meat, now with the Center's money." Then he told Sofie that he had made great sacrifices to come and work among them. " 'For you I came back from Israel,' he tells me," said Sofie. "Who asked him to come? Did I send for him? He picks us up and puts us down like a sack of potatoes when he doesn't like how we are. And we should be grateful? I'll tell you something. He drops us, but we go on. Even after Moses died, the people went on without him," she concluded emphatically.

Said Rachel, "He thinks we murdered him because we insulted him. He never gives a think to the insult he gave to

Itzak. After that happened, Itzak cried for a week." It was Moshe who finally found the formula for persuading Kominsky to drop his idea of a lawsuit. "I told him not to ruin a Center which raised fifteen hundred dollars in one day for the Yom Kippur War in Israel. This he agreed to." Jake's final comment was, "I'll tell you something. I know what I'm saying, not only to hear the sound of my own voice. The Jewish people always had their own way of doing things. Likewise we got our own ways and this he don't conform to. For an educated man, he could learn a few things."

In a number of ways, life did not go on as usual after Kominsky's departure. Olga, his supporter to the end, was so hurt at his being "thrown away" by the Center that she took back the Sabbath candlesticks she had donated, and she stayed out of the Center an entire month. And Itzak refused to continue as treasurer. His eyes had grown steadily worse. Shortly after, he had a stroke.

Moshe was pleased to be president. "Whoever would think that a working man, a paperhanger from a little town in Poland with no education would get to be one day, a president?" Sofie was pleased also that her husband was president. It meant that he had to give up playing pinochle with his friends in order to devote his time to Center work. The kosher kitchen was never mentioned again.

In a tradition that still awaits the Messiah, Kominsky's appearance and promise of redemption had strong emotional resonances among the Center people. They soon realized that they were not yet to be saved, except by their own efforts, and this was not new, or crushing. Kominsky's career at the Center was explicable in terms of several issues that shed as much light on Center culture as on the man Kominsky. His behavior was important, to be sure. He had been insensitive, overtly ambitious, and eventually dictatorial, conduct his constituency would not tolerate from anyone. That he was a stranger in their midst was also important. As president it gave him some advantages: His potency and visibility to the outside world resulted from his outsiderhood. But in fact he was not an indigenous leader. He shared and valued the common heritage that bound him to the others, but he was utterly blind to their way of running their affairs. Basha summed it up when she said, "This Kominsky is like a man who is deaf. He comes across a bunch of people with fiddles and drums, jumping around every which way and he thinks they are crazy. He can't hear the music, so he doesn't see they are dancing."

Kominsky "hoarded mitzvas," as Shmuel put it, and this too contributed to his downfall. He elevated his own importance and power at the cost of others' need to be givers and receive public honor by their generosity. With him around, everyone was put in the "taker" role. Kominsky dominated the stage and used up more than his share of opportunities to be visibile and esteemed. This conduct proved to be more important than he ever realized, for underneath it lay the fact that Kominsky and the Center people had two contradictory understandings of politics and its purposes; he and they behaved in terms of opposing, unconsciously held models that were operant though never articulated. Kominsky's model came from the outside society where efficiency and order were primary concerns. He wished to effect a radical separation between personal elements on one hand, and "doing business," on the other. But this model—so much used in a bureaucratic society that it sometimes seems natural—is in fact culture-bound, appropriate to certain social situations, where large groups of strangers assemble to conduct specific and limited affairs. There impersonality and rationality make for better functioning. But such standards and styles are utterly wrong for intimate relations where people have primary bonds and live together on a full-time basis for long periods. In families, tribal societies, villages, and small communities, for example, leadership is consensual and decisions are organically generated by virtue of shared values and life-styles. The social context in which such relationships are embedded can never be cut away leaving only narrow instrumental concerns. Sentiment and obligation are not to be simply defined out of relevance; obdurately, they cleave to goals, agendas, and rules designed to eliminate them.[2]

For Center folk "politics" was an idiom for seeking visibility and receiving attention. They preferred it to other idioms they might have used because it implied seriousness, Americanism, modernity, power, and democracy, and it had esteemed associations with the outside "real" world. Politics generated opportunities for being seen and honored at the Center. This was the heart of "business" rather than as in other circumstances accompaniment or undercurrent. Voting, holding ning meetings, collecting dues, seconding motions, minutes, and the like were the terms in which the elders could establish and accredit their worth. But in the meetings he conducted, Kominsky regularly shut off these opportunities in favor of getting the Center's business done.

The desire to be counted publicly as honorable is certainly a universal human concern. But some societies lavish more care and time on the matter than others. It would seem that there is often a direct, inverse relationship between people's actual effective power and their passion for publicly enacting their honor.[3] Oppressed peoples whose lives are largely determined by forces beyond their control are often preoccupied with "face," and develop subtle gradations of worth and honor in various terms—precise variations in skin color, minute distinctions of dress, and the like. Economic impotence, social inferiority vis-à-vis other groups, removal from centers of authority and influence are among the conditions leading to a great concern with honor. Socially disdained groups have to find their own standards, generating internal codes for taking each other's measure. Only by doing so can they avoid the devastating consequences of judging themselves in the terms used by people who disdain them, in whose system they will always amount to nothing.[4]

The Center people had two special problems in applying their standards of worth, both associated with their advanced age. In stable societies where the elderly have lived together for their entire life-span, one's accomplishments during the productive years can be used as standards of worth and honor. Those accomplishments are ever-present in the memory of peers who serve as natural witnesses. Everyone knows and remembers what has gone before. The past record of successes and failures is automatically used in valuing the elderly. When people have been uprooted and no longer live among those who witnessed their life, where no future accomplishments are possible because there is not enough time left them, they become completely dependent on their colleagues to voluntarily agree on their worth.[5] Others are needed to attest to one's claims concerning the past. Lacking peers or family who had witnessed their history, Center people for the most part could only turn to each other for validation, and it was usually given grudgingly. Hannah's comments on this were apt. "You notice around here you can always find someone who wants to *kvetch*.* But *halevai*† you get news that your grandson got a scholarship to medical school, you want someone to *kvell*‡ with, all of a sudden eyeryone goes out the window." Sofie agreed sadly but rationalized, "You know why this is Hannah? To sing a song of joy to one whose heart is breaking is to pour vinegar on a wound. What else could you expect?"

To allocate respect publicly to a peer when one feels ignored or disdained takes great character and generosity, perhaps more than can be expected of ordinary mortals. Center people shared each other's griefs and struggles more easily than their joy or successes.

Without natural audiences to be witnesses for their life, Center people were invisible to the outside world, and in some instances, invisible to themselves. Among the very elderly, the engagement with the present was often tenuous. Some had already departed as fully sentient creatures. Buried deep within their own body, they reappeared among the living only occasionally, and then it was as though they were visiting a familiar country in which they no longer made their home. I noticed this for the first time in watching some of the women slowly lower themselves into a chair, touching carefully behind them to make sure the support was where they expected it to be. On seating themselves, they instantly and momentarily fell asleep. Then their lower jaw would fall open as though released by a catch. Quickly they would awaken and their eyes would search desperately for the gaze of another person. At first I thought the urgency behind that search stemmed from embarrassment at being seen sleeping. Later it seemed to me that they needed to reestablish human contact, to be certain that someone else *saw* them. Then they knew this was not a dream, they were awake and still alive. All their losses—of strength, energy, sensory stimulation, and physical contact—fused into a bedrock of fear of losing their awareness of existence—something different from the fear of death. Some people in their midst seemed to fade away, as if the color had bled out of their countenance, leav-

* Complain.
† It should only happen.
‡ Rejoice.

ing behind vague forms. These people no one spoke to, no one greeted or touched. Periodically, they came back to life, in a short, sharp outburst of singing, dancing, praying, fighting, or eating, emerging from behind a veil as fully realized presences. Seen from outside, the contrast was shocking. What it felt like from within was impossible to know.

Even the very active, energetic people came more completely alive when looked at. An opportunity for attention made them shine. An interview, a camera, a tape recorder, or simply an ear, any indication that a record was being made of their existence vitalized them. This hunger for being seen made my work both easier and more painful. It was impossible to do justice to everyone who wanted attention, and even for those given attention, it was never enough. Attention was the scarce goods in this community, the dynamic that gave life its unique form.

Lacking assurance that their way of life would continue, finding no consolation that a God would remember their name, unable to draw upon their own body for evidence of continuing vitality, they turned to each other and outsiders to serve as willing or unwilling witnesses to their dramas of existence. In their collective life, they showed themselves to themselves and proclaimed their continuing reality.

As well as seeking opportunities for appearing and making a public record, they also sought to establish their relative worth, ways of making their honor, vis-à-vis each other. Among them high to low, the opposite of honor was not shame but invisibility. Being neglected was more unbearable than disgrace. When it appeared that Sadie was not going to be either an officer or a member of the Center board of directors, she was near tears. "I am humiliated to have anyone know I am a member, but my name wouldn't appear on any programs. Who would know I belong?" And when she was forced to leave the community for a brief hospitalization she worried terribly that she would be forgotten before she returned. "Write down my name, Barbara dear, in your notes, so you would have it in the record while I'm away," she asked me. When Gita was not asked to sing or to say the blessing at the Sabbath ceremony one week, everyone knew she would soon seize the microphone, tell stories, sing or harangue on any subject as long as possible, to make up for her neglect and to demonstrate her existence in no uncertain terms.

Even people without claims to being of special worth

could "appear" by their own devices—having their name entered in the minutes, making a motion, being a member of the board, holding an office, organizing and running an activity, hanging a painting on the wall, being mentioned by name over the public-address system, being quoted by someone—all were markers of existence and a degree of worth. Evidence could be brought in from the outside, a letter from a child, an award made by an organization, a gift, as documents of existence and means for "appearing." But these acts required getting others to pay attention and thus were risky. Opportunities for being seen were limited and fiercely competed for; giving the attention to one did indeed mean withholding it from another.[6]

A major method for demonstrating one's worth was the raising of funds for philanthropies. Rummage sales, luncheons, dances, entertainments, selling tickets to raffles were commonly used. Women dominated this arena for gaining honor and the tab was strictly kept. I was astonished once when Sonya spontaneously recited to me exactly how much money I had given to her charity over a two-year period, and just as exactly, how much I had given to some of the others.

Other arenas in which the Center elders could calculate worth were more amorphous, particularly doing favors, good deeds, or giving gifts. One's honor was enhanced by giving and correspondingly diminished by receiving. "The poor man and the rich man need each other, the rich man more than the poor" was the saying quoted on the subject. With everyone resistant to receiving, giving was difficult, complicated by the fact that the doing of favors for others had to be made visible in the group to endow honor. And if in the process of giving one shamed someone else, honor was lost, not gained. For a long time I was puzzled when none of the gifts I had given to individuals were brought into the Center. They were gifts that I specifically intended to be available for display, thinking that this would enhance their value to the recipients. I didn't realize that the embarrassment aroused by having "received" overrode anyone's desire to bring into the Center a public mark of friendship with an outsider. But if I failed to display a gift that one of them had given me—a scarf or piece of jewelry or book—I was sharply criticized by the giver. I had denied him or her the opportunity of making visible their act of having given to me.

There were other ways of gaining honor in the community, for example, being "up to adversity," showing a capacity for "suffering well." But as with all other opportunities for visibility, suffering well had to be translated into public display. Others had to acknowledge one's proper suffering, and this they were not usually willing to do. And there was competition for this honor too. Competitive complaining was elevated to an art among them. If it was too strident, one was obviously not "able to take it," and the complaining was then damning. Thus complaints took a particular form; adversity without neediness had to be established, requiring first that one indicated the enormity of his or her pain, then showed how well one had withstood it. If the audience left before this two-phase strategy was complete, it had failed and it lowered instead of raised the complainer's honor.

Honor was always accorded to those who were dignified, but demonstrating this had its difficulties. In the intense activity and noise of the Center, a person with too much dignity might simply be ignored. Being dignified was antithetical to the competition for it in the open arenas. To be noticed honor had to be already well-established by other, clear, irrefutable markers. Very few individuals were consistently referred to as dignified, though this was one of the highest accolades meted out. After dignity, demonstrable learning, intelligence, verbal skill, generosity, and energy were also treated with great esteem. Extreme age, if not accompanied by any loss of clear-mindedness, enhanced the other honorable qualities. Ability in singing, dancing, artistic skill, writing, and telling stories was also much esteemed among them.

The disdained people were the *meshuggenehs*, the crazy ones, and the *am ha-arez*, the ignorant, noisy individuals who continually created disturbances. The crude, selfish, mean people received contempt, while the genuinely senile or psychologically disturbed were ignored and pitied, and this was seen as the worst of all fates.

Honor and worth, it must be noted, did not coincide with leadership or participation. Often those individuals most revered were quiet and somewhat withdrawn from the hurly-burly of group life. Leadership was situationally determined. The leader of one kind of activity was not necessarily prominent in another. This seemed attributable to two factors: role-parsing and power limitation. First, roles and duties of all sorts were finely split so as to be shared by as many people as possible, allowing for greater participation in collective affairs and at the same time diffusing leadership and power.

Second, power was carefully though not always consciously limited among them. A person with the tendency to gather too much influence or control was leveled sooner or later. Center people's independence and antiauthoritarianism were too highly developed for them to allow themselves to be actually led. They were extremely sensitive to any form of tyranny or arrogance. In their religious tradition this attitude was promoted, and it was validated by their own personal histories. They had made a series of independent choices for which they had paid dearly. They had always fought for freedom and that trait was not confined to relations with government authorities or religious officials. They applied it to each other and their daily lives. Because stable leadership never lasted, the groups' capacity for common action was weakened. But from their discord their alliances were built. By refusing to be too impressed by each other—or anyone else—they guarded their own standing in the group too, for if no one was much above them, neither were they much below anyone else. When a leader emerged who was too strong, they formed coalitions and consolidated against him, eventually reestablishing an egalitarian situation. They were in no one's control, just as they were in no one's debt. Thus, they experienced little gratitude and avoided obligations, though this cost them favors and services. But their independence was evidently worth the price.

Considerable strain was generated in their collective life when in the course of time, they grew needier, felt more invisible, needed to establish more clearly than ever their worth and independence. They responded to greater need by generating more ceremonial and political activity, but this was not satisfactory; they had less attention available for each other. They were caught in a descending cycle of diminishing opportunities for visibility and escalating needs for being seen. Perhaps the cumulative tension this created explained the greater pitch at which their crises seemed to unfold over the years.

Center life was a constructed world that served as a frame within which the people could appear—be seen, act, interact, exist.[7] Just as they had made up a culture, they also made up opportunities for appearing in it, giving themselves a stage in which they came into full being, enacting their continuing life. Center politics provided one of the most reliable and satisfying arenas for visibility. In the end knowledge of self is requisite to complete consciousness; consciousness requires reflecting surfaces. Cultures provide these opportunities to know ourselves, to be ourselves, by seeing ourselves. As a mirror, Center politics served its purpose well.

Shmuel and I chewed over the matter of Kominsky's departure thoroughly. I was surprised by his attitude, less critical of the Center people than usual. I told him I thought that Kominsky's behavior had been very demoralizing for the elderly at the Center. "No," he disagreed. "This is how they get to be strong. This is why our Jews stay on, outliving all their enemies. When the enemy comes from outside, this is not so hard. But when the enemy is one of your own, then you are tested, then it is harder and even more important you do it the right way. He was a true enemy to them, but they never humiliated him. He did all that he did to himself. They did not bring him down and they did not bring themselves down. Throw him out, they did, but that is another thing. Now, I'll tell you the funny part. Kominsky was a religious man, but he was not a good Jew. What he does with them there, this was not Judaism.

"There is a famous story about the great Rabbi Hillel, have you heard of him? A heathen came to him and said he would be converted if the rabbi would teach him all of the Torah while he stood on one leg. And he succeeded. He converted the heathen. He said to him, 'Here is Torah: What is hateful to you do not do to your fellow. That's it. All the rest is commentary.' So for all Kominsky's quotations from the Bible, and his *tefillin** and his kosher kitchen, he insults people and when they answer back he gives them a *potch.*† For all that the Jews are so impressed with education and wisdom, and impatient with foolishness, in our traditions a very big difference occurs between being a fool and being simple. Itzak was a simple man, a good enough man, that's all. Is Kominsky's blood redder than Itzak's, he somehow has the right to destroy him? To destroy a man is as though you destroy the whole world. This is from the Talmud.

"Kominsky knew nothing about *koved,* that means honor.

* Phylacteries; boxes containing passages from Scriptures, worn by Orthodox men for morning prayers.

† A jab or hit.

The Jewish sages taught that one gets honor only by giving it to others. A true Jew is supposed to have sympathy, modesty, and benevolence. Did Kominsky have these? I have to give the Center credit for putting him out. They were not long taken in. They know a good Jew from one who is not, even if they couldn't always practice it themselves.

"This is my opinion. Tell me now what you are thinking from all your studies in anthropology."

I explained Victor Turner's notion of a social drama to Shmuel, those moments in social life when events unfold in a classical, predictable sequence—a build-up phase, followed by a climax and resolution. In Turner's scheme, there are four stages: a breach of norms, leading to crisis, followed by redress, concluding with realignment of social relations when a new equilibrium is achieved. Kominsky's career fit Turner's notion well. The first phase consisted of his violation of several major Center norms; interestingly, Kominsky's overfulfillment of the presidential office, his extreme zeal in pursuing business at the cost of human relations, his excessive devotion to his role as spokesman, protector, and giver of mitzvas were norms whose breach consisted of Kominsky's immoderate dedication to them.[8] Repeatedly people tried to check him, teach him their ways with growingly overt measures, but this failed. Grievances with Kominsky enlarged, spread throughout the community, and the second phase began—the crisis—when Kominsky was installed as president. The final and irrevocable breach occurred then, and redress was only achieved by expelling Kominsky and replacing him with Moshe. The drama did indeed conclude with a new arrangement of social relations, Kominsky out and Moshe the new leader. As often happens, final resolution of the crisis involved an evocation of one of the group's most basic general symbols, adherence to which helps provide their unity. The need to support Israel, in this case, unified the members and disarmed Kominsky, who cherished that as a symbol of Judaism no less than they did.

But just as dear to the Center people as the fate of Israel was their equally Jewish commitment to the value of the individual, to their love of personal autonomy, and the allowance for diversity among Jews. Paradoxically, Kominsky proved to be less open-minded than the Center people in spite of his greater dedication to modern American efficiency. They achieved a kind of triumph by standing together against a threat to their unity, distinctiveness, and independence. After Kominsky, they were ready to make a new start. Though their rebellion against him cost them much pain, it gave them real moral power. They had struggled to remain the same and through the struggle clarified their identity.

The social drama was also a *definitional ceremony*, one of many I witnessed during my contact with the Center. Kominsky left behind a few lasting achievements, a few lasting blows to individuals, but his most significant heritage was giving the old people an opportunity to resist him and, in that way, renew their commitment to their beliefs, their ties to each other, and clarify their understanding of their identity by having once more performed it.

"What all this shows me," said Shmuel, "is that the Jews are still not ready for the Messiah. An old story. Whenever people turn to someone for salvation they come to sorrow—if they turn to God or to strangers with wavy hair and blue eyes, it's the same thing. When you let yourself get caught up in someone else's dream, you got to expect consequences."

"You know, Shmuel, I've been thinking about a conversation I had with him when he told me about an incident in his childhood. He was very sick. His mother believed that an old man who was the Prophet Elijah cured him by giving him water to drink that was used to wash a fly-soiled mirror. Have you ever heard of such a thing?"

"This I have not heard of," he answered, "but that doesn't mean it couldn't be. The people in those days had many strange practices, a lot of them. Especially when it came to health, they would use even Gentile charms. I knew some rabbis who said if your life was involved this would be acceptable. Now tell me this, what are you going to do with this information you got about the mirror if you don't understand it? Are you going to put it in your book?"

"I suppose so. This work is in some ways like what we call salvage ethnology. You save all the information, even bits and pieces that you can't fit into the pattern because otherwise it will be lost. Someone else might understand it, in the future, even if I don't."

"So now you want me also to give you things I don't understand? Don't you take on the job of separating the wheat from the chaff? Who is going to do that if not you? What kind of work does that make it? It isn't science. It isn't history. It isn't art. You are cooking together here a *tsimmes** from all these things you pick up. A carrot here, a prune there, in it goes. You could get a full meal from it, but it's not a proper dish."

"I suppose you could call it a tsimmes, Shmuel. I agree it's a curious mixture, not authentic in the sense that it's made out of fragments of the original culture, randomly saved and used. The old ingredients are mixed in with new ones that just happen to be at hand, sometimes renamed by people to make them seem traditional and authentic. But in the end all culture is made this way. It's never legislated. It's what people agree on. You must admit, Shmuel, that this concoction is nourishing even if it isn't made according to the original recipe.

"Anyway, I often collect things when I don't know what they mean, and then a long time afterward, I run across something that explains them. In the short time I've known you you've told me things that become clear like this, after the passage of some time. So I can't always decide what is wheat and what is chaff. I have to make choices as I go along and leave a great deal out, but I don't have any way of telling ahead of time what that will be. Picasso once said, 'When I paint, my objective is to show what I found, not what I was looking for.' That applies to anthropology. Let me give you an example. Some time ago you were speaking about Yiddishkeit. You said it was like your mother, you couldn't curse it because it was your own, a part of yourself, so there was no formula in Yiddish for cursing a mother. Now recently I read somewhere that the only way to make a curse really effective is to include in it the name of the cursed person's mother. The idea of the connection, perhaps even a shared identity, between a Jew and his or her mother is there again. Not completely revealed yet, but more may turn up. Maybe you didn't even know this yourself, but here is an important idea percolating up into your life, probably absorbed in your childhood without your awareness. I could have left it out as chaff, and so could you. For now, I try to keep in the record as much as I can, even if it makes it inelegant.

"Now I want to ask you about something else that Kominsky told me that I don't understand. He spoke about the hidden and the revealed 'just' men who are the foundation of the

* A sweet stew made of whatever vegetables and fruits are available.

world, the Lamed-vav. I think he had decided that he was such a man and that it was time for him to reveal himself when he came to redeem the Center people."

"Yes, all this is traditional," Shmuel answered. "The Hasidim had the belief that the highest form of tzaddikim were the hidden ones. The ones who put themselves out for others were always a little bit suspicious because they could be wanting glory. The hidden one, *nistar*, is for this reason the highest type of wise man and the revealed one, *mefursam*, is not so high, just because of this possibility, so this is why the highest type remains hidden. That means that anyone around you, no matter how humble or ugly, could be such a one. From this you could get the idea that once I told you about. You couldn't be sure you know anybody. Always they can surprise you. So from this you are learning to treat your neighbors with respect and an open mind. Who knows, he might be Elijah, or a Lamed-vavnik.

"In your record you shouldn't leave out maybe the most important mistake that Kominsky made. His kind of Judaism put people apart from each other. If he makes kosher, how many could stay inside the Center? If he puts being observant over being a Jew, what happens to all those Jews who are not? He puts a barrier there they couldn't pass over. I wouldn't deny him that the members in the Center are not efficient. Kominsky was a macher. The others also want to get things done, but in their own way. In between a *luftmensh** and a macher is a mensh. And this he was not."

* A dreamer; one who is not in this world.

CHAPTER FIVE

"We fight to keep warm"

BOBBE-MYSEH

B.M.: One of the things I would like to talk about today has to do with something Sonya brought up last week, the practices people used in the Old World that today we might call superstitions. These are often very interesting and I think it would be worthwhile to record some of them here. Sonya, last week you told me about the evil eye.

SONYA: Yes, I could talk about this. When I was a little girl, I was very pretty, such a shayner maidele,* everywhere I went, people would adimire me. But it began that I got headaches, for no reason. One day before I went out, my mother kisses me good-bye and touches quickly her finger in the ashes, then on my forehead, so fast I hardly noticed. I didn't think more on this until I caught my face in a shop window. I had a black spot where she touched me. 'What is this Mamaleh?' I asked her. 'So you shouldn't get no evil eye,' she said. They believed if a girl was too pretty people would be jealous and give them the evil eye, so you put this mark on them to spoil too much beauty.

MOSHE: And do you think these things get any results?

SONYA: I couldn't say. I could tell you that I didn't get no more headaches after this time.

MOSHE: Maybe this is a reason I should be grateful for all the dark spots I get on my face from old age. At least I don't have headaches.

NATHAN: All this talk makes me glad I converted to an atheist. In the old days you could never be sure you were safe

* Pretty girl.

from demons. Between the cursing and the evil eye and all the things you had to do to protect yourself, you didn't have time to make a living.

B.M.: What were some of the things you could do to protect yourself?

MOSHE: Fortunately, you see, all the demons who carried out these things were not blessed with intelligence. You could fool them very easily. You say, 'kayn aynhoreh,' we put it together quickly, it comes out 'kana hora,' no evil eye. This you mention every time you give a compliment, to show you are not wishing evil on the person. You see, the demons were very jealous. If things went too good for you, they would be mixing in. If you count things, showing for instance, how many chickens you got or how many healthy children, you say, 'nicht eins, nicht zwei,'* the demons won't notice. Also you could say everything backwards, even you say 'evil eye' in Jewish the opposite, you call it 'git oyg,' the good eye. This confuses them. Or if you come around somebody you think wants to do you harm, you spit three times tu, tu, tu, because demons are afraid of spit.

BASHA: You don't have to believe in demons to believe in curses and evil eye. It shows somebody wants to hurt you when they do that. The angry look from someone can hurt you, never mind demons. The same with a curse. Myself, I don't believe in these things, but it doesn't hurt to be careful.

NATHAN: People use these against each other. When you make the 'fig' around someone, it shows everyone you think he is up to no good, they should watch out for him. [He inserted the thumb of one hand into the clenched fist of the other.] This is because demons are scared off by dirty gestures.

MOSHE: That one isn't Jewish. It comes from the peasants.

OLGA: Maybe that's what all the hippies do with the finger in the air all the time. They're scaring off demons.

JAKE: Because hippies are Pollaks, tu, tu, tu. (Several people laughed.)

BASHA: I don't like this kind of joke. Jews shouldn't laugh at anybody's customs, even Pollaks'. You know what they think about our customs, also it looks to them meshuggeneh. There's a saying, 'Religion for one, superstition for another.'

* Not one, not two.

MOSHE: I'm agreeing here with Basha. Where do you draw the line between religion and superstition? This was something my mother and father could never agree about. My father had a big respect for demons, my mother thought this was foolishness. She would do things but always had an explanation different from my father's. So in my house, she always told the children never to sleep with the windows closed. It wasn't healthy. Even if it was freezing, you left open a little crack. Likewise, nobody could go into a room and close a door tight. It was like you wanted to be outside of the family life. According to my father this was also good advice but not for the same reasons she gave. Because the demons didn't like to be shut up, so always a window or door was left a little bit open, not to make them angry. Like Basha, I don't believe in these things but even now I don't sleep so good when the windows are altogether closed.

The same used to occur on Habdala.* On Saturday evenings, my father would light the candle. All the house was coming into a hush. He would put up his hands to the flame and look into his thumbnails to read in the candlelight that showed there what would come to us for the next week. Then he would pour a little wine on the floor. My mother said this was to make our cup less full because we were grieving for the memory of the destruction of the Temple and all the Jews who did not have a full cup anywhere in the world. It was a Jewish custom to do this whenever you had abundance so you shouldn't become forgetful of others in your joy. By my father it was also because the demons liked a little wine, so if you shared with them it might put them in a better mood through the week. (Much chuckling at this.)

OLGA: You could make fun, but it doesn't hurt to take precautions. A lot of strange things happen. The other day, I'll give you an example. I crossed the street over by the Safeway. Very busy. I thought to myself, this is a dangerous street. They should put up a stoplight. The next week I came back, there was a stoplight. Well, I wouldn't say I made it happen, but *there it was.*

NATHAN: My father, as you know, was a rabbi. But he was not an ordinary rabbi. Many people believed he had special powers, especially when it came to finding out who was respon-

* Literally, separation; the ceremony that ends the Sabbath and marks the beginning of the mundane week.

sible for sending someone sickness. People from all around would bring him things, like the yarmulke from a man who had a strange sickness or bad luck, and he could tell from that who was making mischief against him. They thought my father had a magical element that made his prayers and his curses work.

BASHA: *That's true. Some people have the magic, and some don't. I've seen people, like sometimes a nurse or a doctor, they got a magic touch. They just touch you and right away you feel better.*

HANNAH: *Dolly, a lot of them got such a magic touch, right away you feel worse. There are some people around here also, I would say, got the touch.*

OLGA: *How is it, Nathan, that your father, a rabbi, would give out curses?*

JAKE: *In those days, everybody gave curses. You couldn't live without it. A woman there was on our street who could curse like Heifetz plays the violin. The things she would fix up for her enemies! 'May your teeth get mad and eat your head off.' 'May you inherit a hotel with one hundred rooms and be found dead in every one.' 'May you have ten sons and all your daughters-in-law hate you.' 'May all your teeth fall out but one, and that one has a cavity.' 'May your chickens lay eggs in your neighbor's house.' 'May the gypsies camp on your stomach and their bears do the kazotskhi in your liver.'*

BASHA: *This last one you are getting from Sholom Aleichem.*

JAKE: *And where do you think Sholom Aleichem learned it?*

HANNAH: *From Jacob's neighbor? Jacob, I never knew your neighborhood was so important.*

The Passover season was supposed to be a time of rejoicing, but this year a mood of despondency hung over the Center. Kominsky's departure was followed by a period of relative quiet, and quiet for the Center folk was bewildering, even frightening. For all the pain he had caused them, Kominsky had also done them many services and favors, and these were now much missed. Then when the time came for him to renew his license, Jake failed his driver's test. His eyes had got much worse. He had been one of the few individuals with a car and had taken people to doctors, stores, distant bus connections, and the like.

While it was true that he charged them for rides, it was still a great help.

Now there was a rumor that the landlord of one of the big hotels on the boardwalk had received a government grant to refurbish the place. The fifty-six Center members who lived there were afraid that after renovations he would raise their rent. This was strictly illegal, but landlords had found ways around government regulations before. The old people were trapped. No other housing was available to them nor could they hope to increase their income to cover higher rents.

The withdrawal of so much of Abe's time in the Center was a major hardship. Hannah received a small fee for acting as manager. It was her job to open the Center in the mornings when Abe was not there. But she was not reliable and people often found themselves locked out. This was very demoralizing. They hung about outside, looking in the windows in uncharacteristically silent disappointment. They were not even mad, because there was no one to be mad at. Hannah did her best. Abe had no choice. As if things were not bad enough, it was announced that no funds were available for a Passover celebration this year. The most important family holiday in the Jewish calendar would be spent by nearly all the old people in their rooms, alone. Just when it seemed that things could not get worse, word was received that the umbrella organization that sponsored the Center was again considering closing it entirely. This was no rumor. The possibility had been discussed at an important public meeting and the Center people had got wind of it. At last they were informed that if the Center was to remain open, they would have to bring in new members, and quickly.

The crisis was clear. Hard, collective work was their only hope. As well as finding new members, they would have to struggle to keep any of the old ones from leaving, particularly those who had been drawn in by Kominsky's charisma. Just at this time, when unity was most needed, an old quarrel between Anna and Sadie broke out once more, with renewed ferocity, fed by the general anxiety. Sadie was threatening to leave the Center and take her followers with her, and she planned to do so before the board of directors were installed the following month. Ordinarily, Sadie's fulminations would be taken with less alarm. She had said such things before without doing them, and everyone knew she did not want to leave. But now there was so much general anxiety that her threat was taken very seriously. Abe had little energy to handle the quarrel. He was weary, discouraged, and angry that now of all times he was not permitted to devote himself fully to the Center.

Desperate for a solution to this problem, Abe had used an option he didn't like, calling in an outside expert, in this case Dr. Cohen, a clinical psychologist whose services were paid for by city funds. He consulted with Dr. Cohen and they agreed that group counseling would be best, since by now so many of the Center members were quarreling. A series of four sessions was planned, and an evaluation following that to see if they had been effective. Abe gave the psychologist some background on the Center, the members, and their history. Apparently he spoke about the interpersonal conflicts, but glossed the nature and extent of the antagonism between Anna and Sadie, perhaps so as not to prejudice Dr. Cohen, perhaps because he was somewhat embarrassed by it. And Abe knew, as everyone did, that in a sense the quarrel was not, in fact, "discussable," as we shall see. Some strategy was needed, some means for going around it to a solution. A frontal attack would fail, but what that strategy might be, no one could foresee.

Abe had to be very delicate in telling the Center members that an outsider had been called in to help them. The word *psychotherapy* would have to be avoided; to them it was treatment for crazy people. Their pride had to be protected. Appearing foolish, needy, pitiable, old-fashioned, or superstitious before a stranger would be devastating for them. Abe was vague about the nature of Dr. Cohen's visit, suggesting it was a kind of class; they would be hearing a lecture on mental health. He made sure the entire board of directors and all the officers would be there, and hoped for the best.

Shmuel didn't think much of the plan.

"What will happen now is like what always happens," he said. "They will carry on like peasants, shouting, interrupting, not hearing what anybody says, not hearing the doctor, then they will compliment him on his lecture, tell him how much they learned from his class, how they always want to learn—People of the Book, after all—just like they do with your class.

"When they finished with this doctor he wouldn't know

what happened to him. Maybe he will learn something. Anyhow, you could be sure he wouldn't do them any harm, and this you couldn't say for all doctors." Shmuel permitted himself a rare laugh, his thin shoulders bouncing up to the bottom of his enormous ears.

He also filled me in on the background of the quarrel between Anna and Sadie. It began eight years ago, when they "both set their eyes on the same man." The women were physically opposite but well-matched in determination. Anna was one of the small ones—a scarf—always carefully dressed in gaudy, flowing gowns with matching hats or scarves that she made herself. She alone of the Center women dyed the gray out of her hair, wore nail polish and makeup, painting a dark, precise circle above and below her flat lips. She wore no glasses, though she needed them; her eyes were round and blue. Anna loved to dance and required no partner, not even the cooperation of her legs. Somehow standing still and alone in the middle of the dance floor, she created a sense of fluidity and abandon, throwing her head back, twisting her shoulders and hips, snapping her fingers in the air, clasping her hands behind her back, Cossack-style.

Sadie was a great boat. She exuded the unconscious power of a natural force as she stomped across the hall in her heavy flat, black shoes, scowling at obstacles, her black and white braids wound grimly around her head, folding sunglasses snapped up over her bifocals, like the visor of an armored knight entering a tourney.

"This Anna is mostly quiet, what you call a lone fox," said Shmuel. "Rich and stingy, a bad mix. She is smart with her money and she has lived out three husbands, so she got their money also. She owns some apartments, some that people here live in and she charges big rents. For this no one can forgive her.

"As for Sadie, you can see for yourself what kind she is, an ugly mouth, a fishwife, but a *starker*, that means she is a strong one. She raises money for charity and never lets you forget it. She gathers around her all the little bobbes to boss about, doing work for her Jewish Hospital Club. These are women mostly nobody would bother with, until they need them for votes or to buy lunch tickets. Then Sadie can bring them in. So here you got two women, both strong and mean. Nobody respects them, but everybody is a little afraid of them, especially with this fight, nobody wants to get between them."

"If this is such an old quarrel, why is it coming up just now?" I asked him.

"Sadie was in the hospital when the time came to pick the board of directors. Usuaully, she has arranged it so Anna never got nominated. This time Anna saw her chance, so while Sadie was away she got her name entered. Sadie comes back from the hospital and finds Anna is going to be installed. Sadie meanwhile is crazy with anger because while she was away, Anna told some people Sadie was so sick she would probably die. This you don't do to someone, not when they are sick. This they consider very bad luck. So now everyone is mad, but Anna is already voted on the board, so Sadie can't do anything about it. She is telling everybody that she will quit the Center and take all her friends out with her if Anna is installed on the board."

"Why is it so bad to talk about someone sick?"

"Look, I will tell you something that shows you what people are like. Anna, they say she gives the evil eye. You know this is nonsense. But people believe it still. Anna and Sadie, when they had their fight, Sadie gave a *shelten*. That means she gave her a curse. I don't know what she said. These women, what they wish on each other you could hardly imagine. So Anna made this curse on Sadie in front of everyone and the next week Sadie went to the hospital the first time. Now all this puts Sadie in a pickle. She thinks she got sick from the curse, but she doesn't want to say so because then she looks old-fashioned. Anna is not so proud. To get at Sadie, it's worth it to her even if she looks superstitious. So Anna now can just sit without giving a word from her mouth, and Sadie is helpless. This Anna, the quiet one, is not so dumb."

"Do you think that most people believe that the curse made Sadie sick?" I asked.

"Who could say it didn't?" answered Shmuel. "Maybe the curse makes her blood pressure go up. Who knows what causes a person to get sick? Do you?"

"No, and I do believe that people can effect each other by wishing them harm. There's nothing mysterious about it. Bad will and hostility do influence people's state of mind and that certainly affects their bodily health also."

"All right. Now here's the important thing. Anna never

called back the curse. Sadie gave her a chance in front of everybody. She accused her of giving the curse, and Anna didn't say anything. She could have denied it then, but she didn't, so that means she still wanted Sadie to suffer. Now after that, a second time, Sadie goes to the hospital and Anna makes like this is her doing. She puts her bad tongue to work on Sadie while she's sick. She tells people she put Sadie in the hospital again and she could do it whenever she likes. This makes Sadie wild.

"Now if Abe lets Sadie quit the Center, he's got troubles because she could take out a lot of the women with her. Sadie doesn't want to leave, that only punishes her, but she can't stand it the way it's going. A lot of women now are more respectful of Anna. Not so dumb, that one."

"Doesn't this involve the men?"

"No, mostly these things are among the women, concerning jealousy—about a man or money or food. Always somebody is jealous, someone else gets too much, someone else gets too little. Whose fault is it?"

"Shmuel, that's exactly how witchcraft works in a primitive society, especially among people who have no official means to regulate their affairs, no formal punishments, courts, or laws to control deviance." I explained that especially in groups where people are supposed to be equals, witchcraft beliefs are used to cut down those who are too powerful or too wealthy. The inequality arouses general resentment, envy, and fear, feelings that are then attributed to the witch, who, people suppose, likewise has hostile feelings toward them. Jealousy and projection are the key ingredients in witchcraft. Usually the witch serves as a scapegoat, carrying the blame for all kinds of miseries. So you see, witchcraft beliefs serve many purposes at the same time. They account for otherwise unexplained misfortunes, they clarify group norms and define group membership by labeling deviants as enemies. And often the mere accusation—and all the disapproval it carries—is sufficient to bring about a change of behavior in the witch, so it also serves as a social control. "Very often witches are both rich and stingy, just as you have described Anna. What do you think of that?"

"I wouldn't say I'm surprised," replied Shmuel. "It doesn't bring me news when I hear that Jews are just like somebody else, even those who couldn't read and write. Because Jews have Torah, does this make them more than human? Torah could make you smart. Torah maybe could make you wise. But could it make you good if you are not good to start with? No, this is something you are born with. This no religion could teach you."

It was not really surprising to find something resembling witchcraft beliefs operating in the Center. The kinds of societies where witchcraft often operates are those small-scale, egalitarian, often tribal groups very much like the Center in their social organization. Both lacked the clear, centralized, differentiated system of authority and the availability of formal means for enforcing conformity and redressing breaches of norms. Witchcraft is very practical in such circumstances. It works best among intimates—between family members or neighbors. It explains misfortune in human motivational terms, allowing people to project anger and envy onto others while consciously or unconsciously denying responsibility for such unwanted sentiments. It works because among intimates we know that, in fact, the malice of the people we live with can harm us; witchcraft codifies the vague feelings of hostility and guilt that are so relevant and powerful in small groups. Essentially, it is a moral code in terms of which sentiments of ill will on one person's part are recognized as affecting the well-being of another, and as such, witchcraft is built on a world view that has human values as its causal center. All kinds of events, not only social but often natural and even cosmic occurrences, are regarded as responsive to moral relations.[1]

In the Center, as in small societies of intimates—bands, clans, tribes, communes, and extended families—people's ties are complex, highly intertwined, and very charged emotionally. In such circumstances people are extremely dependent on each other, and a quarrel between two individuals quickly spreads, affecting all the others and disturbing relations throughout the collectivity. Such disturbances are difficult to encapsulate and they may simmer indefinitely, flaring up periodically and rupturing the equilibrium of the entire community, sometimes causing permanent harm, sometimes actually destroying the group by driving off whole factions. Thus, all interpersonal relations—even a quarrel between two people—are ultimately public issues and matters of the greatest concern to everyone.

People in these kinds of communities are held to be accountable not only for their behavior but for their sentiments. Where the moral order and the political order are undifferentiated, emotions—expressed and unexpressed—do the bulk of the work of social control, serving the same functions as politics and law in larger societies. In intimate groups, sentiments alone may maintain group solidarity, control deviance, contain quarrels, mete out justice, and enforce and define the body of unquestioned beliefs—the fundamental moral principles—that make a collectivity a culture.

People in such groups, certainly in the Center, expressed their sentiments to each other in terms of an intricate code, consciously and unconsciously manipulated by the members. The code is a verbal and nonverbal vocabulary, sometimes very gross, such as making a gesture, spitting when a disliked or selfish person passed by, and sometimes expressed so subtly as to be unnoticed to outsiders not schooled in its nuances. Among people who need each other as much as these do, and who are deeply connected to each other, with no others to turn to for human association, a shrug, a nod, a frown, a minor slight is a major event, communicating one's standing in the community. Gossip, ridicule, calling names, "aggravating" each other, insulting by compliment and innuendo, suggesting someone may be sick or overwrought can be spoken ("You don't look well") or hinted at by gesture (placing a glass of water before someone who is too excited).[a] These were among the many communications employed in the group to regulate each other's conduct.

Of course, in the Center no one called Anna a witch; this was not part of their vocabulary. Nevertheless, she was used as a scapegoat, and the anger directed toward her was greater than what was meted out to others who had violated equally serious group norms. It was not an accident that Anna had been cast in this role; it was because of her blatant pursuit of self-interest at others' expense. Anna was viewed with general disdain; nevertheless, she was clearly a genuine citizen in the group. There was no apparatus for formally expelling her, and her insensitivity to collective sentiment made her invulnerable to informal means of exclusion. She couldn't be driven off physically, and she refused to respond to expressions of dislike and disapproval. Regulation by sentiment was not working. Anna had become the enemy within. Center people, historically pariahs, were accustomed to concrete enemies. With no Cossacks, drunken peasants, police, or Nazis at the door, Anna was blamed for their present sorrows, quarrels, and pain.

Naturally, individuals varied greatly in the degree to which they believed Anna could have hurt Sadie by cursing her. Some felt Anna was merely nasty, and her curse was only an expression of bad taste and stupidity. But everyone gave Anna a wide berth. Even those who voiced great disdain for such "superstitiousness" admitted they had always heard a great deal about such things. Even the most skeptical could tell stories about neighbors and acquaintances who claimed to have been harmed by a curse.

If this had not been a period of such anxiety and realistic danger, Anna's curse might have been shrugged off. But now, even those who did not believe in the effectiveness of cursing recognized it as a threat. It was truly ominous. For Anna to persist in her ill will toward Sadie at this time was in effect to curse the whole group. But this was not well-articulated; it was a vague fear that could not be put into words. Had it been more clearly perceived, it still would not have been "discussible" because there was nothing to be done about it in the first place, and in the second, no one wanted to be considered superstitious. "Cursing," said Basha, "was for the Old World, not for America, where such ignorant uncivilized things had no place. Besides," she continued, "in America, you couldn't call curses back."

Above all, no one would have discussed cursing in front of a stranger. Even if they had actually known the nature of the psychologist's visit, they would have disguised the real basis of their disturbance. Anna's stinginess was a discussible substitute, though a flimsy one. In fact, Anna's goodwill toward the group was at stake and her stinginess would be used as an adequate metaphor for her antisocial conduct.

When Dr. Cohen arrived, twenty people were gathered around a table in the Center, the newly elected, not-yet-installed board members. Anna, as usual, sat a bit apart, silent throughout the meeting, smiling blandly, her blue eyes bright and masked, her poise impenetrable. Sadie sat as far away from her as possible, frowning, her arms crossed resolutely over her heavy bosom. She was flanked by several of her supporters, the quiet little women Shmuel called bobbes. Plainly, Sadie was determined to have satisfaction.

Abe introduced Dr. Cohen. He reminded many Center

people of their children. He was in his middle fifties, Jewish, American-born of Eastern European parents, educated, literate, clearly well-disposed toward them but utterly ignorant of the parent culture. It was soon clear that he thought he knew more about the Center than he did, and perhaps this caused him to miss specific Center customs and beliefs that he might otherwise have detected. If he had been more assertive and authoritative as a person, it might also have helped. But his responses were so ambiguous and so irrelevant to the people's real concerns that they soon returned to their usual practices—stating their views, performing their self-definitions, challenging, arguing, exciting themselves and arousing each other, exposing, commenting upon, then masking sentiments when they burst out of bounds.

Dr. Cohen could not have been less prepared for what followed. He was a genial man, short, bespectacled, informal. With his trim gray-streaked beard, pipe, tweed jacket, French-cut jeans, and leather Adidas tennis shoes, he was a typical California professional man. In the Center he might as well have been from another planet. Abe announced that Dr. Cohen was a psychologist from the City Health Department, "who has come to learn about us and see if he can help us in some of our difficulties in getting along with each other. You might say he's an expert in arguments."

"In this I think we are the experts," laughed Moshe. "We could give lessons to other people."

"How does this work?" asked Sadie. "Does he give us a lecture?"

"No, not really a lecture," said Dr. Cohen. "Everybody talks, not only me. In the beginning we just get to know each other, then we try to share our feelings, find out what's going on inside other people and ourselves."

"Some people's minds here, you wouldn't want to be inside. It's like a sewer," said Jake.

"We talk about just anything at all?" asked Olga.

"Well, I think it's best if we confine ourselves to the here and now. There's no need to start with the ancient past. We can't do anything about those things. So let's limit ourselves to the people who are here and to what's actually on our minds right now. Is there somebody who would like to start?"

"All right, Doctor. I'll tell you something," Hannah began. "What do you do with somebody who insults you? There's a man here, I wouldn't mention no names. He treats me like dirt. I talk to him but he don't answer. What do you think of such a man?"

"Doctor, this woman is *meshuggeneh*. I don't even know her, and she complains that I don't talk to her," shouted Jake.

"Doctor, this is a *shmegegge** for you," she replied. "He knows me already twenty years. Who does he fool? When he wants somebody to vote for him, suddenly he knows me."

"Now, just a minute, folks," replied Dr. Cohen. "I think that we're doing something here we should try to watch out for. When we call people names like this—shmegegge, meshuggeneh—this doesn't get us anywhere. Now there is something I'd like to explain to you, something that takes many years for us to learn, that is, if I call you a name and you're hurt, well, you don't really have to be. You can say, 'OK, that's the way he feels. He's angry. He wants to call me a name, but I don't have to respond to it.' This is a very difficult concept to learn. It's one of the things we all have to try to grasp." Dr. Cohen delivered his comments with great earnestness.

"You mean to say this is also difficult for you?" asked Hannah.

"Why, yes, certainly," he answered with a reassuring smile.

"You didn't learn this with all your education, but you expect we should?" Hannah rebutted.

"Well, that's why I say it's very hard. I'm only human, too. Just like you, I have trouble when I am hurt and I know it is something I shouldn't let bother me. Then I have to try to examine myself. Why does it get to me that way? When I know this, then it's up to me how I respond. Does anyone here understand what I am trying to say?" he asked.

"How should we know if we understand? Isn't it your job to tell us?" Sonya was obviously uneasy with his familiar approach.

"This is no way to talk to the doctor. A bunch of am haaretz, all of you. Here is a learned man, a specialist. He comes to instruct us and you insult him." Jake jumped to the doctor's defense.

* Idiot, fool.

"Who asked him for instruction? If I need a doctor, I go to my son, the psychiatrist," replied Faegl.

"Sha, sha. Let's hear the doctor!" Moshe intervened.

"Now, that's all right. I am not insulted. I know how hard these things are. In years of experience you come up against this again and again. People want answers, especially from someone they think is an authority. This lady, Faegl? Faegl is having quite a natural reaction. We all have to work hard to accept the idea that answers can only come from within ourselves. Someone else can help, of course, but only as a guide, a sounding board, so to speak, but in the end, no one else can give us answers."

"So why are we here talking to you?" persisted Faegl.

"Let me put it this way. We can help each other help ourselves. One of the things we can do to start is to try to level with each other. If feelings pile up over a long period and people keep them inside, they often fight without knowing why. The first thing that has to happen is that we get our feelings out in the open and examine them. And that's what we've been doing here now, just in these few minutes. Now let's go back to the question of what it means if someone calls you a name. Does it really make any difference, I mean, really?" he asked intensely.

"Certainly, it makes a lot of difference," asserted Basha. "It goes into you like a knife and couldn't stop hurting you because you tell it to. You can't just make up your mind and it disappears."

"Doctor, are you trying to tell me that if a person calls you a name, you should just pretend that nothing happened?" asked Sonya.

"Mr. Weidman, when you lean forward like that, I can't see," said Basha.

"So who told you to sit there? You could move," Weidman replied. General disorder erupted.

"Quiet, quiet, let the doctor continue. You behave like *Kuni Lemmels,"** shouted Nathan. The hushers were hushed in turn, and the din escalated until Moshe banged the table and shouted, "*Soll sein still!*† All of you!"

* Naïve ones.

† Be quiet!

"Let me explain," persisted Dr. Cohen. "I don't mean you should pretend. I mean that inside yourself, you need not let the name stick to you. You have a choice about saying, 'Well, this doesn't really apply to me.' You see, when someone calls you a name, it is not like hitting you. With words we don't hurt each other the way we do if we hit someone. As long as they are only using words, then maybe it is worthwhile to try to pay attention to why the words are acting against you just as if they were weapons."

Dr. Cohen and the Center people had a completely different understanding of the meaning and power of words. Shmuel had first drawn my attention to this feature of Center culture in the course of one of our taping sessions of his life history. He forgot a word he wanted and became very upset. I offered substitutes and finally suggested that we go on without it and return to the subject later. That upset him even more. In part his agitation was due to his fear that this was a sign of senility. But when he discussed it later, it became clear that more was involved. "You understand that one word is not like another," he said. "Just a particular one is needed to do the trick, none other. So when just the word I want hides from me, when before it has always come along very politely when I called it, this is a special torture designed for old Jews. Do you know what a word is to the Jew? Words don't give a name. No, they change things around. This is why we pray, make blessings, make hexes, charms, all those things. When you have the right word, you have power over something. This is why a Jew never pronounces the tetragrammaton. The cabalists believed if you said God's name you would die. This is because it could give you power even over God. When Jabob wrestled with the Angel, what do you think he asked him? He asked his name, because if he knew that, Jacob would be his servant. Everything about a word is important to a Jew, every letter. Rabbi Ismael told one of the scribes of the Torah, 'My son, be careful in your work, for if you mix up even one letter you destroy the whole world.' "

It was not surprising that among Eastern European Jews the power of words was expressed in the practice of giving nicknames to anything or anyone—people, towns, animals, families. They summarized and fixed a single trait, feature of history or accident, character, or appearance for a lifetime. Nicknames lasted like legal names. Sholom Aleichem said they were "like a suit . . . made to order: measured, cut, hand-sewn, and pressed—now wear it well!"

Words, among Jews and shtetl people, were no mere neutral labels; indeed, they were so powerful that one might speak of word-magic. Words could affect what they named, and names contained something of the identity of that which they signified. As Shmuel said, words were alive and they had consequences in the world. In the Center, then, when people called each other names—derisive or laudatory—it had great seriousness. *Gonif, chazer,* meshuggeneh, reb, am ha-aretz, yenta*† *apikoros,*‡ *shnorrer,*** *filosofe, grauber,*†† *yekl,*‡‡ *Kuni Lemmel,* these were permanent summary interpretations of the named one's very essence. Calling names was a significant form of social control among the Center people, and the consequences of name-calling went beyond merely stigmatizing. When one casts a spell or makes a curse, the words themselves are efficacious. There is only a slight shade of difference between spells, curses, prayers, and insulting names in a group that believes in word-magic.[3] Sadie tried to convey some of her feelings about the results of calling people names to Dr. Cohen. The desire to inflict harm was not to be ignored.

"Doctor, sometimes words can hurt as much as if someone would club you," said Sadie. "Words can be even worse than a club. They stay with you when a hit has already stopped hurting."

"This is true. You know the saying, '*Di pen shist erger fun a fayl.*' That means 'the word sticks you sharper than the arrow,' " said Basha.

"Look, Doctor," said Sadie, "there are words and words. Now I'm an experienced person. In my day, I know words from words. I have heard people say bad things and I walk away. "Doctor, I'm not a stupid person." "Maybe I have no education, but I know when you should listen and when you shouuld

* chazer: glutton
† yenta: blabbermouth, meddlesome gossip
‡ apikoros: skeptic or unbeliever
** shnorrer: beggar or moocher
†† grauber: vulgarian or coarse form
‡‡ yekl: greenhorn; yokel

walk away. Now suppose a person says something, it shows she *wants* to aggravate you. I'm a sick woman, so she says something while I'm helpless, in the hospital. She tells people that I had a heart attack, that probably I'm going to die from it. This is like wanting me to die, isn't it? Could you walk away from such a thing?"

"That kind of thing can aggravate a person to death," Basha agreed, and added, "there was a woman here a couple of years ago. Everybody knows her. She was very sick. She went to the hospital and the women talked and talked about her, all kinds of things they said, how she was a terrible housekeeper, how she chased after men . . . and when she comes back from the hospital, she feels worse instead of better. Still they carry on and aggravate her until pretty soon she has to go back to the hospital, and this time she never comes back."

Another form of word-magic in this group as in all small societies, was gossip, a significant means of exerting control over others. When persistent and malicious enough, it was said to be able to "aggravate someone to death." Often this was a mere figure of speech, but cases were regularly cited in which a wife had "aggravated her husband to death" or "children had aggravated their mother to death." Then the meaning was literal. The capacity to harm a person with whom one was supposed to be intimate, by irritating, shaming, nagging, or rejecting, could be escalated to the point of causing sickness or even death. "Death by aggravation" was also used to arouse guilt, as an accusation against an intimate who was causing one ill health. But this accusation could only be practiced in relation to those who were basically trusted, and who were responsive emotionally to one's complaint. A stranger or enemy would not be regarded as capable of creating this emotional condition.

Gestural accusations of aggravation were also made by Center people against each other. Sonya silently popped a nitroglycerin pill into her mouth when anyone shouted at her, thus suggesting the person's conduct was a threat to her composure and her health. Jake, who everyone knew had a bad heart, gasped and pounded his chest when it suited his purposes. Hannah staged dramatic exits, saying her blood sugar was getting out of control, when she was displeased or upset by people's conduct. Wordlessly, but eloquently, these gestures said, "You'll be the death of me," "You are responsible for my condition," "If something happens to me it will be on your head." These mechanisms were premised on the acceptance of mutual responsibility, for only among those who feel truly and properly connected to each other can the arousal of guilt serve as a regulatory mechanism. These are strategies of intimacy that have no power over outsiders who can simply choose to ignore them.

"But you see," said Dr. Cohen, "these things don't have to be aggravating when we can get our feelings out in the open and understand each other. We can find out why people are hurt and angry enough to behave this way."

"Doctor, please, listen to me. I know who she's talking about . . . this is not how it happened," shouted Faegl.

Again an uproar developed.

"People, listen, please." Dr. Cohen raised his voice for the first time. "Please! I have noticed that it is very hard for people here to listen to each other. Basically, I think we all want to do that. There's enough time, everyone can be heard."

"This is my turn, Doctor. You heard what I told you. A certain woman is aggravating me. How could you help yourself against her? Can you give me an answer to that?" Sadie demanded.

"I cannot give you a simple answer offhand," he answered. "Does anyone else here have anything to say? Maybe we can hear from some of the others who haven't spoken yet. How would some of you handle this situation?"

"You should give her back like she gave to you," shouted Jake.

"Mr. Weidman, you're leaning forward again. I can't see," objected Faegl.

"This case of Sadie's is just something you have to put up with. What else could you do? This is how people are around here. I don't know why I keep coming back. Such commotion makes me sick. I'm allergic to this place, but I always come back," said Hannah with a shake of her head.

Hannah here was lamenting her inability to "harden her heart" enough to stay away from the Center. She, like most Center members, was not capable of really denying her connections with the others, despite strong ambivalence. "Hardening the heart" against each other was another of the Center people's means of controlling things. It required them to dramatize their intention not to care, and thus to punish people they felt had treated them badly. It was a kind of emotional boycott, ranging from absenting oneself to silence, which among these verbal Jews was an eloquent act. Jews, as Leo Rosten has put it, are "let down by 'coldness.'" Taught from their earliest childhood that to respond to others is an obligation, among them to fail to show feelings for others is to be lacking in compassion, *rachmones,* one of the most prized virtues, an attribute of God. Indifference to others, especially to their miseries, is "to fail in one's duties as a man." Paradoxically, a hardhearted response is less hardhearted than no response at all.

Thus, for Center people to demonstrate aloofness and indifference to others was a drastic measure, meant to be a very strong censure. It was based on the underlying hope that others would not fail to understand the extent of the misery giving rise to such extreme conduct, and repent, bringing about response by non-response. But there were drawbacks to the way this was used in the Center. It punished the one who practiced it by cutting him or her off from human contact almost completely. And it was an attitude that had to be publicly displayed. In the hubbub of Center life there was always the danger that others would not notice absence or coldness. So it was not uncommon to see people sitting on the sidelines and refusing to speak or participate in collective activities, demonstrating that their hearts were hard against the others. Or, more dramatically, a man or woman who was hurt could be found seated on the benches outside the Center, positioned conspicuously so that those entering could not fail to notice they had no intention of going into the Center. Heart-hardening was premised on sentiments of concern and attachment, another intimate means for regulating each other's behavior in the absence of more formal, impersonal mechanisms.

The ultimate means for control among groups of intimates is always that of complete, physical rejection—ostracism. True, lasting ostracism was virtually unknown in the Center. Since rejected people almost never actually moved out of the neighborhood, there was no way of avoiding regular encounters with them, an embarrassment for all concerned. Nevertheless, ostracism was an unspoken, underlying threat. When ostracized people have nowhere else to go, expulsion from their group may be tantamount to physical death. Among Center people expulsion meant social and cultural death. The mere existence of this possibility gave a bite and gravity to the mildest expressions of rejection between members, hinting at an invisible, unspeakable fate. When people have the choice of leaving a group and going to live somewhere else in a comparable collectivity, they need not put up with unbearable behavior or treatment.

But Center people had to remain together at all costs. They did not have to like it, and they did not have to like each other, and this they made very clear, dramatically, frequently, but always stopping short of uttering sentiments that could have brought about a response such as, "Well, if you don't like it here, why don't you leave?" They had, as a result, great though enforced toleration for deviance, and this was nearly an articulated norm. Perhaps the situation had been similar in the shtetl, where intense in-group struggling also appears to have been common and accepted as a fact of life. After all, a pariah people, then and now, do not have many of the options available to others.

"Please, people," pleaded Dr. Cohen. "Let's hear from some of those who are quiet. We must give everyone a chance to talk, even if it's hard for us. Yes, sir, what is your name? Could we hear from you?"

"My name is Nathan Rabinowitch, spelled R-a-b-i-n-o-w-i-t-c-h, if you want to put it down somewhere. Well, I don't have much to say on this. I try to keep away from these women. How they behave, I don't want to have anything to do with, cursing and carrying on. Two women, like this I say, a plague on both their houses."

"Nathan, what kind of a way to talk is this from a rabbi's son?" asked Moshe.

"You see, Doctor, I myself am an atheist," Nathan continued. "My father was a rabbi, that's true. So people ask my opinion. Not because they want to hear what I have to say. Nobody listens to what I say for myself, so mostly I keep quiet."

"I think we all recognize that everyone here has something worthwhile to say," replied the doctor. "Everyone of us is a valuable, unique individual, whose opinion is worth hearing, for its own sake, the son of a rabbi or the son of a butcher."

"Doctor, don't say this," said Jake. "There are people

here you don't want to hear from. People with no education. Doctor, do you know that Abe wants us to put on the board of directors a woman, I wouldn't name no names. She can't read or write. What kind of people are we if this is our board of directors? It shows the world we got no respect for ourselves."

"This is a democracy, Jake. We don't give literacy tests. Anybody elected goes on. Don't tell Abe how to run things. He knows what he's doing," said Moshe.

"I'm sure Abe knows what he is doing," answered Dr. Cohen. "But you all do, too. You talk as though you think you'd fall apart without him. You can take care of yourselves."

"Without Abe, we would kill each other," retorted Faegl.

"Doctor, you really are telling us that everybody here is alike, everybody is worth the same thing? You believe this?" asked Nathan.

"No, that's not what I mean. I mean that though there are differences between people, that does not imply that some are better and some worse. This is a subtle distinction, I realize that, but important. We all have to try to learn that we don't always have to judge differences in terms of who is superior and who is inferior. We can try to accept the fact of our differences, and that means while we are all individuals, still we are of equal value."

"That's true, that's what we believe in America." Basha was very definite.

"A *nechtiger tog*!* You look around, you got to notice that all are not worth the same, America or not, this even a child knows," said Faegl.

"Doctor, I didn't get to finish," yelled Sadie. "You talk about fair, but you didn't let me have my say."

"Quiet, Sadie. You had your say," yelled Moshe.

"Doctor, you see how people carry on? Have you ever been in such a madhouse?" asked Jake.

"I can't stand this commotion. My heart starts up. You will all excuse me." Leah smiled politely, pulling on her gloves, and rose, waving aside protests against her departure and pleas that she stay.

"Look, people," insisted Dr. Cohen, "there's something I think should be said. It's that all of us here, we are all getting older. Nobody has mentioned this yet. When we get older,

* What nonsense! Literally, a nightly day.

things are a little different than they used to be. Things happen and make us a little more irritated than when we were younger, for example, the noise of our beloved grandchildren. We want to be around them, but it's difficult. Children can't help being noisy, and we can't help it being hard on us. It's the same with our friends. They also do things that irritate us, things that once we would have overlooked. But we just don't have as much tolerance as we'd like, and this is something everyone has to face in time."

"These people here have been this way all their lives, Doctor. This is why I can't stand to be around them," replied Hannah.

"Abe, I came here for a lecture. I can't even hear the doctor for all this shouting. I can't make anything out of this. What's going on?" asked Sadie.

"So why are we wasting our time? No doctor can help us. The doctor tells us we carry on like this because we are old. Is this something he could cure?" asked Olga.

"I didn't come here to be cured. Who is sick? If I'm sick I go to my son, the psychiatrist," said Faegl.

"Now there's something we should explore," Dr. Cohen broke in. "Let me tell you what I think is happening here. When people are together a lot, like all of you, and when you don't tell each other your real feelings—what's bothering you—you can't get along. This is part of being mature, and people have to do it, no matter what they are or how educated or how old. It's very hard work to keep growing and learning."

"Dr. Cohen, we are not getting anywhere. I will tell you what is going on here, to make a finish to all this walking around the bush." Sadie had decided to bring matters to a head. "Doctor, tell you me, what do you think of a person who sends you a curse? A woman who curses—is this a lady? This is much worse than calling you a name. What would you do with such a one as that?"

"I don't like to hear such talk, Sadie. This is not what we do! In the Old Country people cursed. But this is America. In America we don't do these things," asserted Basha.

"Doctor, she says we don't do these things," replied Sadie. "But look for yourself. This happens right in front of us. A woman, I wouldn't mention her name, she does not behave herself. She cursed me and then she wishes me dead when I am sick. Doctor, you are a learned man, a professional. I want you to tell me. What do you think about a woman who curses?" persisted Sadie.

"What kind of talk is this? What goes on with you here?" Basha was furious and stood up so suddenly she knocked over her chair with a clatter. "This is the twentieth century, America. We don't believe in curses anymore. In America we are educated people. The curse comes from the grandmothers. No more!"

"Exactly what do you mean by a curse? I think this is something perhaps we should explore," said the doctor.

"No, this isn't a good subject. We don't get anywhere by going into these things." Moshe was very firm, but Sadie pressed on.

"Look, Doctor. Myself, I don't believe curses could actually hurt you. But the curse means someone wants you to suffer, doesn't it? Suppose a woman cursed you, God forbid, and everyone heard that she wants something terrible to happen to you. You tell her that's no way to behave, but she doesn't answer. That means she *wants* to bring you down. Who could sit at the same table with such a one? It shows no respect for yourself. So, you avoid her and mind your own affairs, and then you get sick and have to go to the hospital, and while you are away, she tells everyone you are going to die. While you are lying there sick and helpless, she is telling everyone this."

"Now you talk like a *prostak*.* All it shows is that such a woman is not a nice person. It doesn't mean she hurts you," said Sonya.

"Do you tell me that I should sit on the board with one who curses me? *Tu, tu, tu.*" Sadie made the spitting sound over her shoulder. "Does the Center show any respect for me if they don't put her out? I have no choice. Because of this I am withdrawing myself as a member, after nine years of work here. Naturally, my friends don't want to see me treated this way. They come out with me. All my life I've worked for Israel. I made Jewish charity lunches for twenty years. But I can't stay here no more. I hate to do this because it will pull down the Center if I and my friends don't come back. No more lunches for Israel, no more fund-raisers for the Center, nothing. But I can't lower myself by staying in this situation."

* Ignorant boor.

"Sadie, for eight years you are mad at this woman. Why do you go out now?" asked Moshe.

"Because while I was away, sick in the hospital, she starts talking about me again. That is something I can't forgive."

"Do you mean that these two women have been angry at each other for eight years?" asked Dr. Cohen. "Surely there are more immediate concerns to talk about. We gain nothing by going back into past history. These things are behind us."

"Does it look behind to you? To me, it looks right here at the table," replied Olga.

The doctor's remarks were generally ignored. Obviously tense and frustrated, he began to massage his forehead. Sonya followed her custom: Seeing a man in distress, she placed a glass of water in front of him. He seemed not to notice.

"The woman was voted to the board, Sadie. You couldn't interfere with that," said Moshe.

"What kind of person is that to be on the board. She can't read or write. She doesn't belong here. We should kick her out," said Jake. Once more everyone began talking at once.

"Silence!" bellowed Moshe. "I am the president here. I don't put up with talk of kicking people out. She got a right to be here like everyone else. Sadie, you should forget all this. You behave like a *yachne*."*

"I have had enough of this. I have to think of my health." Sadie spoke dramatically. She seemed near tears. "If that one stays, I go. All these years I have worked for Israel, I don't know how much money I have raised. I give big affairs for the Jewish Hospital benefit. I bring in new members which the Center needs to survive. So is this the treatment I get in return? All those years of slaving for my people, and who appreciates it?"

"Why is everyone so on edge? Can't we talk about these things peacefully?" Dr. Cohen implored.

"Doctor, you wanted us to open up," Basha reprimanded him. "All right. Now we are opened up. You got what you wanted. Does this help anybody? You think we got to know each other better? Here we are. This is us. Where does it get us?"

"I think it does help to open up, even though it is sometimes painful," he answered. "We can and we must express our

* Loudmouth, gossip.

emotions, but that does not mean we have to fight. It's possible to tell each other about our angers or hurts without shouting."

"You should tell people you're mad in a nice way?" Faegl asked. "If you could tell them nicely, you're not mad. When you got feelings, they come out how they come out."

"Doctor, I must leave. All this fighting makes my blood pressure go higher. I can't take it no more." Nathan rose to go.

"So you see, this woman is harming other people, not just me," said Sadie. "This has gone on long enough. I am going to tell you who is doing this thing to me. You could ask her yourself if she wants to make me sick."

"No! Naming names doesn't do anybody any good. Now you are behaving as bad as she is. Worse even. If you name her, *I* am going to leave." Sonya was adamant and Sadie was silent. "This goes too far. No names, Sadie."

"Enough talk about leaving here!" shouted Moshe. "This is a time when the Center needs everybody. We harm each other this way. We do the work for our enemies. We have our differences here, but we all want the Center to survive. These are very bad times for us. We need all our members or we close down. And we don't think only of the Center. We got to think of Israel. We raise a lot of money for Israel here. Sadie is right, she worked hard and we all work hard. We got to put our fights aside. We got in common that we are Jews and that we support Israel. That's enough."

"This woman who curses doesn't support Israel," shouted Jake. "She has a lot of money, but she never gives anything to anybody. She is a miser, no better than a Cossack, for all she thinks of her people."

"Moshe is right," said Basha. "We are fighting for our life, and other people's lives, not just our own. Now Sadie, if you really love Israel as much as you say, you won't hurt it that way. Next week you are going to give a luncheon. It will be a big success and we need it. Everyone here wants to come and support it. You have some tickets still? Anybody here who hasn't bought one, you could sell them one right now. There's no one in this room who doesn't want to come. Isn't that right? Sonya, you have a ticket? Anna, would you like to buy a ticket if you don't have one already? Naturally, Anna, everybody here knows you want to support Israel, like the rest of us. We are all Jews, and we are taking care of each other. Nobody is going to do this for us. There's nobody in this room who didn't lose family in the Holocaust. Why are we left? So we shouldn't forget our Jewish way of life. Otherwise we finish off Hitler's work for him. Sometimes we forget this asks of us *sacrifices,* all kinds, money, and other things. This doesn't have anything to do with one person. It's for our parents. It's for our children. It's for history. So for that reason I think everyone in this room who loves Israel should buy a ticket for the luncheon, even if they don't go."

Basha's speech produced a silence, the first of the afternoon. In the hush that followed, people nodded and sighed, including Anna. She fished three dollars out of her purse and pushed the money across the table toward Sadie. "A ticket for your luncheon, please." She spoke very quietly and expressionlessly. Sadie took the money with a frown and a nod, and handed the ticket and fifty cents change back to Anna.

"Don't forget to mark down that Anna's coming to your lunch, Sadie," said Moshe. "You should put it in your records so you don't forget." No one missed Moshe's point.

Basha was delighted that her strategem had worked. "Anybody else here doesn't have a ticket? We want this to be a big affair. We show the world what a handful of us here can do for Israel by working together. Sadie will be very proud the day of the lunch, everyone will come and see how hard she works for her people. She's been doing this all her life and she's not going to throw it away. Now, I would like to buy a ticket for Dr. Cohen as my guest. He's sat here through all our complaining. He should also come and see how we make a celebration. Will you accept, Doctor?"

"Why, thank you. I'll try to come, I'd be delighted. Now, our time is up. I think this was a useful session. We made a very good beginning. We all got to know each other a little bit better. This work is difficult, but we all have to stretch ourselves to keep adapting, all our lives, young or old. Good-bye, everyone. Stay well, have a good week." He smiled warmly, gathered his things, and waved good-bye.

"Thank you, Doctor. This was a fine class. I am sure we all learned a lot," said Olga. "He's a nice Jewish boy, if only he would get rid of all that hair on his face, he would be good-looking."

"Also very intelligent," said Sonya, after Dr. Cohen left.

Basha was embracing Sadie, now surrounded by her friends, relieved and cheerful that they would be able to work in the luncheon next week. Anna, smiling as serenely as ever, nodded to Moshe and me and left.

I had promised Shmuel that I would bring him my notes and comments on the therapy session, and tell him whether or not he had been right in his predictions. I went over my notes carefully before going to his house, trying to anticipate his reaction, which I was sure would be critical. It would be nice to be able to give him an account that cut through the din and name-calling and made some sense. That was, after all, my job. It was clear that in the session two quite different belief systems were juxtaposed, conflicting on a number of basic points. The model used by Dr. Cohen advocated an honest, self-revealing exposition and exploration of emotions, holding that to be an intrinsic good, conducive to improved intrapsychic and interpersonal functioning. It was based on the assumption that an honest encounter would lead to heightened knowledge of self, of others, and eventually to greater acceptance of one's own and other people's negative emotions. One of its premises was that individuals would not use the information thus unearthed against each other. Presumably defense and attack, blame, criticism, and accusations would be gradually dropped as people came to know each other more deeply, and compassion might follow this fuller understanding.

But the Center people held a different view of negative emotions. Such feelings were not acceptable, in themselves or others. Their self-esteem was based on the maintenance of honor, decorum, and dignity. Loss of control was regarded as an embarrassment and sometimes as shameful. And their solidarity was too fragile, their mutual trust too thin to support disclosure to each other of their great hurts and needs. Furthermore, they held themselves accountable and responsible for good behavior; emotions, inner states, motivations were not included in their code of honor. They were not the significant determiners of reputation. Negative emotions were properly private concerns, unless they made themselves manifest through someone's unfortunate loss of control. The Center people approached the therapy session as another opportunity to demonstrate their moral qualities. They were not prepared to expose themselves beyond a certain point. The vulnerability and defenselessness implicit in too great a revelation were likely to give someone else privileged information about themselves, thus putting them in another person's power.[4] People might use this information to elevate their own standing, appearing to be knowledgeable about members' affairs, and receiving attention at the same time. For the old people, the therapy session was an occasion that allowed them to proclaim a self-selected, highly controlled image for presentation to the outsider, peers, and themselves.

Among people already so helpless, so vulnerable, so needy, the loss of control was extraordinarily threatening. Their efforts were directed at convincing others, and then themselves, that they were in charge of their life. It was not only that self-control made the appearance of dignity possible, but also enabled them to maintain their standing as people of honor. Underlying this was the unspoken, enormous fear of senility. Clear-mindedness and self-possession were signs of being intact. They regarded any indicators of senility, decay, and dependence as more alarming than an illness that might terminate in death. A forgotten word, an outburst of temper, a non sequitur, a misplaced object, a lapse of judgment or reasoning were all scrutinized as ominous portents that the process of decay was beginning. At odds with this desire for self-control was their attraction to intensity, interpreted by them as an indication that one was still fully alive. A set of opposing pulls thus existed. Passion was a sign of continuing strength and involvement. Fierce activity and feelings proved that their powers were intact. They were read as evidence of vitality and used to counter the dimming of physical sensations that everyone experienced to some degree. As Abe put it, "The flow of adrenaline tells them they are as alive as ever." Thus, the old people were in a double bind for which there was no solution—pulled toward poise and dignity by one need, and pulled toward outburst and passion by the other.

Moreover, it seemed that Center elderly had inklings that there were no ready, certain methods for assuring that once publicly exposed, their quarrels would remain encapsulated. The old fight between Sadie and Anna had been contained for a long time. Until now, they had managed to keep it from becoming the basis for establishing two entrenched, permanent, opposing factions. When Sadie threatened to "name the name" of the one who had cursed her, she came perilously close to opening what might be an irreparable breach. She was prevented from this by Moshe and Basha who fully realized that such a possibility was an imminent danger.

Dr. Cohen and the Center people also disagreed about the significance of history in their present affairs. The doctor's insistence that their discussion be limited to the "here and now" made no sense to them. They had a long, complex, common history that was ever-present in their interactions. Eighty and ninety years of struggle and survival were not to be lightly relinquished, even momentarily. They could not imaginatively set aside the living reality of their social life over time. Some individuals may do this in therapy, or perhaps strangers do so; psychotherapy encounter sessions are not generally designed for people who have lived together over protracted periods. Ordinarily in such sessions, strangers are assembled for a few hours a week, for a year or at most a few. In these circumstances, people's treatment of each other and their use of privileged information can be closely supervised by the therapist, acting as protector of suitable norms. Indeed, often one of the norms regulating group therapy is that individuals not meet outside the group while treatment is ongoing. It is assumed that therapy sessions are special and artificial circumstances that allow members to practice new modes of interaction to be applied later in natural contexts. But when group members are intimates, and in this case the members' only intimates, the risk of exposure and misuse of information is inordinate.

Furthermore Dr. Cohen believed that all people were capable of change, of giving up old psychological patterns and learning new ones. The Center folk thought that adults "are who they are, period." Their character had long since been fixed. They did believe that learning and growth were possible and desirable, but intellectual, not emotional development was what they strove toward. Underlying all this was their conviction that now in old age they had the right to be themselves, just as they were. It was past the time when they should modify their behavior to please others. They were too alone and there was too little time left to make it worth their while for them to bend to social expectations overmuch.

Too, the doctor held that all people were essentially of

equal worth, while Center people recognized clear, important differences in human worth; some people were simply better than others. While they did believe in the American values of democracy and equality, seldom did these concerns override their appreciation of differentially valued individual merit. Some of the differences they acknowledged were ascribed, derived from neither character nor conduct. Thus a rabbi's son deserved respect even though he was an outspoken atheist. Similarly, they respected the doctor because they viewed him as an authority. His efforts to set this aside mystified and annoyed them. When he "shared his own struggles," thus modeling his equality with them, they were put off. They wanted him to demonstrate his superiority.

And of course, Dr. Cohen and the Center people had quite different views on the uses and nature of words. For the doctor, words were employed to convey neutral information, whereas for the old people they were intrinsically powerful, and in some contexts, even supernaturally effective.

The therapy session brought to light some of the internal inconsistencies within the Center people's ideology that had nothing to do with contradictions between their and Dr. Cohen's notions. Center folk wished to be modern, rational, and without superstition, yet in fact most believed in the operation of magical forces in general and in particular took cursing seriously. These conflicting ideas coexisted, one an overt ideal, the other a persistent, uncomfortable covert norm.

The contradictions at play in the session were rife. Yet perhaps no more so than one might find in any culture. As Max Gluckman, Victor Turner, and other anthropologists have often shown, a group's ideology is never completely systematized or internally integrated. People mobilize one norm for one occasion and an opposing norm for another, unperturbed by their contradictory premises. In crises, these conflicts may become evident and require some manipulation or temporary reconciliation. Always, people or factions use such discrepancies in situations for their own purposes, but usually the beliefs themselves are not revised or discarded as a result of internal contradictions.

Another internal paradox was at work in the session, having nothing to do with Dr. Cohen's presence. Center people held the cherished ideal that Jews, as One People, were bound to each other by religious and historic ties; their common beliefs—and enemies—required them to demonstrate their unity and accord, by living together in peace. Yet Center folk experienced their connections with each other most convincingly and easily through the expression of anger and conflict. Anger is a powerful indication of engagement between people, the very opposite of indifference. It may be regarded as the most dramatic proof of responsiveness and caring. It is also a mode of relationship regularly used by people to allow them to deny that they are helpless victims of circumstances. By demonstrating opposition, per se, one is asserting that he or she has some degree of resistance, autonomy, and power over oneself and possibly others. It is a basic form of remaining attached. And among people who are not inevitably bound together, anger may become a refutation of the possibility of separation. Anger is a form of social cohesion, and a strong and reliable one. To fight with each other, people must share norms, rules, vocabulary, and knowledge. Fighting is a partnership, requiring cooperation. A boundary-maintaining mechanism—for strangers cannot participate fully—it is also above all a profoundly sociable activity.

In fighting with each other, the old people established a negative identification, proclaiming who they were by asserting who they were not. By treating their fellows as antagonists they emphasized the distance and differences among them and so were saved from seeing themselves as reflected in their peers, most of whom they regarded as pathetic, weak, and lonely. As long as they fought, they knew certainly that they were "not like those others."

And too, it was dangerous to acknowledge their full neediness in friendlier terms, since ties could be eradicated at any moment. Each week and day, people were snatched away. It was safer to quarrel with one's friends, denying the fullness of their mutual needs, yet remaining together, linked by intense emotional ties.

In fighting, too, they displaced their generalized anger from its proper targets—their children, fellow Jews, the government, history, luck, and time itself—and directed it at those around them. Their denial of commonality protected them psychologically but gravely damaged their solidarity. Still it spared them an excruciating reappraisal of one of their most essential claims—that they belong to and are esteemed by a family, a culture, and a society. The more intense and convincing the evidence of the shortcomings of their fellows as the real source of their unhappiness, the better were they protected from acknowledging their anger toward those to whom they could not, and dared not, address it. Their amour propre and their sacred symbols were thus preserved, but at the cost of group cohesion and harmony.[5]

The Center folk claimed to want peace and harmony above all, and regularly lamented their quarrelsomeness. They hated their inability to conduct their affairs peaceably and wanted desperately to be dignified. The old people were frustrated and perplexed by their quarrelsomeness, and so was I. Until recently anthropologists have been schooled to believe that unity, stable relations, social harmony, and the avoidance of quarrels and conflict were the conditions naturally sought by societies. All social processes were ultimately directed toward maintaining equilibrium, I had believed. This assumption and the members' own distress at their fights colored my early responses to Center conduct. For a long time, as I sat watching the dramas of discord unfold beneath the motto painted on the proscenium of the stage, "Behold How Good It Is for Brethren to Dwell Together in Unity," I was puzzled and appalled.

Day after day, week after week, year after year, I witnessed people hurting each other in small ways and large, disrupting their own ceremonies, making each other sick and agitated, irritated and enraged, cursing, naming, shaming, gossiping, and aggravating each other into sickness, if not actually to death. In time, I became increasingly aware of the connection between that motto and another one, painted on a placard across the room: "Cast Me Not Out in My Old Age but Let Me Live Each New Day as a New Life." No wonder these people were desperate and antagonistic. How could it be otherwise in their circumstances?

More time went by and another ingredient entered my interpretation of these dramas. In part they served as definitional ceremonies, contrived to allow people to reiterate their collective and personal identities, to arouse great emotion and energy, which was then redirected toward some commonalities, some deep symbols, and stable shared norms. These ceremonial fights were more than mere catharsis, though like catharsis, much heat occurred and little changed. Indeed, part of the purpose of the ceremonies was to allow things to stay the same, and to allow people to discover this sameness in the midst of furor and threats of splitting apart.

Often such ceremonies were crystallized around an innocent outsider. Ostensibly the Center folk entered into the stranger's agenda for a class discussion, a religious event, a lecture. The outsider provided the format and was treated superficially and briefly as a mediator in their quarrels. But inevitably he proved inadequate, and his purposes and plans were aborted as he displayed himself not sufficiently knowledgeable about their culture, desires, beliefs, symbols, and local history. The old people's means of controlling one another were ritualized reiterations of the profound connections among them, of their power over each other, hence, their power over their own destiny. When such ceremonies concluded, the outsider was usually left bewildered, sometimes offended, but often fascinated by Center people's energy and strength, realizing only that something important but mystifying had occurred.

The therapy session was understandable as a Turnerian social drama, but with a little twist of its own, the avoidance of true crisis. The first stage involving a breach of norms revolved around the malconduct of the two women protagonists, who by persisting in their maliciousness, were threatening the existence of the Center. The crisis stage would have occurred if Sadie had resigned, either as a result of Anna's installation as a member of the board of directors, or if Sadie had been allowed to "name the name" in the therapy session and Anna had persisted in her refusal to retract the curse. At this point Sadie would have resigned immediately, taking her followers out with her. But in fact, Moshe and Basha had managed to avert this. Redress was accomplished when Anna was permitted to make a gesture that symbolically affirmed her allegiance to all Jews, and by inclusion, Sadie. This saved Anna's face and dramatized her willingness to state her good will toward the Center, putting that loyalty above her bitterness toward one of its members. It was not a major reconciliation, but it was sufficient. And Moshe warned Sadie in telling her to "be sure to write it down," that it would have to count; at least superficially, she would have to forgive Anna. The reintegration process began at once, the crisis had been postponed and the solidarity of the Center would hold for the time being. As a social drama, it can be said that in the session a real change occurred; it was an event with a beginning, middle, and end, not an endlessly repeating cycle. Social relations had been realigned; Anna at least on a shallow level was accepted back into membership by her gesture of somewhat less than voluntary repentance. The fissioning of the group was prevented by the redress of the breaches.

In another light, as a definitional ceremony, the repetitive features of the affair were more striking. The therapy session—typically for Center definitional ceremonies—ended not with a genuine resolution, because the difficulties touched on were not resolvable. In one way or another, Center ceremonies concluded by the reiteration of the people's most general, basic commonalities, referring to Judaism and Israel, and occasionally the perpetuity of the local group. By the conclusion of such events, the members had reassured themselves that they would not dissolve as a group, and that they would not actually ostracize or destroy their fellow members, despite their hostile feelings. It is a truism but worth restating that conflict is often a form of cohesion.

Eventually, I recognized in Center fights a particular cultural style, and I could identify a working equilibrium underlying people's raucous, passionate lungings and lamentations. Quarrels were contained. Deviance was punished. There were regulations, common beliefs, rewards, and punishments. Disorder was their peculiar idiom for expressing the basic social processes that govern all ongoing collectivities. Despite ambivalence and pain, their collective life was vital, durable, and patterned. Disorder was not anomie, tumult was not chaos.[6]

Here was a community, then, sewn together by internal conflict, whose members were building and conserving their connections using grievance and dissension. Anger welded them together, fulfilling many purposes at the same time: asserting autonomy over themselves and their circumstances; demonstrating responsiveness to each other; clarifying the community's membership boundaries; displacing resentment from absent, vague targets toward nearer, safer ones; and denying that they shared a common, hideous fate.

It was not merely my interpretation. Some of the Center people, too, recognized the positive functions in their disorderly behavior. Shortly after the therapy session, Olga had said, "Just look how we all carry on. Leave it to the Jews to get into an argument. Why do we have to behave like this all the time?"

"In the first place, because we are Jews," replied Basha. "In the second place, what else should we do around here? You remember what Sholem Aleichem said? 'We fight to keep warm. That's how we survive.' "

A few days before I was going to see Shmuel I went to a Center meeting and was pressed into staying for lunch. Perhaps because I was anticipating having to defend them to Shmuel, perhaps because I was especially tired, I found myself disenchanted with the Center people. They seemed more contentious than usual. There was endless hassling about the food. People at the tables farthest from the kitchen clamored loudly because they would be served last. Jake didn't like the dessert and tried to sell it to his tablemates. Sam stuffed all the rolls he could reach into his pocket.

Sadie stomped out in a rage because the chicken was gone and she didn't want fish. When it appeared that someone had eaten Manya's salad, she burst into tears. Anna had brought her own silverware with her, since she, like most of the old people, found it very difficult to cut her food—however soft it was—with the tiny plastic forks and knives they were given. She refused to lend her implements to Leah whose arthritic hands made it nearly impossible for her to hold the flimsy plastic. How could I have found this place, these selfish, petulant, aggressive people interesting or charming? How could I recommend them to Shmuel who knew them so much better than I? When I had once referred to the in-fighting among them as their way of maintaining their moral order, he said he saw nothing moral in it and certainly nothing orderly. He was right. No wonder these people's children stayed away from them. Everyone kept urging me to eat. The food was tasteless.

My irritation grew when bowls of oranges and apples were passed out at the end of the meal. At our table the fruit was snatched up immediately, leaving only three bruised apples. Two women elbowed each other for the best ones, then looked at me somewhat sheepishly, noticing that I would be left with the bruised apple. I said I didn't mind, and took it with me to eat on the way home. But it was completely rotten inside and even though I was hungry, I had to throw it away.

That night I dreamed I had traveled to Poland. I arrived in

a deserted city and found myself outside the door of a hotel. Carlos Castaneda opened it for me, motioned me to enter, and pointed to some hieroglyphic writing on the wall. I understood that it was my task as an anthropologist to decipher it and bring it to light, as Carlos had with Don Juan's codes. On a table was a bowl of apples. I removed one, polished it on my sleeve, and held it up to the hieroglyphs. Reflected on the shiny surface of the apple, I could read the message. But when I awakened, I no longer knew what it was.

I forgot about the dream until I went back to the Center several days later. Inexplicably, things seemed normal once more and I wondered what I had been so upset about when I was last there. Then I understood the message on the apple skin. The selfish women at my table for lunch were themselves too bruised to graciously accept a damaged piece of fruit. The meal had been free—a windfall—but its conclusion had threatened another disappointment and that was too much to bear. These people themselves were too much like rotten, unwanted fruit. Their struggle for the better apples was a small way of repudiating their own condition. For people in such straits as they, nothing is impersonal. Their condition swells until it fills the world. Solipsism is a certain mark of those too long abused. A rainy day is an unkind attack, a broken zipper a manifestation of the hostility of the universe. In many ways, these small challenges can be turned into triumphs. Such misfortunes, minute in other people's lives, were enormous in theirs. Their affairs were not miniature to them, though in the larger arenas of the outside world, they would appear so. Our activities swell to fill the frames in which they occur. To those inside, they are always complete and consuming. Thus, local politicians consider their own comings and goings to be as momentous as those of the ministers of nations. And for the same reason, my four-year-old son sobs inconsolably when his Popsicle falls off the stick.

The bruised apple often served as a mnemonic for me, reminding me that however vital and joyous and angry the Center people were, however adept at asserting their independence, disguising their hurts, protecting their pride, they were deeply injured by their situation. Without this clear realization, their actions were unintelligible. I had this in mind a few days later when Basha showed me how cleverly she had cut up her shoes and inserted a piece of elastic to allow her corns and bunions to bulge out. I was able to marvel with her. Her cleverness was perfectly evident, and so was the genuine significance of this piece of work. From such scraps and rags and ingenuity whole worlds and whole lives could indeed be fabricated.

When I arrived for my visit with Shmuel he knew all about the session with Dr. Cohen, having "circulated through the benches."

"Now tell me, what do you think about all that?" he asked me. "Do you still call it a therapy session? Do you think anybody got better mental health from it?"

"Well, I wouldn't say it was a normal therapy session. I don't think anybody 'got better' or changed. I think they used the session as a means of staying the same and staying together. You might say the therapy was the metaphor. It was like the Graduation-Siyum in that way—they made the occasion into what I consider a definitional ceremony."

I explained to Shmuel what I meant by this, how I saw Center people as enacting their identities, and constructing their own myth.[7]

"You think because they claim something in public, they actually believe it? They don't know this is make-believe? Now you are insulting them."

"Let me put it this way, Shmuel. The literary critic Kenneth Burke once described ritual as a way of 'dancing an attitude.'" I went on to describe how when people in a preliterate society do a rain dance, for example, they don't think they will actually cause it to rain. They are enacting their desires. He suggests we think of it more as "dancing with the rain," a kind of prayer. It is belief but the sort one finds in the theater, achieved by a willing suspension of disbelief. Mircea Eliade, the religious scholar, talks about this in rituals. People put on masks or costumes, and by using symbols, transform their reality. Very little is needed to do this. Sometimes a person can transform himself into a bird and "experience" the power of magical flight merely by wearing a single eagle feather, or even drawing a feather on his body. Eliade says, "One becomes what one displays." There are worlds of difference between lunacy, lies, and imaginatively creating an alternative reality.

"And do you suppose the doctor also got people to imagine they were cured?" Shmuel asked impishly.

"I don't know if he would have called it therapy. The people who were there might call it a discussion or class. You would probably call it a brawl. Perhaps it could be called a political event. And no doubt for a number of people, it was entertainment."

"These people come together, curse, shout, and in general act like peasants in front of an ignorant but well-meaning stranger," Shmuel protested. "They put eventually some money in the *pushke** and you call it a ceremony, very original. No, in this I couldn't go along with you. You are altogether too indulgent. Where are your standards? When you find this behavior 'interesting,' you ask nothing of them. It does not show them respect and it does not show respect for yourself. Are you going to bring up your sons to think this kind of carrying on is acceptable? No, you wouldn't do it for them. You shouldn't do it for anybody. These are my people. I recall to you what Jeremiah said of such ones: 'Their tongue is a sharpened arrow/They use their mouths to deceive/One speaks to his fellows in friendship/But lays ambush for him in his heart.' If you want to look at this inside Jewish tradition, you got to be more strict in your judgments. You couldn't say I'm wrong about them. 'They wear themselves out working iniquity.' "

"Well, Shmuel, even if you find so much commotion unacceptable, not everybody does. Abe just told me something you might think about." I tried to conceal my delight in this news that I was sure would make Shmuel reconsider in his righteousness on the subject.

"It seems that a woman nobody knew, a South American Jew, had stopped in the Center during one of their 'commotions.' She died shortly after and in her will left the Center five hundred dollars because she found the old people so wonderful, so full of life. They're going to use the money for Passover, so there will be a Seder in the Center after all."

"I suppose fighting is better than being in a coma like you see with a lot of old people," he said. "If that's what they have to do to keep going, what can I say to you? It's not for me."

"Basha made a remark that I really enjoyed. She quoted Sholom Aleichem, 'We fight to keep warm. That's how we survive.' "

* Little can in which money for charity is collected.

"This is just like them. It happens that is not from Sholom Aleichem. In my opinion it is a sad thing. You see, we Jews have such a great culture. It would be better if they could use it the right way. When they mix everything up like this, they don't show respect for it. I know, I know, you think it doesn't matter so much if they get the names right. To me it matters, because scholarship is about truth, not only ideas. Little truths, big truths, it doesn't matter. On the other hand, maybe I give too much importance to culture. This matter about what difference culture makes I have been thinking about all my life and still don't have an answer.

"This was always very puzzling to me, even as a child" he continued. "I saw already that we had a great culture, and I saw the difference between the Jews and the peasants, but always we were in trouble, not them. How did we come to this? That I couldn't understand.

"My thoughts always at Passover turn back to these things," he said. "In spring it was the finish of those terrible winters. People seem to become more tender at this time, the tight cords of the heart let go. I would walk out into the woods and see that river like a shining ribbon across the green fields, the wildflowers so small you had to lie down on the ground to see them, the smells of the wheat fields, mushrooms and berries calling to you when you walk through the woods, whether you want it to or not, taking you up in happiness. In springtime I think always of my beloved brother who had the misfortune to be a gifted artist. He left our town the Passover before I was twelve. He couldn't help himself. He loved beauty and saw it everywhere. Whether it was the beauty of the Jews or Gentiles made no difference. You see, this was a hardship for a Jewish boy to have this gift, finding a desire for art when the love of images is forbidden to him. Those who have a gift for music or words are not so afflicted. But those who are born to see and make pictures have another story. Such a one was this brother. In time he left for Paris, his mouth bare of French, his pockets not overstuffed with money, but his drawings spoke for him and he enrolled in the School of Fine Arts. In all his life he never tired of creating beauty. All that was around him became enriched, including myself."

"You lived with him in Paris for a while, didn't you?" I asked.

"I went there and saw what he was doing," he replied. "I

wanted to go to work to help support such a talent, but he was not one to nibble on his future greatness, letting others do for him. We lived together there, so poor we had one pair of good trousers between us. Whoever had the need that day, that one would take the trousers and the other stay home in bed. For him those were the happiest days. I have in my mind a picture of him sitting with the sun on his forehead, singing rich Polish songs with his hands flying up and back like swift white birds over the work he made.

"It was this brother who in his own way brought me a new awareness of our Jewish culture, even though he was himself less taken with it than any of us."

"How did that happen?"

"This brother of mine, and the other one, also older than me, were both revolutionaries. They had to smuggle in books from the bigger towns and cities. And this literature they had to hide from everybody, the officials, the rabbis, their families. No one was supposed to read secular books, let alone revolutionary books. You could be arrested for that. But they had ways! They would smuggle pamphlets in their shoes, cut out pages from the religious books and put others inside. They would pretend to be chanting from the prayer books, but inside they had these other books they were reading. I knew something funny was going on. Then one day, my oldest brother leaves behind such a book. Was it by accident? I don't know. Anyhow, I fall upon it like a great treasure. Already it emerges to me as a new life. In Jewish, it was Karl Marx. From then on, I did not play Bible; the Talmud began to fade out for me until much later, when I was old enough to know the value of it. I went on from that to Dickens, Cervantes, and the great Russian literature.

"It was this," Shmuel said, "that brought me to understand some things about our Jewish language and literature, how it is different from others. Our writings bring us out of the morbid parts of life by laughter. The Jew has a joyful life regardless of the oppression he walks through, because he is a good swimmer. He always comes back to the surface. He tries to reach the other side, with his humor and irony. Great humor is based on pain and grief. And in this, the Jew proved to be the expert. To me, finding this other literature was a way of finding how Jewish life is written about.

"But all that is behind." He sighed heavily. "My brothers,

my parents, all are gone. From fourteen children, only my sister and me are left. Of that big family, why are we only here? I often ask this. Are we the best ones? Why are we the lucky ones? I can't find an answer. It causes me great sorrow to think that we were allowed to live only because we were adventurous. Why should this be rewarded? It's not a necessary thing to be rewarded for taking chances. Does this make a better man? I ask you, what kind of God could explain this?"

"Shmuel, do you think the reason you ask so much from the Center people is because they are alive when the others are not? Could it be you have high standards for them because you want them to show themselves to be better than the ones who were left behind?"

"I couldn't answer this for you. I can't find any morals in it. The same thing occurred to me even when I was a boy walking in the woods before Passover. I would look at the chestnut tree and think how it is different from us. It is not cultured. There is no preaching in it. It blooms in the spring, that's all. It was made that way. Man is not so natural. He lives by morals, but he never keeps them. Later I thought about this more so. What does our culture give us? Culture is not a simple idea. Germany, for example. There was in its way a rich culture. Rich in philosophy, poetry, in music, in art. But as long as there is a nation that can bring so much harm to the living, that nation is not really cultured. This is not only for the Germans but for all mankind.

"We think in our time we made a lot of new discoveries, we crossed the threshold into progress. We did cross the threshold, the threshold of cruelty, of brutality. We have not evolved as much as we think. Our inventions got better, that's all.

"Like the chestnut, we stay the same. It is our nature. We try to bring order out of things, but we are hopeless. We have pretensions, but we are not getting anywhere. Man cannot find order in his own bosom, that goes for the Jew and the Gentile. Now the Jew never did cruelty to others like the Germans, but he never had the chance. Do we know if his culture is strong enough to make him safe from greed and cruelty? The Jews have not been tested in our day. Because if our culture does not do this for us, then you have to ask, what is the good of it?"

CHAPTER SIX

Teach us to number our days

BOBBE-MYSEH

OLGA: *This is such a terrible day for me, I don't know how I will manage. Such a shock I had. This woman Gita, I have known all my life. She was a landsman, even if she was not my type. To find her like that, my heart nearly gave out. Wandering around on the boardwalk early in the morning, all covered with filth. She didn't recognize me.*

MOSHE: What did you do?

OLGA: The best what I could. I sat her down on the bench and wiped her around with my hankie. Finally I got ahold of Abe. He called the paramedics. She had some sort of stroke. She looked like she didn't eat for days.

BASHA: Has she got family?

OLGA: She got a son in Detroit. In her purse there was a letter she wrote to him. She told him to come and get her, she wasn't feeling right. But even if she sent it out, it wouldn't do no good. She hasn't seen him for years. If she doesn't make it, then he'll come and visit. A couple weeks ago she made her own arrangements. She gave Abe her blue dress, the one for dancing with the silver braid, and along with this some money, so Abe could make sure she had a nice funeral, with a bus to take people to the cemetery and refreshments. He should see that they put on her the blue dress.

MOSHE: With a son like this, she won't have anybody to say Kaddish for her. That's a sad thing.

NATHAN: Whose children these days will say Kaddish? When my father saw how it was going with us, his children all unbelievers, he adopted his nephews. They were still religious, *he made them his "Kaddishim" to say the prayers and keep his name going.*

BASHA: *In this country we know already, we can't depend on the children. We gotta make our own life, from the inside to the outside. In this time if you don't concentrate on what you got left, you sink under.*

RACHEL: *I second this. A lot of people don't realize how we got to look out for ourself in old age. We think life is only for the children, then we're alone. We got to face the world in a new way. This means you find your own kind, so you can be comfortable, otherwise you are lost completely. For some people old age is a terrible ordeal because of the loneliness. But if you manage to find yourself you take a big step. You stop thinking about death. When you have every day something to do, you begin to live all over again.*

OLGA: *Everything in old age is like what it always was, only more so. You got to keep moving. You couldn't let yourself stagnate. If you fall behind, it's very hard to catch up again. If we would let ourselves go we could be like those old men who play cards all day and hang around the shuffleboard. The women gossip and take trips to Las Vegas. This they call the Golden Age. It would kill me in a week. You got to keep a breath of air in your mind, keeping new ideas circulating or you could suffocate.*

SONYA: *For myself I find a lot of life in here at the Center. It's a pleasure to come to these classes, or to Esther's or whoever is giving one. I seek education, any little thing I can learn, to me it is a treasure. What have I got to do? I can't read no more. I can't see enough to make new friends because if a person would meet me one day and the next day come up and say hello, maybe I don't recognize them and they get insulted and go away. So in here I come with all my heart and soul.*

LEAH: *The main thing is not to let yourself get depressed in old age. After I lost my husband and my daughter, I remained for a whole year in the house. One night I sat down and took inventory. My dead loved ones wouldn't want me to live a life like that. I wasn't being true to them. So I got up and got dressed. I said, I must go out into the fold again between my people.*

HESCHEL: *On this we could talk all year. All of us here are experts on how to survive old age.*

MOSHE: *Heschel, you don't come often. When you come you always sit quiet. Now on this you have got an opinion, you could tell us. Especially with your experience, you know a lot of how to survive.*

HESCHEL: *I got opinions, but what good would it do to tell them? I would be the first one to say, I am not objective. If I would tell you, it would change you. You won't be anymore the same. If I tell you and you are still the same, why should I bother to talk? I would only waste my time.*

MOSHE: *Time, you got.*

HESCHEL: *So, I'll tell you how I survive, but you won't like it. Every time I say anything about it, people shudder. But you couldn't get away from it, the thing I am talking about. The word is 'pain.' Pain is the avenue to getting a soul, getting quality from yourself. This is how you get a life that's really on the essence.*

You got to go about pain the right way. You couldn't escape, so you go into it. Then it melts. You get from this the whole thing, the idea of life itself and the result is you're able to take pain in and ignore it because you're so full of living. When you learn to do this—and believe me, it took me a very long time—you get a clarification, I would say.

Now if you would like to hear a little more, I could give you an example. When I start to talk about pain it leaves me. That's why I don't like to talk so much. All that I got to say is painful, and when I tell somebody about it, then I feel better. But that's no good. It comes back to you when you're not looking, whoosh, it jumps out from behind the stove and grabs you. So when the pain comes, I am patient. I shut up, active silence; I bear it, wait, even overnight, but I mean I bear it, I don't take a tranquilizer, a sleeping pill, some schnapps, or watch television. I stand before it, I call the pain out. After you go through this you discover you got choices. You become whole. This is the task of our life. I want to live this kind of life, so I can be alive every minute. I want to know when I'm awake, I'm altogether awake. When I'm asleep, I'm asleep.

HANNAH: *This sounds to me like something masochistic.*

HESCHEL: *It's not masochistic. It's not stoical. In fact, if you want to know, it's Jewish. One of our prophets said, "In quiet confidence, shall lie your strength." In this way you can make of suffering something positive, because it's part of human life. Dostoevski wrote about that. He said, "I want to be worthy of my sufferings." And believe me, he suffered.*

HANNAH: *Good, he suffered. He was one of the biggest sufferers. He was also one of the biggest anti-Semites.*

BASHA: *Being a Jew and a sufferer go together. When we stop suffering, we get rich and secure, we stop being Jews. We become like everyone else, living for enjoyment only. Without it we don't know what our purpose is.*

JAKE: *Suffering gives you purpose, the purpose to get free of it.*

HANNAH: *Look now how our children live. My granddaughter joins Jews for Jesus. Like Esau, these children throw the heritage away for a bowl of cereal.*

FAEGL: *The grandchildren are not so bad as the children. My granddaughter takes Yiddish in college. She asks me all the time about life in Romania. She's more interested in this than her mother.*

JAKE: *Some get it and some don't, like the smallpox. We couldn't inject in them Jewishness when they don't want it.*

MOSHE: *You see, when things get quiet, Jews drop away. You remember when General Brown said those things about how the Jews were running this country? That was an uproar. Jews were coming out from everywhere; before they couldn't be bothered. Security and success are our enemies as much as Hitler. With them we start to forget our Jewishness, we marry Gentiles, we put ourselves out of business.*

BASHA: *That's right. My daughter complains to me, why do I always send my money to Israel? Why don't I buy myself a nice sofa, a good mattress. "Mamaleh, you're old, give yourself a break. Buy yourself some nice things before it's too late." Do I need luxury at this age? If I want white rugs I could visit her house.*

HESCHEL: *In old age, we got a chance to find out what a human being is, how we could be worthy of being human. You could find in yourself courage, and know you are vital. Then you're living on a different plane. To do this you got to use your brain, but that's not enough. The brain is combined with the soul. Do you know what I'm talking about? I don't think you could get to this understanding too young, but when you get to it, then you couldn't go before your time, because you are ready.*

MOSHE: *Nobody wants to go, no matter how ready they*

think they are. I'll tell you a little story about Methuselah. When he arrived finally at the age of nine hundred and sixty-nine, his son began to worry, when would he be ready to die? "Pa, it's your birthday today. You're nine hundred and sixty-nine, Pa, so what about it?" "So soon, mein kind?" the old man answered, "so soon?"

The celebration of Jacob Koved's ninety-fifth birthday was planned to be a grand affair. Abe, Jacob, and his family had invited over 150 people, relatives, friends, and Center members, who would gather to honor him. The plans were made even though Jacob was very sick. For three months preceding his party, he had been hospitalized in intensive care and three weeks before, at his request, he was removed to the home of his son Sam so that he could be "properly taken care of, out of the unhealthy atmosphere of a hospital." Before, Jacob had always resisted living with his children, and people interpreted this change in attitude as indicative of his determination to live long enough to come to his birthday party. The old people were aware that Jacob had resolved to have the party take place whether he was able to attend or not. They were impressed, first, because Jacob had the autonomy and courage to assert his opinions over the recommendations of his dictors—evidently he was still in charge of himself and his destiny—and second, because Jacob's children were so devoted as to take him in and care for him. But most of all, they were struck by his determination to celebrate his birthday among them. The elders were honored and awed by this. Everyone followed closely the daily developments that preceded the celebration: details concerning Jacob's health, the menu for the party, the entertainment—all were known and discussed at length.

As the party grew near, much talk concerned the significance of the specific date. It was noted that the celebration was being held on Jacob's actual birthday. His parties were always on Sunday, thus the date and day coincided only every seven years. Surely this was no accident. March, in itself, was especially important. In the Hebrew calendar, it is a month of major holidays. Moreover, they said, in March Moses was born and died. He was supposed to have died on his birthday.

A week before the event, there was talk that Jacob had died.

Many who were in touch with him denied it, but the rumor persisted. Two days before the party, a young woman social worker and close friend of Jacob's told some of her friends at the Center that she had dreamed Jacob died immediately after giving his birthday speech. She also told them that Jacob's sons were advising him against coming to the party, but that he would not be dissuaded. He had resolved that nothing would keep him away.

The atmosphere was charged before the party had even begun. Abe was worried about the old people's health and the effects on them of too much excitement. There were those who insisted that on the birthday they would be told Jacob had died. Jacob's friend Basha said, "He'll come all right, but he is coming to his own funeral."

And what were Jacob's thoughts and designs at this point? His intentions were clear in some taped interviews he made with his son Sam and his granddaughter. In these, common elements emerged: He was not afraid of death, but was tormented by confusion and disorientation when "things seem upside ways," "not the way you think is real." Terrible thoughts and daydreams beset him, but he explained that he fought them off. "I have always been a fighter. That's how I lived, even as a youngster. I'd ask your opinion and yours, then go home and think things over and come to my own decision." In one of the tapes, he described his battles against senility and his determination to maintain coherence by writing, talking, and thinking. He concluded, "I was very depressed in the hospital. Then I wrote a poem. Did you see it? A nice poem. So I know I'm still living and I have something to do. I got more clear-headed. I controlled myself." Jacob had always controlled himself and shaped his life, and he was not about to give that up. "I'll never change" were his last words on the tape.

It was difficult for Jacob to hold on until the party and to write his speech, which seemed to be the focus of his desire to attend. Its contents were noteworthy in two respects: First, he made a financial donation that provided for five more parties whether he was there or not; and second, he stated that whereas on all his previous birthdays he had important messages to deliver, on this one he had nothing significant to say. Why, then, the desperate struggle to make this statement? The message, it seems, was that he could and would deliver it himself, that he was still designing his life and would do so to the end. The preparations for and circumstances in which the speech was delivered conveyed and replicated its message.

Under normal circumstances, Jacob's birthdays were major events. All the other members celebrated birthdays collectively; all those born each month had a joint party. These were simple affairs. Only Jacob had an individual party and this reflected his unusual standing in the Center. He was a patriarch; though less active now, he remained a major figure whether present or not. He had been president for many years and even after he left the nighborhood to live in a rest home, he returned regularly and had been named president emeritus. He was one of the oldest people in the community and the most generally esteemed. No one else had managed to provide leadership for so long a time without becoming entangled in factions and disputes. He regarded himself and was generally regarded by others as an exemplar, for he had fulfilled the deepest wishes of most people and he embodied their loftiest ideals.

Jacob was conscious of being a leader and a teacher. He meant his life to provide the others with an example, particularly concerning the matter in which he approached growing old. Jacob's attitude toward aging might be called professional; it was a genuine career.[1] To it he brought the same consciousness, intensity, hard work, high clear standards, and demands for growth and success that he applied to himself through the years preceding his retirement. Indeed, the word *retirement* was misleading in referring to his life between age sixty-five and ninety-five. There was no leisure there, no relaxing of his commitment to strict, valued, long-range goals, no sense of being irrelevant or useless. Simply, he was no longer paid to do some of the things that he had always done and continued to do. After sixty-five, he was a professional elder, and one could say that the high point of his career in this capacity was realized the day of his birthday party.

The story of Jacob's life, rich and varied as it was long, was dramatized and summarized the day of the party, in the prepared ritual and its unprepared outcome. Many of the biographical particulars were fairly typical of most Center members, and predictable. In other ways, his life was atypical. His ideals, his human relationships, choices, actions, his intense engagement with his tradition went beyond the norm, representing in purer, clearer terms the most cherished of Center people's values. Jacob's past and present were a case study of morality and triumph. His ideological, social, and economic struggles were characteristic of many of the members, but his success was unique. Jacob's story, then, was more than one man's life history. It was also a moral tale, and as such bears looking at in some detail.

Jacob was born in 1880 in a small Ukranian town, the third child in a family of eight. His father was employed by a road construction company and was often away from home. Like all Russian Jewish boys he was taken to cheder to learn Hebrew at the age of three. From the beginning he disliked the rigidity and narrowness of his religious education and was relieved when, at age nine, he was enrolled in a secular school.

Even as a young child, Jacob was aware of and revolted by class inequities. His little town was socially segregated, and he was distressed that because he belonged to the middle class, he was not allowed to play with the shoemaker's boy on pain of punishment by the rabbi. Jacob's mother managed an inn. His father was eventually made a partner in his road company. Between the earnings of both parents, the family was comfortable. Jacob's secure, stable family life ended abruptly with his father's death when the boy was twelve. The company camp in which the father worked was sealed off when cholera broke out. Hundreds of men died there and were buried in a mass grave. Jacob's mother was determined to remove her husband's body to a Jewish cemetery and sold nearly everything the family had to pay for the opening of the workers' grave. She sorted through the corpses until she found her husband's body. Now penniless, she sold the house and moved to Odessa where she attempted to support her family. After all the household belongings were sold, there was only enough money for her to take four children with her. Jacob and an older sister remained behind until she could send for them.

Jacob managed to eke out a meager living for himself and his sister by teaching Russian to the Jewish children in the town. After several months, he had even saved a small amount toward the fare to Odessa. But he was tricked out of his money by a stranger who offered to buy him a cheap ticket. Jacob soon found himself penniless and without a ticket, on a train far from home and Odessa. After many harrowing adventures in the course of which he was jailed, became a hobo, slept in synagogues, begged for food, and rode the rails, he made his way to the city and was reunited with his mother and siblings.

In Odessa, Jacob tried many jobs and for a time was an apprentice to a metalworker in hope of learning a trade. For four years he was driven mercilessly, half-starved, and worst of all he learned nothing. He had slept on the floor of the unheated shop all this time for nothing. When he ran away and found employment in a sheet metal factory, he was aghast to find that after four years of suffering, he had not learned enough to be a sheet metal craftsman. A craftsman had to know pattern cutting and he did not. Worse, there seemed little chance he would ever learn. Of the thirty men employed in the factory, only one had such knowledge, and he jealously guarded his position by hiding his work, always doing it in secrecy. One of Jacob's tasks was sweeping the factory at night after the others had left. This gave him the opportunity he needed. He studied the discarded pieces and from these scraps reconstructed the process of pattern layout, working furtively through the nights for several months. The acquisition of this skill was to be a turning point in Jacob's life—the source of his independence and freedom many times over in the future. The work suited him. It satisfied his aesthetic desires and talents and his respect for manual labor, a respect that soon grew into a fully developed political philosophy.

It was the eve of the Russian revolution, a time of great philosophical and social ferment. Jacob found the working conditions in which he labored intolerable and though at sixteen he was the youngest man in his shop, he organized a strike. It failed, the men were fired, and undaunted, Jacob managed to acquire some tools and set up a small cooperative sheet metal shop in his mother's kitchen.

Gradually, Jacob was indoctrinated into the principles of socialism and began to attend, then himself organize political meetings. Many times he was beaten and clubbed down in demonstrations that were broken up by mounted Cossacks. During this time, Jacob's life was completely devoted to work, politics, and avoiding the police. This continued until 1900 when Jacob was drafted into the Russian army and stationed near Warsaw. He resumed his illegal political activities in continual fear of being detected, since now as a soldier discovery meant death. In the army he managed to use his skills as a metalworker to allow him the freedom of movement and time needed for his continuing political work.

Eventually, Jacob was arrested for a minor matter, but his safety was assured when he found favor with the wife of the commanding officer who admired his craftsmanship. She ordered a very complex metal ornament of her design and watched over Jacob until it was done, interceding with her husband for the young man's safety on more than one occasion. The revolution of 1905 found Jacob a civilian and he returned to Odessa where he resumed work as a labor organizer.

The next years were marked by regular riots and widespread starvation. Jacob was jailed several times. When money was donated by the rich of Odessa and America to be used to provide food for the masses of people who were starving, Jacob persuaded one of the founders of a relief organization to allow him to set up soup kitchens for the poor. The authorities doubted that this would work. Jacob persuaded them to give him twenty hours to try. From one morning to the next he ran about feverishly, and when the time had elapsed his kitchen was serving breakfast to two hundred people. Of all his many accomplishments, this was perhaps the single event in which he took most pride. He continued to do relief work until he was tipped off that he was about to be arrested again. Jacob fled to a small town near Odessa and hid out there. A politically active young woman, Rivke—who was to become his wife of forty-five years—smuggled food to him. They fell in love and he persuaded her to marry him—but on her terms: They must leave at once for America. The evening of their wedding they escaped to Finland and from there booked passage to Milwaukee, where Rivke had a brother.

Their story in America is familiar. They arrived in the United States without any knowledge of English, found themselves in a strange country, surrounded by baggage, with no place to sleep, and only fifteen dollars between them. Rivke's brother was of little help and once more Jacob's resourcefulness and determination came into play. Soon, they had a room with a sympathetic family and Jacob had a job as a sheet metal worker. At once, he began night school and studied English. He immediately became active in the union. The couple saved every cent and bought steamship tickets in monthly installments for the family left behind. Within a year, all the couple's brothers and sisters had been brought to America. Jacob and Rivke housed and helped establish them, and matters went well until the crash of 1907. This threw Jacob out of work just as his first child, a son, was born. Since employment was not available, Jacob managed to go into business for himself and for the next dozen years his fortunes ebbed and flowed. Many times he prospered and many times he lost everything and began again from scratch. He was fleeced, cheated, and he made many mistakes. But the story was consistent—he always pulled himself out of defeat, used his craft, cleaved to his beliefs, worked for the union, and remained tightly tied to his family.

In 1918, Rivke's brother became ill and was advised to move to California. Jacob, Rivke, and their four sons soon followed. Jacob once more established his own business and ran it as a cooperative, in accord with his beliefs. In time, he drew his sons into it and they worked together until he retired at sixty-five.

Jacob and Rivke were exceptionally successful in transmitting their values to the sons. None of the boys was given a religious education, but all felt deeply connected with secular Judaism and were active in the Jewish community. And they in turn transmitted this to their children. All the sons were highly educated and became successful businessmen or professionals. They established themselves in the city where their elderly parents lived, and stayed there. The sons married Jewish women and drew their spouses and children into the tight-knit family. The family remained close even after Rivke died in 1950. At family gatherings Jacob always quoted her last words, taken from a letter she arranged to be found after her death. Speaking to her husband and children she said, "All your life you should hold to your friendship with each other; guarding your health; not pursuing great wealth; leading a normal life; doing good deeds for mankind; helping as far as you can the needy."

"These were words to live by," said Jacob. "They contained all of the Torah on one foot."

After leaving his business at age sixty-five, Jacob began a second career, organizing elderly Jews into voluntary groups and community centers. For a time, he moved to Miami and continued his work with the elderly there. When he returned to California, he discovered the Aliyah Senior Citizens' Center and devoted himself to it with vigor. There he met Bella, a widow whose children were already married into the Koved family. Jacob and Bella married, weaving the family together with yet another strand. They took an apartment near the Center, which "became their second home."

Before long, Bella grew ill and the apartment was too much for Jacob to manage alone. The couple moved into a luxurious home for the elderly, which Jacob found sterile and cold. Eventually, Bella needed hospitalization and they were separated until her death, a few years before Jacob's.

Jacob was a symbol, as T. S. Eliot has put it, "a symbol perfected in death." Worker and a Socialist, he was also a man who had succeeded in the world. He was immersed in a form of Judaism the Center members identified with, secular Yiddishkeit and the Jewish cultural-ethical tradition. He supported the Center and so did his sons and their children, demonstrating their respect for Jacob and his followers, signifying to the members the hope of continuity and providing them with some visibility in the larger world outside.

At every Center gathering arranged by Jacob, parts of his earlier life were brought in—the same parts that most Center members had also experienced. Jacob made generous financial contributions toward sustaining the physical continuity of the Center as an institution, along with his contributions to the cultural continuity of its people.

Jacob was not only a symbol of and force for continuity, but also he was to Center members a symbol of the possibilities of aging well. Extreme age had not cost Jacob clarity of mind, determination of purpose, or passion in life. All this he maintained with an air of gentleness and dignity. Tolerant and generous, he aroused no envy; Jacob was a symbolic and literal focus of Center culture and of the people's fragile solidarity and continuity.

All these historical, biographical, and cultural threads came together the day of Jacob's birthday. The weather was exceptionally fair and several hours too early celebrants came streaming toward the Center down the small streets and alleys. That the day was set apart was clear from people's appearance, the women in white gloves, holding perfectly preserved purses from other decades, wearing symbolic jewelry, unmistakable, often expensive gifts from their children—golden medallions bearing grandchildren's names, "Tree of Life" necklaces studded with real pearls; Stars of David; and the golden letter "Chai," Hebrew for life and luck. All were announcements of connections, remembrance, and esteem. Glowing haloes from scarves and bright hats colored the women's expectant faces. Men wore tidy suits polished with use, over frayed, starched shirts.

The Center hall, too, was festively decorated and people were seated formally. At the head table was the Koved family and around it the dignitaries. Jacob, it was learned, was behind the curtain of the little stage, receiving oxygen, and so the ceremony was delayed for about half an hour. At last he came out to applause and took his seat. Jacob's son Sam was the master of ceremonies. Music called the assembly to order and people were greeted with "Shalom," Hebrew for peace. Jacob was presented as the guest of honor, followed by introductions referring first to the whole Koved family as *mishpocheh*,* then extending the term to include all those assembled; all present were an extended family. Each member of the Koved family was named, including the absent ones, along with their profession, academic titles, and degrees, generation by generation. Sam greeted the assembly on behalf of "Pa, his children, his children's children, and even from their children." The broche in Hebrew was followed by the traditional Jewish toast, "L'chayim," to health and life. Then Sam set out the order of events in detail, including a specification of when Jacob's gift to the Center would be described (during his speech), when dessert would be served (with speeches), and when the cake (after speeches). The announcement of procedures was intended to achieve coordination and invite participation, and the audience was appreciative. People applauded for the academic degrees and for the regrets from family members unable to attend, and recognized all the implicit messages—of continuity, of tradition, of respect from younger generations, of educational accomplishment, and responded to the sustained dramatization of filial devotion and intense familism that characterized the whole ceremony.

The meal went smoothly, and no unusual developments were evident to the assembly, but privately, when Moshe came over to congratulate him, Jacob whispered that he wished people

* Extended family.

would hurry and eat, "*Malakh-hamoves** is near and hasn't given me much time," he said.

As dessert was about to be served, Sam took the microphone and began his speech in which he recounted some biographical details of Jacob's life and certain cherished characteristics. He emphasized his father's idealism and social activism in the Old Country and in America, and spoke at some length about the courtship and marriage of their parents. Though their mother had died twenty-four years ago, she remained a strong influence in keeping the family together, he said.

He continued, "You know, Pa doesn't think a birthday is worth celebrating without raising money for a worthy Jewish cause." Thus, the event had a more ambitious purpose than merely celebrating a mark in an individual life. This was not a birthday party in the ordinary sense—it was a metaphor used because it came from the American experience and thus symbolized the people's membership in a secular, modern society; as a simple birthday, it had little significance to them. None of them had ever celebrated their birthdays in this fashion. Indeed it was customary to commemorate the day of one's birth on the closest Jewish holiday, thus submerging private within collective celebrations. More important, Jacob's party was called a simcha, a *yontif*,† a mitzva—elevating it to a blessing, a special holiday, and an opportunity for performing good deeds. His birthday, then, became a cultural celebration and an occasion for doing good works that expressed the celebrants' identity with the widest reaches of the Jewish community, including Jews in Israel and needy Jews everywhere in the world.

During Sam's speech Jacob was again taken backstage to receive oxygen. People were restive and worried, but Sam assured them that Jacob would soon return and the program continue. Eventually Jacob took his seat, leaning over to tell one of the young people in English, and Moshe in Yiddish, that he had little time and wished they would hurry to his part of the program, for now he said, "Ich reingle sich mutten Malakh-hamoves [I am wrestling with the Angel of Death]."

The progression was interrupted briefly when his sons recognized Jacob's difficulty in breathing and gave him oxygen at

* The Angel of Death; God's messenger.

† A yontif is a festival day, often a religious occasion.

his seat. A pause of about ten minutes ensued. The momentum of the ritual lapsed while people watched Jacob being given oxygen. Moshe and Abe were worried about the impact of this sight on the old people. The previous year someone had died among them and the old people had been panic-stricken. But now all were rather quiet, talking to each other softly in Yiddish. At last, Sam took the microphone and spoke extempore about his father's recent life, filling the time and maintaining the ritual mood until it became clear that Jacob was reviving.

Sam went on to explain that since leaving the hospital Jacob had "embarked on a new career, despite his age." Jacob was teaching Sam Yiddish and had agreed to stay around until Sam mastered it completely. "Since I am a slow learner, I think he'll be with us for quite a while," he said. This too was full of symbolic significance, suggesting that new projects were available despite advanced age, and that the knowledge of Yiddish was being passed on to the next generation.

Sam went on, extending his time at the microphone as he waited for a sign that Jacob would be able to give his speech. By now Sam was improvising on the original format for the ritual. He made his announcement of the gift of money, half to the Center for cultural programs, half to Israel.

Still Jacob was not ready, so the microphone was turned over to Abe, who developed some of the same themes, again and again touching important elements. He, like Sam, referred to Jacob as a stubborn man and to the Jews as a stiff-necked people, tenacious and self-determined. He reassured the assembly that they were important people and would be remembered, that outsiders came to their Center to share their simcha and appreciate their unique way of life. They like Jacob would be studied by scientists one day, for a better understanding of the indivisibility of mental and physical health, and to see how people could live to be very old by using their traditions as the basis for a good and useful life. Abe concluded by emphasizing Jacob's most revered qualities: his devotion to his people, his passion for social justice, his learning and literacy, his courage and dignity. He was an example to them all. "And," he went on speaking slowly and with great emphasis, "you, too, you are all examples."

At last the sign was given that Jacob was ready. Abe announced the revised sequence of events: Jacob's speech in Yiddish, then in English, then dignitaries' speeches, then the cake. Jacob remained seated but began his speech vigorously. It was characteristic that Jacob's Yiddish was free of anglicized words, distinctly articulated and syntactically correct; this respect for the language was understood by the old people to bespeak Jacob's respect for his heritage.

After a few sentences he faltered, slowed, and finished word by word. Here are selections from his speech in translation:

> Dear Friends: Every other year I have had something significant to say, some meaningful message when we came together for this yontif. But this year, I don't have an important message. I don't have the strength. . . . It is very hard for me to accept the idea that I am played out. . . . Nature has a good way of expressing herself when bringing humanity to the end of its years, but when it touches you personally it is hard to comprehend. . . . I do have a wish for today. . . . It is this: that my last five years, until I am one hundred, my birthday will be celebrated here with you. . . . whether I am here or not. It will be an opportunity for the members of my beloved Center to be together for a simcha and at the same time raise money for our beleaguered Israel.

The message was powerful in its stated and unstated content, made even more so by the dramatic circumstances in which it was delivered. Jacob's passion to be heard and to complete his purpose was perhaps the strongest communication. He was demonstrating what he had said in the earlier interviews, that he sustained himself as an autonomous, lucid person, using thinking, speaking, and writing as his shields against dissolution and despair.

Jacob finished amid great applause. His and the audience's relief were apparent. He sat quietly in his place at the table, folded his hands, and rested. Just as Sam began to read his father's speech in English Jacob's head fell forward gently, then back, and his mouth opened slightly. Oxygen was administered within the surrounding circle of his sons as Abe took the microphone and asked for calm and quiet. After a few moments, his sons lifted Jacob still seated in his chair and carried him behind the curtain, accompanied by Moshe, Abe, and the rabbi.

Soon Abe returned and reassured the hushed assembly that

a rescue unit had been called, that everything possible was being done, and that Jacob wanted people to finish their dessert:

> Be assured that Jacob knew the peril of coming today. All we can do is pray. He's in the hands of God. His sons are with him. He most of all wanted to be here. Remember his dignity and yours and let him be an example. You must eat your dessert. You must, we must all, continue. We go on living. Now your dessert will be served.

People ate quietly. Regularly Abe came to the front to reassure them, with special firmness when the fire department siren was heard outside. He explained at length all the steps that were being taken to save Jacob, and concluded:

> He's very delicate. Your cooperation is very beautiful. Jacob wants us to continue. You heard his speech. We all have a date to keep. Out of love and respect for Jacob we will be meeting here for the next five years on his birthday. We will be here, you will be here, whether to celebrate with him or commemorate him. They are taking Jacob away now. The hospital will telephone us and we will tell you how he is doing.

People complied and continued eating. There were many who quietly spoke their certainty that Jacob was dead and had died in their midst. The conviction was strongest among those few who noticed that after the rabbi and Moshe left Jacob behind the curtain, they went to the bathroom before returning to their seats. Perhaps it was only hygiene, they said, but it was also known that religious Jews are enjoined to wash their hands after contact with the dead. Hence, the gesture was read as portentous.

The room was alive with quiet remarks:

"He's gone. That was how he wanted it. He said what he had to say and he finished."

"It was a beautiful life, a beautiful death."

"There's a saying, when the fig is plucked in due time, it's good for the fig and good for the tree."

"Did you see how they carried him out? Like Elijah, he died in his chair. Like a bridegroom."

"He died like a tzaddik."

"Moses, also, died on his birthday, in the month of Nisan."

Order was restored as the dignitaries were introduced and

sounded the same themes in their speeches: Jacob's work among senior citizens, the honor of his family, his exemplary character, the beauty of Yiddish life, the worth and permanence of the Center, the strength of its members, and the like. A letter to Jacob from the mayor was read and a plaque honoring him proffered by the councilman. Then a plant was given to his family on behalf of an organization, and this was regarded as a signal that ordinary gifts were possible and appropriate. Jake took a painting of his off the wall and presented it to the family. Leah gave the family a poem she had written honoring Jacob, and Basha brought up the flowers from her table. The tension of the ritual lapsed completely in the face of these spontaneous gestures. People were repeatedly urged by Abe to take their seats. Jake asked what would be done about the birthday cake now that Jacob Kosed was gone. Moshe rebuked him for being gluttonous. With great difficulty, Abe regained control of the people, reminding them sternly that the ceremony had not concluded. There remained one dignitary who had not yet spoken. This, Abe pointed out, was insulting to the group he represented.

Abe was improvising here, no longer able to utilize the guidelines of the birthday metaphor. The ceremony threatened to break apart. In actuality Abe was worried about letting people go home without knowing Jacob's fate. It would be difficult for him to handle their anxieties in the next few days if they were left in suspense. And no one wanted to leave. The circumstances clearly called for some closure, some provision of order. The last dignitary began to talk while Abe was wondering what to do next. Then the phone rang and everyone was quite still. Uncertainly the speaker persisted, though no one was listening. Abe came forward and announced what everyone already knew.

> God in His wisdom has taken Jacob away from us, in His mystery He has taken him. So you must understand that God permitted Jacob to live ninety-five years and to have one of his most beautiful moments here this afternoon. You heard his last words. We will charter a bus and go together to his funeral. He gave you his last breath. I will ask the rabbi to lead us in a prayer as we stand in solemn tribute to Jacob.

People stood. About a dozen men drew yarmulkes out of their pockets and covered their head. The rabbi spoke:

We have had the honor of watching a circle come to its fullness and close as we rejoiced together. We have shared Jacob's wisdom and warmth, and though the ways of God are mysterious, there is meaning in what happened today. I was with Jacob backstage and tried to administer external heart massage. In those few moments with him behind the curtain, I felt his strength. There was an electricity about him, but it was peaceful and I was filled with awe. When the firemen burst in, it felt wrong because they were big and forceful and Jacob was gentle and resolute. He was still directing his life, and he directed his death. He shared his wisdom, his life with us and now it is our privilege to pay him homage. Send your prayers with Jacob on his final journey. Send his sparks up and help open the gates for him with your thoughts.* We will say Kaddish, the mourner's prayer. *Yitgadal veyitkadash shmeh* rabba . . . "Sanctified and magnificent be Thy Great Name"

The ceremony was now unmistakably over, but no one left the hall. People shuffled forward toward the stage, talking quietly in Yiddish. Many crossed the room to embrace friends. Strangers and enemies embraced as well. Among the old people, physical contact was usually very restrained, yet here they eagerly sought each other's arms. Several wept softly. As dictated by Jewish custom, no one approached the family, but only nodded to them as they left.

There were many such spontaneous expressions of traditional Jewish mourning customs, performed individually, with the collective effect of transforming the celebration into a commemoration. Olga reached down and pulled out the hem of her dress, honoring the custom of rending one's garments on news of a death. Someone had draped her scarf over the mirror in the women's room, as tradition requires. Moshe poured his glass of tea into a saucer. Then Abe took the birthday cake to the kitchen. "We will freeze it. We will serve it at Jacob's memorial. He wouldn't want us to throw it away. He will be with us still. You see, people, Jacob holds us together even after his death."

Finally, the Center had emptied. People clustered together on the benches outside to continue talking and reviewing the events of the afternoon. Before long, all were in agreement that Jacob had certainly died among them. The call to the rescue

* In Jewish mysticism as represented in the Cabala, a person's soul or spirit is transformed into sparks after death.

squad was a formality, they agreed. Said Moshe, "You see, it is the Jewish way to die in your community. In the old days, it was an honor to wash the body of the dead. No one went away and died with strangers in a hospital. The finest people dressed the corpse and no one left him alone for a minute. So Jacob died like a good Yid. Not everybody is so lucky."

Over and over, people discussed the goodness of Jacob's death and its appropriateness. Many insisted that they had known beforehand he would die that day. "So why else do you think I had my yarmulke with me at a birthday party?" asked Itzak. Moshe commented, "After a scholarly meeting, it is customary to thank the scholar. Jacob was a scholar and we thanked him by accompanying him to Heaven. It's good to have many people around at such a time. It shows them on the other side that a man is respected where he came from." Sofie's words were, "He left us a lot. Now the final chapter is written. Nu? What more is there to say? The book is closed. When a good man dies, his soul becomes a word in God's book." It was a good death, it was agreed. Jacob was a lucky man. "Zu mir gezugt [it should happen to me]," said several of the old people that afternoon.

Two additional rituals followed Jacob's death: funeral and memorial. The funeral was attended by most of the Center members who had been present at the party. As promised, a bus came for them and took them to the cemetery. A month later, a shloshim was held at the Center.

At the funeral, the young rabbi began the ceremony by reiterating his earlier comments, concerning the "electricity" he had felt emitting from Jacob just before he died, describing how Jacob had used his remaining strength to make a final affirmation of all his life had been about. He added, "At the last moment of his life, Jacob—surrounded by all the people he loved—believed in God." A number of Jacob's friends disagreed with this. Hannah was certain that Jacob died an agnostic, but she was not going to argue about it. "If it makes the rabbi happy, let him believe it," she said.

Several eulogies were given. In Sam's he said: "In our traditions there are three crowns—the crown of royalty, the crown of priesthood, and the crown of learning. But a fourth, the crown of a good name, exceeds them all."

At the graveside, the rabbi led the customary memorial prayers, closing with a psalm:

> *Lord, what is man, that Thou has*
> *regard for him?*
> *Or the son of man, that Thou takest*
> *account of him?*
>
> *Man is like a breath,*
> *His days are as a fleeting shadow.*
>
> *In the morning he flourishes and grows up*
> *like grass,*
> *In the evening he is cut down and withers.*
>
> *So teach us to number our days,*
> *That we may get us a heart of wisdom.*

Impulsively, at the graveside, without benefit of direction from funeral officials, many of the old men and women came forward to throw a shovel of earth on the grave, sometimes teetering from the effort. Each one carefully laid down the shovel after finishing, according to custom. Then they backed away, forming two rows, to allow the Angel of Death to pass through. They knew from old usage what was appropriate, what movements and gestures suited the occasion, with a certainty rarely seen in their present life.[2] Moshe, one of the last to leave, pulled up some grass and tossed it over his shoulder. This he explained later, "to show that we remember we are dust, but also that we may be reborn, for it is written: 'May they blossom out of the city like the grass of the earth.' "

By the time of the shloshim an official interpretation of Jacob's death had been forged and shared. He had become a saint by then, and was to be honored. Several disputes were avoided that day by people reminding one another of Jacob's spirit of appreciation and acceptance of all of them and his wish for peace within the Center. The cake was eaten with gusto as people told and retold the story of Jacob's death.

Funeral and shloshim were the formal and collective dimension of the outcome of Jacob's death. In private casual conversations people said things they had not and probably would not express in public, particularly about matters that they knew might be regarded as old-fashioned, un-American, or superstitious. In confidence, several people expressed wonder and some satisfaction in what they regarded as the divine participation in the event. Said Olga with a chuckle, "You know if the Lord God, Himself, would bother about us and would come around to one of our affairs, well, it makes you feel maybe you are somebody after all." Said Sofie, "I wouldn't have believed if I didn't see with mine own eyes. Myself I don't really believe in God. I don't think Jacob did neither. If a man talks about the Angel of Death when he's dying that don't necessarily mean anything. Everybody talks about the Angel of Death. It's like a saying, you know what I mean? But you gotta admit that it was not a regular day. So about what really went on, I'm not saying it was God working there, but who can tell? About such things you could never be sure."

The subject was also pondered at great length in the Living History class. Moshe quoted a psalm in which King David prayed to God "to know the measure of his days. The request was denied because God decreed that no man shall know the hour of his death." This troubled the group. Did Jacob know the hour of his death? Could it be that God granted Jacob what he had denied King David?

The young social worker's dream in which she had anticipated the time and manner of Jacob's death, was also much discussed. Dreams, they agreed, had to be carefully evaluated, for they may be sent by God or the demons, and as such were not to be taken as prophecy on face value. Itzak said that perhaps the young woman should have fasted on the day after the dream, since this gives assurance that a dream will not come true.

And why, they wondered, had a young woman had the dream? She knew nothing of these matters. Why had it not come to one of them, who understood the significance of dreams? After an hour or so of disagreement only two points were clear. First, that the news of the dream had received widespread circulation before the birthday party, and second, that it added to people's readiness to participate in a memorial instead of a party. It made what happened more mysterious and more acceptable at the same time. Did it convince anyone that God had had a hand in things? Perhaps the general view was expressed by

Moshe who on leaving said, "Well, I wouldn't say yes, but on the other hand I wouldn't say no."

The impact of Jacob's death went beyond the immediate circle of Center members. The dignitaries in attendance at his party had been included in the moment of intense community that followed Jacob's death, and were duly impressed. Before leaving, one of the non-Jewish politicians told the people around her, "I have always heard a lot about Jewish life and family closeness. What I have seen here today makes me understand why Jews have survived as a people." This praise from an official, a stranger and a Christian to a group that has always regarded Christians with distrust and often fear, was a source of great satisfaction, a small triumph over a historical enemy, and an unplanned but not unimportant consequence of the event.

The whole occasion was reported in the local newspapers and soon picked up by papers all over the country. Members of the audience were given opportunities to tell their version of what happened when children and friends called them or wrote them, "Were you there that day . . . ?" The impact on the Center members of the dispersion of the news to an outside world, ordinarily far beyond their reach, was to give them a temporary visibility and authority that enlarged their importance, expanded their social horizons, and intensified their communication with the world around them.

In our society, in our times, aging well is not common. Many life phases are particularly hazardous these days, adolescence and childhood certainly. Old age is even more trying and far fewer individuals are up to its special tasks and challenges. Since more and more people are living longer and, it often seems, with decreasing satisfaction, it behooves us to look carefully at those who age well for clues, pointing to some of the factors that go into success, for if the best predictions hold, as a society we may expect to live not only longer than ever before but in more isolation and in more severe economic straits than those which beset the Center elderly. What inner and outer resources will we draw on? How will we manage?

As a group, most of the Center members were aging well. It is not possible to know how many people like them there are in the country—people of extreme old age, with very limited means, alone, independent, participating in an active social life and enjoying a culture built out of a cherished common past, contributing to their continuing sense of purpose and vitality. This achievement seems hardly ordinary. But the Center people were not ordinary. Good health, resilience, endurance, imagination, courage, and a childhood passed in a society that treasured its children—these were among the ingredients that contributed toward their success in aging, in what combinations and proportions it is not possible to know. And, it must be said, luck played a part.[3] Though it cannot be explained or predicted it must always be entered into the record.

Looking now at Jacob's life to identify some of the specific features that account for his success, it is at once clear that luck contributed a fair share. Jacob was naturally favored with great energy, good health, intelligence, and talent. In addition to these fortunate personal endowments, he was lucky in his successful marriage that produced four healthy, intelligent sons. Jacob had his share of bad luck too, and his life did not follow an even upward course. He had been a political refugee, was jailed, struggled through the major upheaval of immigration, had had to learn new occupations, to relocate many times, was cheated out of his business by his partner, went bankrupt, made and lost money again and again. Through all his reverses and mistakes, he had no regrets, and he rebounded with more perspective and energy from each setback.

Jacob's autobiographical writings document his active struggle at every stage of his checkered career to integrate conflicting pulls between family obligation and worldly success, and between worldly success and social-political ideals. He struggled also with the contradictions between his internationalist beliefs and his nationalism, in the form of Zionism and American patriotism. And he managed to embrace contradictions generated by his agnostic, even antireligious attitudes, on one hand, and fervent identification with cultural-ethical Judaism, on the other.

These conflicts, it must be stressed, Jacob *integrated*. He did not simply resolve and dismiss them—for indeed the contradictions are real. The one who chooses to remain alive to the intrinsic worth of all these opposing beliefs must continually renegotiate their alliance. Jacob was able to tolerate ambiguity and perhaps this trait was a critical contributor to his successful old age. He was not alone in successfully managing such ideological complexity. Most Center members also struggled with oppositions between their beliefs in nationalism and internationalism, and between religious and cultural Judaism. And the few who had been economically successful struggled too with difficulties arising from the accumulation of wealth and a commitment to socialism or communism. These conflicts, then, were not generated by Jacob's individual psychology or peculiar life history. They were the collective dilemmas of a whole population, engendered by their cultural membership and the historical circumstances they had encountered. It may be that an active engagement with ideological conflict played a part in the ability of the Center elders to age well. It may have given them experience needed to achieve the complex, even paradoxical attitude toward aging, so thoroughly articulated by Jacob and to some degree practiced by all Center members. What precisely was that attitude that marked Jacob as an exceptionally successful elder?

Jacob's conceptions about and approach to aging were complex and dynamic. He knew how to intensify the present, how to deepen his satisfaction in small rewards and pleasures, how to bring the past into his life for the continuity that gave it intrinsic meaning; yet he never remained fixed on the past nor used it as a negative standard in terms of which to view the present. He knew how to look at the inevitable destiny the future held and accept it without moving toward it with unnecessary speed. Too, Jacob could provide new standards and desires for himself as the old ones became unattainable, generating from within appropriate measures of accomplishment and worth, in a continual process of discarding and creating. Aging in this manner is serious life work. It required a dynamic equilibrium and led to an integration of internal and external forces. Jacob's aging work was continuous with his prior experiences in coping with paradox and conflict.

This acceptance of ideological complexity, the understanding, even delight in dialectical argument and multiple, relativistic perspectives, the use of sometimes sardonic, resigned humor about life's inevitable flaws has cultural antecedents, both in Talmudic debate (pilpul) and in the literature and folklore of the shtetl.[4] The approach is exemplified in the figure of speech "On the one hand . . . but on the other hand—" so characteristic of Jacob and most Center people. For Jacob and for them there was always another way to look at things; closure, simplicity, certainty in outlook were disappointing—small failures, since everyone knew truth is provisional, and knew, too, that as long as there is debate there is possibility, sociability, and excitement. Jacob's attitude toward aging was rooted in this tradition, exemplified in a Yiddish proverb he was fond of quoting: "He that would avoid old age must hang himself in youth." This intransigent realism tempered by a mocking, undefeated acceptance of life was woven into a philosophy of aging by Jacob and many of his peers.

A final factor contributing to Jacob's success in aging, and a major one, was attributable to his love of writing. In this, too, his work was continuous, for he wrote all his life, expanding the quantity, use of different genres, and content of his products greatly after age sixty-five.

Jacob's writings consisted of two nearly book-length autobiographies, one covering his life up to the age of sixty-five, the other from age sixty-five to ninety-four, and a collection of essays, speeches, letters, short stories, a travel diary, and poems in English and Yiddish, amounting to several hundred pieces. From age eighty-nine on, he regularly used his birthdays as occasions to reflect upon his life and revise his interpretation of its sense and worth. He wrote pieces for the rites of passage in the lives of his children, relating their history to his own. Several pieces were reminiscences of his childhood, his parents and grandparents. He was also inspired to write by external events, for example, moments in the history of Israel, developments in Jewish history, especially the Holocaust and the destruction of Eastern European Jewry. Some of his pieces were occasioned by the death of friends and family members. Some marked Jewish holidays and others were written for celebrations held at the Center.

Jacob was fortunate that literacy was a traditionally valued activity in his culture, and brought him public esteem. In Jewish tradition, old age is regarded as an appropriate period for the study of Torah and for reflection. That Jacob studied himself and the world around him was his variation on a conventional cultural theme. He used his writings to teach, with the hope of passing on to his descendants an account of his history and philosophy. And he wrote in order to clarify his thinking and stave off occasional periods of depression, anxiety, and fears of senility. Above all, in the writings he organized his conception of himself and the meaning of his life.

Jacob's writings also revealed a passion for continuity, in its various forms: vertical, over time, as he wove his past into the present and shaped it in order to pass it on to his children; lateral, across individual boundaries, as he passed his work on to others of his age group. He created for himself personal continuity by integrating all the phases of his long life into a single, narrative account, contemplated by a single sentient being, aware of having been other beings at other points in the life cycle. And he incorporated external historical events into his life account, thus establishing continuity between himself and the times in which he lived, meshing inner and outer history into a unified tale.

In these writings, Jacob constructed a sacred story, a personal myth, which took up the ultimate eschatological questions, "What has it all meant?" "Why was I here?" In traditional, religious settings, answers to these questions are provided collectively. In our secular world, the individual must provide his/her own, and this Jacob undertook. For him, the work was obviously urgent, and this was not surprising. When a man is facing death, when he does not believe in God and has no reason to believe his way of life will be perpetuated, when the world does not consider his wisdom and experience germane, discontinuity is so extreme as to constitute a threat of total nothingness. What Sir Thomas Browne said in 1658 is still true: The threat of oblivion is "the heaviest stone that melancholy can throw at a man."

The desire for temporal continuity, the wish to be remembered, was only one of the tasks served by Jacob's writing. The struggle to find internal continuity was as important—expressive of the powerful human impulse to order. Through autobiography, "man creates by the very act of seeking, that order he would have . . . [looking for] a oneness of self, an integrity or internal harmony that holds together the multiplicity and continual transformations of being . . ."[5]

In his autobiographical work, Jacob was not only constructing a myth, an orderly and moral tale about himself, he was constructing a Self. Through the heightened awareness and consciousness provided by self-reflection, he was crossing the delicate but crucial threshold between merely being and being a man, a sentient human being, *knowing* himself to be. In order to accomplish this, one needs reflecting surfaces. Rituals often provide them, especially those that define the Self through changes in social station and life phases. Audiences, listeners, witnesses are essential for self-awareness, even when a person is his or her own mirror, at once subject and object, speaker and listener in the same story. This is precisely what is done in autobiographical writing, the individual equivalent of the collective dramas I have called definitional ceremonies. In view of the difficulty Center people had in listening to each other, in view of the shortage of good listeners—meaning younger people and members of the outside world who could retell the tales they heard in the Center—it was no wonder the old people talked and wrote so much about themselves and displayed themselves whenever they could, literally "making a scene."

In constructing a Self, Jacob—and the other old people—sought to define a coherent experience of "I," a sense of continuity with one's past selves. This is not inevitable, as James Fernandez points out.[6] It must be actively sought and maintained by examining, selecting, interpreting, and connecting elements from one's inner and outer history. To experience the Self as a stable, continuous being through time, across continents and epochs, despite dramatic physical changes, is especially important to the old, burdened with such vast and disparate memories. Reminiscence is no mere escapist desire to live in the past, as some claim; rather it should be regarded as a major developmental task for the elderly, resulting in the integration that will allow them to age well and die well.[7] The discovery of personal unity beneath the flow and flux of ordinary life is the personal counterpart of myth-making, the ceremonial displays that characterized public life in Center culture.

Throughout his writings, Jacob repeatedly could be seen making bearable his periods of anguish and confusion by finding them explicable. And, to paraphrase Susanne K. Langer, one can bear anything of which one is able to *conceive*.[8] Without our conceptions, our sacred symbols, lacking a vision of coherence and continuity, we become utterly vulnerable and disoriented. When we contemplate and construe our experiences, building up an explanation for Self and the Universe, we make Cosmos out of Chaos, and this, said Einstein is the "only way man has of making the universe stop pounding and washing away at this little light of consciousness." When his eyesight had failed him, when passivity and defeat threatened, when his body no longer moved as he wished, Jacob's mind and fingers served him still. He continued through the writing to be the engaged, lucid man of purpose that he had always been.

Jacob's confrontations with some of the regular difficulties facing the aged were especially interesting in this context: his despondency over illness, his revulsion at the home for the elderly in which he lived for a short time, his dismay at the loss of contact with younger generations. Regularly, he admonished the elderly on the necessary ingredients for a positive response to old age—humor, realism, the preservation of tradition, the necessity for continual learning and adapting to change.

The attitude was exemplified in one of his pieces, which he called "Ten Commandments for the Elderly." It combined resignation without defeat, showing an impeccable perspective about the situation of being old. The last commandment best illustrates this:

> Dress neatly and don't try to save your best clothes, because after you leave this world you won't need them anymore. Keep your head up, walk straight, and don't act older than your age. Remember one thing: If you don't feel well, there are many people who are feeling worse. Walk carefully, watching for the green light when crossing. If you have to wait a minute or two, it doesn't make any difference at your age. There is no reason to rush.

Jacob's passion for continuity was a leitmotiv, woven throughout the body of his writings. This passion goaded him on despite the weariness he felt as he began his second autobiography at ninety-four. In it, he reminded himself of the reason for fighting apathy—to leave his life story for his children.

"So, Jacob Koved," he wrote, "pick up your pen, don't be lazy, for time runs too swiftly while we humans fall behind. There is a saying in Hebrew, 'The day is short and the work is long.' So I will begin my work now, and I hope the Angel of Death will allow me to complete my work before he performs his."

The writings, he concluded, should be read at family and Center gatherings after his death. And when these readings occur, he stated, "I, in my new home, will feel both happy and serene, being with all of you in spirit as I am now in body." With the writings Jacob provided his own memorial. His final notes constituted his legacy to the children, in which he urged them "to try to draw out the thread of our family, in order that your children and grandchildren will have some understandings of their origins." Here, Jacob went beyond assuring his own personal continuity. He bequeathed the *concept* of perpetual continuity, not merely as an individual memorial, but as a permanent process, to those who follow him.

Jacob's birthday was planned to provide continuity—between Jews throughout the local community, between the local community and Eretz Yisroel, between Jews of the past, present, and future. And by his plan to donate funds to provide birthday celebrations for five years after his death, Jacob was attempting to give sufficient continuity to the Center for it to endure as long as any of its members were still alive. The Kaddish prayer, recited spontaneously in response to Jacob's death, was of course unplanned;* but it too contributed to Jacob's purpose of dramatizing and assuring continuity. The Kaddish, known as the mourner's prayer, significantly, says nothing about death.† It is a prayer about continuity in which the name of the departed may be "bound up with all the company of righteous Jewish men and women," with the ancestors and those who will yet be born. The continuity of remembrance is assured for the dead by the children's Kaddish prayers. And a community of mourners, an *Edah*, is created among those who recite the Kaddish, thus continuity is provided between all who have ever grieved for a loved one.[9] For nonreligious and religious alike that day, the Kaddish expanded and concretized the significance of Jacob's death. The prayer "bound up" Jacob Koved with the ancestors and as well with each person's private, particular griefs. Individual deaths were equated with all who had ever died, who would ever die, so that among them a unity was established.

This was a miraculous moment, the kind that Susanne K. Langer calls a "transformation," "when symbol and object seem

* Strictly speaking the Kaddish should not have been said, but rather is supposed to be reserved for graveside and memorials.

† Kaddish is an eschatological, messianic prayer, most often associated with death and memorial services.

to fuse and are experienced in a perfectly undifferentiated whole." Such moments cannot be willed. Though rituals strive to achieve them, they are rare. They carry participants beyond words and word-bound thought, "altering . . . conceptions at a single stroke." At these times, symbols do not merely point to things beyond themselves. They "call into play imagination, emotion, and insight," briefly, suddenly, making present the meanings of symbols, known to us not by intelligence and reason but in experience.[10] Those present when such transformations occur are filled with wonder and gratitude, and are likely to experience the intense camaraderie Turner has called "communitas." Participants are drawn into an unseen but vivid reality that is the deep purpose of all religious rites. Far from the secular celebration it started out to be Jacob Koved's death was a sacred moment, a triumph of understanding and belief. Almost at once the mortal man Jacob, his life and death, became mythic, illuminating the lives of all those in attendance, demonstrating the continuity between one human being and Humanity. Myth and ritual are important because they connect our private lives, the human condition and the mythic condition. More than an eternal tale, they tell us about ourselves.

The Kaddish prayer provided the occasion—not uncommon in sacred rituals—for bringing the past into the present. Originating in the most basic layers of childhood, rooted there with the earliest emotions and associations, the Kaddish had Proustian powers for arousing deep involuntary memories, those surges of remembrance that are not merely accurate and extensive but bring with them the essences and textures of their original context, transcending time and change. This happened to Basha when she experienced herself as a child in saying the Sabbath prayer, and to Moshe when he recited Kaddish the day Jacob died. As he chanted the ancient words, he relived the first time he had heard them and once more felt himself as the small boy wrapped snugly in his father's tallis, standing close to him against the cold, weeping and swaying over an open grave on a bright winter morning.

All immigrants acquire a second culture, often after childhood. Even among second- and third-generation immigrants, a second culture may exist, preserved and practiced in the home, distinguished from the customs of the outside society observed away from home. The first culture, the one associated with childhood, family, and in the case of a bicultural society with ethnic origins, is often the most emotionally powerful. Rituals drawn from that context have the capacity to carry one back to earliest times and selves with nostalgia and great yearning. By means of ethnic rituals, the past is maintained in the present; these rituals can rearouse the kind of experiential remembering that Adam Mendilow calls "hermetical magic." Ethnic memories are "sealed outside of time . . . allowing all of life to be experienced as a single moment . . . pinpoints of great intensity . . . antithetical to the diffuseness of life."[11] For the old people the Kaddish was associated with the Eastern European past, for the younger people it was part of their ethnic identification associated with family and home. For all it was a moment of the kind of mythic timelessness that allows for an experience of the indestructible parts of self and tradition, parts beyond change and history, eternally valid.

In dying when he did, Jacob gave his last breath to his people and they gratefully received this as his final gift to them. But, hinting as it did of divine collaboration, his death could have been alarming and frightening, particularly so by occurring in the middle of a ritual. Ritual after all is supposed to provide reassurance, a sense of order and predictability, yet here were awesome intrusions, disruptions suggesting the very opposite of pattern and form.

Paradoxically the very elements of unpredictability made the ritual more persuasive rather than less. These elements came in traditional garb. Prophetic dreams and the Angel of Death were familiar notions. And these were precedents for the timing of Jacob's death in the accounts of the tzaddikim, and the deaths of Elijah and Moses. Thus conceptions existed for handling them, and if most people involved claimed not to believe in the religious dogma, neither did they overlook the possibility that religious explanations discarded long ago might warrant reconsideration on this occasion.

Had there been no intimations of the supernatural, the death would probably have been frightening, suggesting that Jacob's mortal powers were beyond what we normally regard as possible. The hints that there were other forces at work, besides Jacob's will and beyond his control, made a religious experience of one that might otherwise have been more bizarre than spiritual.[12] Despite the interruption of the party and the radical change of course, the celebration that finally occurred had the very sense of inevitability and predictability of outcome that is the underlying, unstated goal of all rituals.

Jacob's death revived the idea, or at least the hope, that sometimes people die meaningfully, properly, and purposively. Death is often felt as the final manifestation of helplessness, accident, and disorder, but here it seemed apt and fulfilling. Too often, death flies in the face of human conception, reminding us of our ignorance and impotence. It finds the wrong people at the wrong time, it mocks our sense of justice. But here it did the very opposite and made such obvious sense that it appeared as a manifestation of a higher order and morality.

Jacob's death couldn't change the hard realities. But if people lived only by hard realities, there would be no need for rituals, symbols, or myths. Their power is that they may change our very experience of the world and ourselves. Jacob's death rites may be considered an extraordinarily successful example of ritual—establishing continuity of many kinds—cultural, biological, and spiritual. At the beginning of the day, the obliteration of a man and his way of life seemed unquestionable. At the end of the day, that certainty had given way to other possibilities.

Shmuel and Jacob were dead. Center people would go on without them, but their ranks were greatly diminished by these losses. There would be no replacements. Both had been men of stature in their world, highly developed individuals of remarkable independence and strength. From the same social and cultural tradition, both Yiddishists, Socialists, workers, yet opposites in many ways. One a leader, the other a critic; one a man of action, the other a thinker; one a Zionist and atheist, the other against nationalism and a believer in spite of himself. Jacob died a culture hero, amid ceremony and drama; Shmuel quietly slipped away and was not widely mourned in public. The contrast in the appearance of the two men was also striking: Jacob, very tall and pale, stately, stiff in movement, gaunt-faced, square-jawed, his eyes hidden behind thick lenses; Shmuel, tiny, ruddy, lithe, bushy-haired, eyes naked and often mischievous, likely to suddenly sing, chuckle, or weep.

I missed Shmuel often, never more than in the days after Jacob's death. There was so much I wanted to ask him. In my imagination, we conversed and argued, as was our custom after important Center occasions.

"Shmuel, I can't help but feel somewhat sad that your death was so little noticed while Jacob's was given so much attention. You deserved more honor and gratitude."

"Now you are talking like one of the bobbes," he answered. "Haven't you learned from me that one thing has nothing to do with the other? 'Az ikh vel zayn vi er, ver vet zayn vi ikh?' [If I would be like him, who would be like me?] You know how I feel about exaggeration. In my opinion, Jacob was a good man, a fine man even, he should rest in peace, but his death was an exaggeration. His birthday party, the same. A party is one thing, but a simcha for all Judaism, this goes too far. A man is a man. This is his highest work. It takes away from him to make him a hero."

"Shmuel, I think you could look at it another way. Jacob's death was a cultural celebration. It gave people an opportunity to experience their unity with each other, with the past, with Jews everywhere. It enlarged the private significance of one man's death and made it something that everyone could participate in. And by giving the donation for parties for the next five years, Jacob was assuring people here that they would not outlive Center celebrations. He allowed them to be certain they would continue as a group beyond his departure and as long as they lived."

"That part, I would say was very original," he replied. "Other things were not correct. It is not Jewish tradition to say Kaddish until the person is buried. A lot of the talk afterward was all mixed up, bobbe-myseh. Elijah did not die in his chair. He went out by a whirlwind that took him into Heaven. Moses also died on the seventh of Adar. It was not Nisan. This they changed around to suit the occasion."

"But isn't it true that some tzaddikim died in their chair and anticipated their death? And wasn't it true that Moses died on the day of his birth?"

"Not only Moses but many righteous men. In the Talmud it says that righteous men are allowed to complete their years exactly from day to day and month to month. 'The number of thy days I will fulfill,' saith the Lord.' "

"But, Shmuel, you can understand why people would

weave these materials into a myth in order to explain the event, to give it meaning. Surely trying to make sense of it in terms of their own traditions can only be admired."

"You could admire it if you want. Don't ask me to. It's the same thing that always bothers me, how they are always making up everything. Not letting things be themselves. I suppose as usual you are finding something in your anthropology books about people dying like this?"

"I will tell you one thing that struck me, Shmuel. There is an account of the death of old people among the Polar Eskimo that I remember reading. When a man or woman has decided that their life has been completed, they may hold a public ceremony. There is food, dancing, and festivity. The old person is surrounded by loved ones, friends, family, his best dogs. At a sign from the old person, a rope is fastened around his neck and his favorite child rubs noses with him, then hoists him to his death.[13] The dying person is the hero, the death not an intrusion but a fulfillment of his life."

"It's not Jewish custom, but I would have to say that it's better than dying unconscious and alone in a hospital or old age home."

"I read another interesting book about ceremonial death that you might enjoy, by a historian who writes about death in the Middle Ages. Evidently, there was a custom among medieval knights to prepare their own death ritual. They would preside over the event, summoning to their deathbed parents, children, neighbors, then make a simple speech, receive communion, and die. The historian calls this a 'tamed death.' It was not romantic or dramatic. Death was part of the household activity, as was birth. It wasn't banished from the domestic circle as it is among us. It was familiar, accepted, and the dying person always remained at the center of the occasion, directing the ritual as he saw fit."[14]

"Now this is not so strange to me," he replied. "You have read about Malakh-hamoves? This is the Angel of Death in Jewish. Not necessarily an enemy. Not like we have it here, with the skeleton and the scythe. He could appear places quietly and go away again. He was God's messenger, not Satan's. One myseh tells how he came to fetch a man who on that day was a bridegroom. The bride argues against this, telling him that the Torah exempts a man from military service to remain home with his wife for a year after marriage. If the Angel took her husband, this would go against the Torah. The Angel went back to God with the problem because it seemed to him like a good argument. He wouldn't make this decision on his own. The Angel was well known to the Hasids. The Baal Shem Tov he visited several times. When he was very sick, the Baal Shem Tov said to his disciples, 'See, there he is, the Angel of Death. He always flees from me, but now he has been given permission to come and he flaps his wings and is full of joy.'

"Now if you want to think of Jacob like one of those myths you admire, you could say it wasn't so much that he wrestled with the Angel at the birthday party. He more likely made a bargain. Jacob won from him a little time, enough to make the speech. If the paramedics could have revived him, he wouldn't have kept his part of the bargain. If I believed in such things, I would say Jacob and the Angel had an understanding."

"I like this interpretation, Shmuel," I answered. "I often feel that the Angel of Death is present here, among the people I'm with, not as an enemy but as a member of the family. Not long ago, I sat with Leah on her narrow bed in her tiny room at the Kosher Guest Home. She told me that the day before her granddaughter had died, leaving her without any living family. She spoke about her bitterness at being left behind. 'I am cursed with such health, so I remain after everyone I love is gone,' she said. I think outliving one's children must be the heaviest burden a person can carry. Yet she was not defeated even by that. As we sat on the bed, she reminisced about her childhood and the fullness of her life. She was prepared for death, but was not anticipating it by diminishing her life now. As we talked, I felt as though another presence sat on the bed with us, quietly, without threat, the Angel, with his wings folded. When people have made this peace with death, they live with greater consciousness. Every day, every moment becomes more complete in itself. It makes people impatient with trivia, decorum, deception, because every moment counts, for good or ill."

"You speak as if you are already familiar with the Angel?" asked Shmuel.

"Yes, Shmuel, I know him well. I lost both parents, all my grandparents, and recently Ruth, my beloved friend of twenty years, who was like my sister. We were together almost every day for eighteen months while she was dying. I learned from her about the nearness of death intensifying every aspect of life. It is to her that I will dedicate the book I'll write about you, Jacob, and the Center people."

"I think this attitude you are talking about, paying such attention to life, is what we mean by 'a heart of wisdom,' " he replied. "In the psalm it says, 'So teach us to number our days, that we may get us a heart of wisdom.' "

"I had a dream the other night when I was writing up my notes about Jacob's death, Shmuel. A man of great wisdom, a doctor, told me I had a fatal disease. 'You cannot remedy it,' he said. 'There is nothing I can do for you except to give you this advice: Do your work as well as you can. Love those around you. Know what you are doing. Go home and live fully. The fatal disease is life.' "

"This is very interesting," Shmuel said. "The Jews do not have much of an idea about an afterlife. Everything is how you live here. You should be good to others. You should pay attention to your history. You should always be wide awake so you can be responsible for what you do. God wants more of the Jews than to survive. The Jews must *choose* to be alive. So for once, I would have to say you had a very Jewish dream."

CHAPTER SEVEN

"Jewish comes up in you from the roots"

BOBBE-MYSEH

BASHA: *Men are helpless. No matter how strong they are, the truth is they can't take care of themselves.*

NATHAN: Of course. How would they learn this? When my wife had her stroke, I thought we would starve. I had a kitchen so big an ox you could cook in it. But I didn't know how to cook an egg. My wife couldn't talk, she couldn't laugh, she could only cry and eat. We counted on the mama for cooking and for finding the food. When they couldn't, it was the end of the world for them. The first thing I remember about my mother was her crying when she came home dry. We were so poor that she had to be a wet nurse. My father was away in the army. Like a cow, she sold her milk. At night she came home to my baby brother and gave him bread soaked in water. He cried and she cried, but what else could she do?

SONYA: While we are talking about women, I would like a say. In my family we were all brought up very modest so we don't talk a lot about it, but the big trouble was always sex. It's hard to imagine what those women went through. Like Nathan, I remember my mama also with pain. I must have been about five years old. My sister just died, a very slow death, and we didn't have enough food for her. The whole city cried. She was a beautiful girl, about twelve years old. Already there were six of us and my mother didn't want no more children. I heard a funny sound and crept out in the middle of the night. My mother was lifting up a heavy barrel full of pickles and dropping it again and again. Somehow I found out it was to get rid of her baby, so she would have a miscarriage. You know how many marriages this ruined, because even if she loved her husband, *she wouldn't let him go near her. In those days they had abortions, like I wouldn't describe them here. My mother's sister died of that, she had fourteen abortions and eight children at forty. They knew none of the children would have a chance in life if they kept on that way, so she wouldn't go to her husband anymore. From this he lost his manhood. I heard her tell my mother that if she wasn't a Jew and it wasn't against the law, she would hang herself.*

OLGA: *There were a lot of hard parts, but for me the worst part was always the dowry. This was disgusting. For the family, the biggest disgrace was if the daughter didn't get married. My father, thank God, was more enlightened. One day one of those* shadchens* *came into the house, sniffing a good fee because there was two pretty young girls there. With my mother she started in haggling about prices for my sister and me. My father came into the room and started to yell. "Where do you think you are, a stable? Do you think we're selling horses here? You want this one or that one for a better mount? Get out and don't come back!" He threw her right away from the house.*

BASHA: *Sometimes it was the mama who was more enlightened. My mother, she was old-fashioned as could be, very quiet, you couldn't buy from her a word. But she wanted her girls to have education. When we were children, she sold her braids to get us money for school.*

MOSHE: *While we are talking about women we should bring in how important they were in keeping up Judaism. I would say the women had more to do with preserving Jewishness than the men. This is not maybe a popular opinion, but it is how I am seeing things. The father had the job to bring the boy to circumcision, then to cheder, then to Bar Mitzva. But it was the woman who was the guide. Always quietly, without a big fuss. Remember, it was the women who saved Moses and raised him up in secret. Always, it was the woman who gave the moments of life into the family, in the holidays, in the tragic moments. She could do this because she was allowed to express herself more than the men. She was more free with her emotions, and to a small child, this is the most important. A man's religious expression was in the crowd, in the shul. Uneducated she was, but the woman did the rituals. She had the wisdom. She knew how to live with all the men prayed and talked about.*

* Matchmaker, marriage broker.

BASHA: *Barbara, darling, I will explain to you. You know Judaism is really what happens in the family, and this makes it something a woman knows best. A lot of these men aren't religious. We all overthrew a lot of that, especially the men, when they came to this country, even before. But what came into the family through the woman, you couldn't overthrow.*

NATHAN: *You see, that is something we don't know as children. All we hear is to follow the rules. When I was fifteen years old, I stopped going to synagogue altogether because we revolted against the praying. We threw out the good things with the bad.*

RACHEL: *I would like to come in on this. What the girls had is different from the boys. Now what ideas Moshe and Nate got, they come to through the schooling. We girls had another kind of a religion. We couldn't doubt too much because we didn't know enough. You could say, from this we were always in a positive way. You see, all this is from what's going on in the family. That's the root of being Jewish. Jewish comes up in you from the roots.*

Now you could say we girls were more superficial. We couldn't question things. "That's just how things are supposed to be." God said it. We girls had what you could call domestic religion, that means it comes into you through the rituals. I will explain to you. We had a grandmother who gathered us seven girls around. The two boys went off early in the morning to pray. For us, we had to say the morning prayers. I couldn't understand the Hebrew words, the meanings of it, because we were girls and we never went to school. But I understood the expression of the little grandmother. She was so beautiful, so tiny and white. And we gathered around her before we are going to have our breakfast.

Now I knew the Hebrew words already by heart, I knew about the washing of the hands, the prayer for the bread, keeping separate the meat and milk, all these things Grandmother taught us. But not what anything means. But it was our habit and it was beautiful. God wants it so, that's all. After breakfast comes the ritual of dividing up the work. This the grandmother does in Yiddish, because this we must understand. That speech she makes after breakfast also was the way God wanted us to do, made very carefully, as carefully as the prayers, so that one girl doesn't get more to do than the other, all arranged according to her age. That was her wisdom. And this wisdom, we are believing, comes to her through God. Grandmother made such a nice division, in such a beautiful way, not commanded, but just like she was a part of God, even though it wasn't in Hebrew.

Now I did not like to wipe the dishes because the towel was so rough, it didn't feel good, and I did not know how to explain this to Grandmother. The towel was thick, tough, because everything had to be sturdy, not refined like if it would be in a rich house where they got everything soft. So I rebelled against that. The job was not well done. I'll never forget that, how my grandmother, she took me aside one day. She did not reprimand me in front of everybody. She began first all around with praises. "Rucheleh," she says, "you know you are a beautiful girl" (and maybe I was), "Rucheleh, you know you are carrying a holy name. And according to your name, you have to be perfect." Well, she gave me all that until when I looked at her, my spirit was rising and rising, higher and faster until I forgot all about that sturdy towel and my hatred for it. The towel, it was straight from the peasants, you could make rugs from it. But after that speech, I was transformed into a different person. The towel became soft as fine linen and I loved to wipe the dishes. And always before me, when I was wiping the dishes was the name of the holy mother Rachel, and I thought, 'She's right. I am that woman.' That, that is what I call domestic religion. It makes the adrenaline flow. It changes your entire view on things.

I think the boys didn't have it that way. They knew what the sacred words meant so they could argue and doubt. But with us girls, we couldn't doubt because what we knew came without understanding. These things were injected into you in childhood and chained together with that beautiful grandmother, so ever since infancy you can't know life without it. The boys in cheder could learn the words and forget them, but in this domestic religion, you could never get rid of it. This is not like with Nathan. You could not just put it aside when you don't agree anymore. When it goes in this way, I describe, Jewish comes up in you from the roots and it stays with you all your life.*

Basha had decided that she could no longer live on her own. A series of blows had demoralized her: an obscene phone call, her purse had been snatched, her new dentures could not be made to fit properly causing her endless digestive problems, then she lost her Social Security check and took this as a final sign that she was no longer able to take care of herself. If she waited much longer, it might be too late—she might become really dependent and she dreaded her friends' pity more than leaving them and the community. Sonya scolded her. "Look here, Basha. I don't like this attitude of yours. I've known you for thirty-eight years and you were always a brave woman. You're giving up and there's no excuse for it." But Basha was resolute. She was going to an old age home twenty miles away and would probably never see the Center again. From time to time a few friends would find ways to visit her there, and phone or send notes, but she knew this was all she could hope for in salvaging ties that had endured for three decades. She had had her hair washed and set in a beauty parlor for the first time in her life just before she left.

A few days before her departure, Basha invited Olga, Sonya, Hannah, and me to her room for tea. She had packed nearly everything. The room was oppressively clean. Basha was not ordinarily a neat housekeeper. Her room had been crammed with the material remains of her own and her parents' lives. Photographs of everyone but her father—who had been unwilling to "become an idol" by having his picture taken—hung on the walls, alongside a night school certificate, an award for completion of a course from the Singer Sewing Machine Company, and her Graduation-Siyum diploma. Books, newspapers, greeting cards, buttons, and scraps of material had mingled unselfconsciously on every surface.

Basha's room was really one big kitchen. She had arranged this when she first moved in by removing a partition that separated the cooking facilities from the sleeping-sitting room. The space was dominated by a table and chairs and in the center of the table, a fine brass samovar that Basha's mother had managed to hold on to through a lifetime of movement and adversity. Basha had kept it out to use for this afternoon. In one corner of the room was a narrow couch-bed and in the other Basha's old iron sewing machine with its splendid worked iron treadle. "This machine goes with me wherever I go," she had told me when I first visited her. "In the middle of a room, it makes of it a home. With this machine you could change everything, making from a shmatte a Purim gown. You sew on a ribbon here, a feather there, pretty soon you're done up like a queen."

Someone from the thrift shop that supported a Jewish hospital was coming out to take the machine away later on in the day.

We had all dressed up for the occasion. Olga swept in in a flowing black cape. "For what else would I use it if not here?" she asked. "Lately no one has asked me to the Grand Ball." Sonya wore a bright red jumper that accentuated the straight delicate lines of her back and neck. She brought a plate of organic squash latkes, which were received with pleasure. Basha politely rejected my box of fancy cookies. "Too much refined sugar for us, dolly, maybe you could give them to some of the ones at the Center who could not afford luxuries." I should have known better. They did not approve of spending money on delicacies and Basha was not about to accept anything from me just because this might be my last chance to give her something.

Everyone made much over Basha's new hairdo. Pleased and proud, she refused our compliments. "A dressed-up potato is still a potato," she quoted in Yiddish. "You shouldn't be taken in by an old lady."

We talked a lot that day about Jewish women, about our mothers and grandmothers, and about how it seemed to all of us that the old women of the Center were managing better than most of the old men. They asked me about my grandmother, my mother's mother. I told them that my pleasure in their company originated in my love for her, and that I had noticed that those of my friends who were most attracted to the elderly had had early, happy contacts with their grandparents, particularly their grandmothers. My grandmother was very similar to these women and she looked like Basha.

Sofie Mann, born in the Ukraine, had raised me. As a child, I remember thinking that she had always been old. She liked being old, liked her "drapes" as she called her wrinkles, liked being stout and thought her long hair made her look dignified. She was a *bobbe*, a grandmother, and a *balebosteh*, a matron or householder. Only bobbes could tell folk stories well and make proper traditional foods, she thought. Wisdom, humor, and certain slowly acquired skills were the natural rewards of aging for her. Sofie felt her innate qualities were standing her in good stead as she grew older. Her common sense, her great, comfortable strength, her good health and her inner poise were sources of pride. Somewhere in her background, one of her Jewish forebears must have mated with a peasant, she said jokingly, and this accounted for her endurance. She claimed to have been born in a cabbage field, "that's Jewish fruit." Her mother, she once told me, delivered her in a field, all alone. She wrapped Sofie in her shawl, rested awhile, then picked up the infant and her bundles and continued on her way to town. "This was a good start," she said.

In 1880 a marriage was arranged for her with Jacob, a stranger. He was a taciturn, determined man and emigrated with her to America. That year they left their Russian shtetl—the name of which no one has recorded or remembered—and never returned. Without relatives or friends in the New World, without skills or business experience, education or knowledge of English ("Like babies we were," she said), they managed to survive, then succeed. At first Jacob and Sofie were peddlers, eventually owners of a small grocery store. Five of their children lived to maturity. Two received a college education. All had musical ability and were given training; three became professional musicians. The children understood Yiddish but only spoke English. None learned Hebrew or received any formal religious education.

During the American depression, Jacob and Sofie's house was overflowing with people. Their married children lived there, worked, and the grandchildren were cared for by Sofie. It was probably the happiest time of her life. She loved the full, noisy house. She found time during this period to go to night school to learn to read and write English. More educated than many of her childhood girl friends in Russia, Sofie had been taught to read and write Yiddish. She learned to speak and read English in time but never really mastered writing. She knew America and foresaw that one day her grandchildren would be moving away; she would have to write to them in English, so she persevered. Her grandchildren enjoyed helping her with English, her children were less patient. They always wanted her to be modern and urged her to wear stylish clothes and cut her hair so that she wouldn't look like such a greenhorn.

As the years passed, Jacob grew more silent and morose and less certain of himself. We had always thought of him as the absolute head of the house. On Sabbaths and holidays, he was referred to as The King. Only he knew Hebrew; only he could pray. Little by little, we all grew less afraid of his stern looks, more sorry for him, especially after he retired. Then he was physically around the house more, but he was not a presence. There was little for him to do but pray, but he was not a deeply religious or learned man. He had no friends. He wasn't needed.

Sofie was doing what she had always done, taking care of people and the house. In contrast to Jacob, she enlarged in every way. She grew stouter, jollier, cried and laughed more, talked freely about her childhood. It was hard to account for the difference between them, but I remember feeling that Jacob, whose life was not confined to the house, watched us enviously, not knowing how to get "in" to the family. He hung about and read the paper as Sofie cleaned, cooked, sewed, knitted, sang, baked, visited sick neighbors, saved pennies for the poor, and taught the grandchildren her skills and stories. On Friday mornings she was fairly feverish with excitement, killing and plucking chickens and baking the braided Sabbath loaves, dancing to "The Russian Hour" on the radio, whirling a laughing child or two across the kitchen floor spotted with feathers, blood, and flour. She never sat down, and she thrived.

Sofie seemed to have been born a grandmother. The photographs of her, beginning in her girlhood, show the same calm, ready dignity, the unconscious patience that never left her. Always the long gray and black braids were twisted into a bun held by enormous hairpins. She seemed to have been corseted even as a young woman. The photographs do not reveal her capacity for pranks and foolishness. Very little is really known about her. Her maiden name is not known, and even her birthday is lost, as it was celebrated on the nearest Jewish holiday, the traditions of the race absorbing her individual history. In all the photographs she wore black dresses and ropes of fake pearls. But I remember her in cheap cotton starched dresses, and over those an apron—uniform, armor, and vessel, banks for ponds of soft, vast flesh that I peeked at when she struggled into her flannel nightgown each night. It made me sad to see her big yielding body marked by the tracks and notches of her whalebone corset stays. The aprons were as soft as the dresses were stiff.

Sofie had the capacity of transforming the world for those she loved. Her great gift was her ability to stand between the outside and the inner domain of home and children, protecting them against real and imagined dangers. She had a way of seizing small adversities and making them into adventures. This in particular she did through her penchant for storytelling. Entertainment, instruction, consolation, and distraction were provided in these stories for all who needed them.

As a child, I was a notoriously bad eater, and Sofie took this on as a personal challenge. We spent hours and months, sitting in the breakfast nook in the kitchen of the house on Taylor Road in Cleveland, spread before us the special morsels that she prepared to tempt me. We looked out the windows together, past our yard to the houses on the hill. For each bite I took, she gave us entry into one of the houses, and told a different story each day, about the people who lived inside.

These accounts informed my entire life, more than any teacher or book or country I later encountered. Sofie Mann, without her maiden name, without her own birthday, without education, undifferentiated from the stream of her people, Sofie knew and taught me that everyone had some story, every house held a life that could be penetrated and known, if one took the trouble. Stories told to oneself or others could transform the world. Waiting for others to tell their stories, even helping them do so, meant no one could be regarded as completely dull, no place people lived in was without some hope of redemption, achieved by paying attention. Boredom was completely banished by this approach, a simple essential lesson that decades later was to be the most basic message I tried to convey to my own students. None of this did Sofie say. She simply lived as she always had. The stories carried her through the monotony of her work, the pain of perpetual fatigue, through loneliness, eventually through blindness and crippling. And all this prepared the way for my work at the Center. Even now, when I walk along the street, my own, or one in a foreign country, or on the boardwalk near the ocean, I look deeply into the rooms, the faces, greedily and gratefully entering, owning what I behold.

What Sofie knew so did some of the Center people. Perhaps her storytelling was part of shtetl kitchen life. Perhaps that is why her maiden name was lost, why no one even called her Sofie—she was "Ma," or "bobbe," or to my grandfather, "Mrs. Mann." Years later, Shmuel told me about his practice as a child —the practice Sofie had shown me as a child—of making a peephole in a window covered by frost. One winter day, I cried because I could not see outside and thought that meant no stories could be told. Sofie laughed and warmed a penny in her palm, then pressing it against the pane, she made a small, round opening. This framing suddenly transformed the view; the street, now focused and contained, became a magic scene. The houses on the hill rose and twirled about, animated by our gaze, dancing on chicken legs like the home of Baba Yaga, the Russian witch.

The best stories came on the days when I had a cold and was allowed to stay home from school. Then Sofie and I were alone all day, in the big, cold house on Taylor Road (coal was too expensive to heat a whole house just for two). Then she would tuck me into the big bed in the front room where at night three grown-ups slept. And from the closet floor she would bring stacks of old magazines, and from the drawer one of Grandpa's huge hankies. The chicken soup was put on in the kitchen below. She lugged her huge sewing machine into the room. The stories pulsed out steadily, accompanied by the *pocketa pocketa* of the pedal, her feet riding up and down on invisible currents throughout the afternoon. Outside the snow settled evenly and in time the soup delivered up its primal odors. The world was ample, timeless, and complete.

Many years later, Sofie and I shared a room again. Now it was my room, time and fortune having divested her of home and husband. She was a perpetual visitor in her grown children's households. I liked having her sleep next to me, though my mother thought an adolescent girl should have a room to herself. Sofie, toothless, shorn of braids, status, property, and independence, tossed and grunted on her bed like a beached porpoise. Sometimes she would awaken and we would begin whispering in the darkness, gathering in all our past, telling the stories again, forestalling everything that waited outside the room. When her eyes and legs were gone, in extreme old age, the stories were with her still, lasting as long as she needed them.

Jacob died ten years before Sofie, and was not much missed. He seemed to have actually departed long before. During the latter part of their life, Jacob appeared to shrivel while his wife, Sofie, expanded. There was the suggestion of a similar reversal taking place among the old men and women in the Center community.

The women in Basha's room listened to my description with great interest. "You could say I'm not one hundred percent objective," said Sonya, "but I am of the opinion that maybe things get better for old women and not so much for the men." The others generally agreed, and I did, too. In nearly all circumstances, it seemed to me, the Center women as a group were the more capable, active, and authoritative people. There were a number of remarkable and outstanding individual men, but it was clear that their personal characteristics accounted for their distinctiveness. Collectively, most of the men were quieter, vaguer, more sad than angry compared with the vitality and assertiveness of the women. The women effectively ran the Center on a day-by-day basis, and they dominated the community. They seemed, as well, to manage their private life more successfully.

Of course, there were far more women than men. Women outlive men, and increasingly so as age advances, but it is impossible to say precisely why, given our present state of knowledge. Some still-mysterious intertwining of biology and culture consistently favors women and permits them to outlive their male companions.

The scarcity of men could have given them advantage or disadvantage in terms of the leadership in the Center. Their relative rarity might have brought them into prominence. They might have banded together to give each strength and support in dealing with those of their problems not shared by the women. But this was not the case. Instead, the men were isolated from each other and overwhelmed by the women, before whose greater numbers and more intense vitality they paled.

All the old people, men and women, occasionally gave lip service to the notion that men in general were more important than women, but behavior suggested otherwise. Only two regular Center events brought out the alleged male superiority and female subservience: the Sabbath ceremony and the serving of food. In these areas, the women and men fell into the stereotyped sexual roles.

The roots of the situation lay in the common history of the Center people and their childhood experience with the roles of men and women in the shtetl. Patriarchy was a dominant force in the shtetl, replicated in family and community with perfect consistency. Religion was the concern of everyone, but the specific responsibility and privilege of the men. Women were extremely important, absolutely essential as facilitators of the men's activities. The woman was to bear and socialize the children and provide a harmonious home, conducive to the men's study and prayer. The woman had the exacting job of carrying out the dietary regulations according to the men's instructions and interpretations. Whenever possible, women worked outside the home, enabling their brothers, sons, and husband to spend more time in religious study, providing the support system, the mundane base for the primary undertakings of the men.[1]

In her own right the woman was nothing. Her prayers were not necessary except for her own satisfaction. They did not benefit the community, therefore it was considered a waste to educate women. (Indeed, Rabbi Eliezer said, "Whoever teaches his daughter Torah teaches her obscenity.")[2] But to the extent that the woman fulfilled her supportive role, she could achieve great esteem. Folklore extolls a woman who sold her hair for the money that freed her husband for study. Another tale tells of a woman who sold her soul for her husband (but this story may be apocryphal, since there was debate as to whether women actually had souls).[3]

The shtetl woman realized herself through others—children, men, support of the needy. She had only three positive *mitzvoth* to keep (she observed the same negative commandments as men) and their substance illuminates the traditional role of woman's nature and place: She must purify herself in a ritual bath after menstruation so as not to pollute her husband and her community (*mikva*); she brought her household a taste of Paradise by lighting the Sabbath candles in the home on Friday evenings (*bentching licht*); she must burn a bit of dough when baking bread ("taking *challah*"), representing a sacrifice to God made in the household oven ever since the destruction of the Temple.[4]

All these commandments pertain to the woman's biology and her position as homemaker and keeper. But it would be a mistake to assume that this ideal picture of the woman's life in the shtetl exhausted her possibilities. In all societies, women and men transcend, change, distort, enlarge, and otherwise make habitable restrictive roles, and as we shall see, the shtetl woman embellished an alternative sex role that was later parlayed into a flexible adaptation, highly suited to the exigencies of old age.

The ideal social role of the woman in the shtetl—performing her household and religious duties in a quiet and self-effacing manner—specified not only her duties but the manner in which they were to be performed, that is, the kind of person she was supposed to be: submissive, docile, decorous, retiring, modest, patient, and utterly devoted to her family, without ambitions or aspirations of her own.[5] In fact, an additional, contrasting sexual stereotype was developed by the women, almost an underground role, generated not by design but out of the practical necessities of her work outside the home, and particularly in the marketplace. This role, less overt and not formally vaunted, was nevertheless accepted and admired. It was a *contingent* sexual role, arising in response to and maintained because of its situational appropriateness; within it lay a set of possibilities mined by the Center women in later life.

What were the attributes of this role? First, the shtetl housewife was required by circumstance to be a pragmatist. She needed business acumen and great energy. She needed to know how to deal with government officials and peasants, and as a result often had a superior command over the vernacular languages—usually Russian and Polish—than her pious male relatives. She was the intermediary, often more than the men; she navigated the conflicting, dangerous waters between home, shtetl, and the outside world. She had to manage the household, earn the budget money, regulate time, funds, and attention within the family, make countless practical decisions, allocate labor, and organize and integrate family schedules, articulating the familial with the public demands.

In addition to her activities in marketplace and household, the shtetl woman devoted herself with intensity to community work. She attended to the sick, shared home duties and child care with other needy women, collected money for brides without dowries, fed visitors and strangers, raised money for orphans, made clothes for Palestinian refugees, and worked on behalf of poor and needy Jews all over the world.

It was clear that the baleboosteh needed to be purposive, robust, intrepid, and efficient. Jokes and stories about this stereotype abound, deriding her as fishwife and shrew. No doubt some of these women were domineering, shrill, and implacable. But this was forgiven, since it was felt that woman's nature inclined her to great vigor and volatility. Naturally she was seen as given to outbursts of emotion and was expected to be more expressive than her male counterpart. She was, after all, closer to natural forces, while men were regarded as more innately spiritual.[6] And because women were viewed as weak and imperfect, their complaints were more acceptable. A woman was fortunate in having at hand explanations for her failures not available to men: After all, what could be expected from a poor, uneducated, sinful woman?

If there was available to shtetl men an additional, contrasting contingent and worldly role, parallel to that of the women, I have not been able to find it, in literature, folklore, ethnographic descriptions, or in the improvised solutions of old Center men. Perhaps men were more limited by the religious obligations that constituted the core of their sexually stereotyped role. This would not be surprising since their religious activities were of more community concern than the women's.

The ideal Jewish shtetl male, in physical type and demeanor, could not have been more different from the baleboosteh role of his wife. He was expected to be dignified, soft-spoken, poised, reflective, and gentle; his hands were soft, his eyes weak, his brow furrowed, his skin pale—indicating the many hours devoted to spiritual questions and religious study.[7] With an ideal *and* contingent role available, women, it seems, had more options than the men, more flexibility, more opportunity to express their individuality and adapt to circumstances. And it was the contingent, the underground female role, prefiguring women's future accommodations in old age, that equipped them with the flexibility and pragmatism that ultimately served them so well.

Sexual stereotypes aside, there were other consequences of the shtetl's radical separation of the responsibilities of men and women. The domination of the home and marketplace by women was certainly not unique to this society. Wherever that occurs, it offers to women the possibility of considerable accumulation of power and influence. When shtetl men withdrew from the mundane world and left to the women those presumably lesser duties of "running things," they lost all but titular control. Ultimately, everyday decisions shape everyday life and these were made in terms of situational needs by women. The men made the important decisions: when the Messiah will come, what the Torah means, and what are the attributes of God. The wife decided how much money to spend on clothes, whether or not to pawn the family candlesticks to apprentice the son, when the daughter would marry, and whether it was better to buy fish or chicken for the Sabbath meal. None of this altered the basically patriarchal form of the society. This common development (called a cryptomatriarchy by one anthropologist)[8] is often the butt of jokes, but the laughter is aroused by the embarrassment of instant recognition.

The world of the shtetl shaped the Center men and women. Their shtetl childhood provided them with the basic materials on which they drew in formulating responses to the New World. They encountered some radical changes in their youth in this country; among the most significant was the substitution of a different set of duties assigned to men and women. In the New World, religion quickly gave way as the center of life. Work and money were now the ultimately serious affairs and as before, the most important concerns were assigned to men. As soon as possible women were pulled out of the labor market, since in America a man didn't want his wife to work. In America, immigrant women were soon confined to the home.[9] They became more dependent on their husband, more isolated from public life. In the absence of extended family, community, or economic activities, they contacted the outside world indirectly, through husband and children. The baleboosteh's qualities of strength and competence, energy and autonomy, were not to find adequate outlet during her middle years, and only in old age did these women rally and demonstrate once more some of the features associated with the roles in the shtetl.

To be sure, the older values on and about men had not disappeared; men were highly regarded and sought after by the women in the Center community. Women with men, whether long-term spouses or newly acquired boyfriends, were considered enormously fortunate and viewed with envy and pain by the single women. Men exerted a drawing power on the women. It was not unusual for a single woman to attach herself to an amenable couple, sharing the man's friendship, thus forming a stable triad. Competition among women for men's favors and company was fierce, and strong jealousy was common, sometimes breaking up female friendships of long standing. The men were closely watched and fussed over. However, it could not be said that they were usually the primary leaders or even the consistently dominant people in most Center activities.

In group discussions, men were not deferred to by women, and since they did not usually talk as loud or as much as women, they exerted little influence on the flow of talk, though "serious" discussion had been one of the exclusively male prerogatives in the shtetl ideal. But in the Center, it had by now become clear to everyone that the men were no brighter, no more well-educated, no more perceptive than the women. (Perhaps this was always known but more carefully concealed when people were younger and more patient with harmless deceptions that preserved self-images and social stereotypes.) Except for occasional pieces of specialized religious knowledge, or statements made by the two men who were rabbi's sons (wise, by definition), it was not assumed that the men had anything worthwhile to contribute merely because they were men. Women were more outspoken and assertive in all forms of verbal expression, abundantly producing essays, stories, poetry, and songs. Only two men in the Center group wrote regularly, though among Old World Jews specialization in literate activities was exclusively male.

Center events that required physical endurance were likewise female-dominated. Only a couple of men attended the exercise class. Men came to dances with women but were usually left to themselves. They tired more quickly than their female partners. Men were passed around somewhat since every woman wanted to have a male partner for at least one dance. But the woman often appeared inhibited by her male partner, dancing with him decorously, then becoming more animated after depositing him on one of the benches lining the hall, where he would sit smiling, clapping to the music, nodding his head, tapping his feet, and waiting for the next woman to sweep him away for a dance. Meanwhile, with undiminished enjoyment, women alternated "being the man" in dances that called for a male partner.

In governance, where one would certainly predict male domination, the pattern recurred: The real work was done by the women, though men had de facto supremacy. Organizational tasks, record-keeping, program and class arrangements, the planning of agendas, collecting of fees and dues, and performance of maintenance and administrative jobs that amount to running things were carried out by women. Men were invariably ceremonial leaders, and all the important leadership positions were held by men: the Center president, president emeritus, treasurer, and the director. (The single exception was a woman who, for one year, had served as president; her unusual characteristics—enormous intelligence, energy, wealth, and sophistication—overrode the norm of masculine officials.) All important male leaders were allied with or married to important women whose direction and influence were unmistakable. One of the most important activities in the Center—charity in the form of raising funds and gathering food and used clothing for Israel—was entirely female-dominated.

Center men were used symbolically by women for various purposes. It was a common sight to see Olga, for example, enter the hall, marching across it accompanied by a male companion, bearing herself proudly, almost with disdain, asserting publicly her superiority in being "attached," then leaving her escort on the benches as she entered the fray, unwilling to be encumbered. On leaving, she would stop for him, and depart as she entered, on his arm, grandly, donning the man as she might her gloves. Center males often appeared to be passive tokens manipulated in the more significant interpersonal exchanges between women.

Sadie and Anna, old rivals, vied for Nathan's favor long and hard. When he finally showed his preference for Sadie, she seemed to lose interest. Though she proudly sat next to him at Center activities, her most animated conversations took place with her women friends, and Nathan was more or less ignored.

As a group, the men seemed more worn out and demoralized than the women. How can this be explained? Do the same biological factors that cause men to die sooner than women contribute to their earlier debilitation? Certainly, there seemed a definite difference between the sexes in terms of energy, probably reflecting some complex combination of physiology and culture. One may only speculate about the part played in that combination by different early social and sexual roles of men and women. It seemed as though the old men of the Center were enacting the only role that had been available to shtetl males: the idealized scholarly persona—dignified, remote, self-absorbed, reflective and grave, given more to thought than action. The elderly females of the Center, in contrast, had as models two shtetl roles: that of the idealized woman sketched by tradition—subservient, restrained, home-bound; and the contingent, improvised "underground" feminine role. The latter, which I have called the baleboosteh role, was a response of shtetl women to their existential circumstances as custodians of the mundane realm. The Center old women now, like their shtetl forebears, were strikingly vigorous, resourceful, indomitable, often rude and brazen, antiauthoritarian, outspoken, and submissive to no one. They exuded a presence, a sharp-tongued dynamism expressive of their determination to get by and make do, regardless of external pressures.[10]

The old women were especially powerful in verbal assault and defense. These were seldom subtle, erudite, or complex as were some of the men's displays of verbal skill. The women were experts at sending words like missiles to the very heart of error, piercing a situation, turning it around or standing it on its head. Abe once remarked in public that Center people were not really religious. "Not religious?" protested Basha. "Because we don't go to shul? Since when is finding God in your heart instead of a building not religious?" Often through songs and poems, the women defended themselves and attacked others. Required to listen in an attitude of feigned politeness, Faegl smiled grimly one Sabbath afternoon as Sadie took the microphone and "for the entertainment of our members," sang a song she had composed.

Our lovely member, Faegl Crown
She's always happy. This one seldom frowns.
A lot of people fail to understand
How hard she's always working for the Promised Land.
Sometimes it's hard for people here to see
Because she pushes hard, and with her cutting tongue
is very free . . .

Faegl retaliated the following week, criticizing Sadie with similarly lightly masked insults. The members enjoyed these cycles of song duels, applauding those they thought the cleverest in delivering their barbs.[11]

I remembered with enduring awe Sonya's response to Abe when he announced that I had just returned from an international conference in which I had presented a paper about the Center. "Now all of you here are becoming known to scholars all over the world. Our lady anthropologist has given a paper about us at a very important meeting. Isn't that wonderful?" he asked. In a very quiet voice, Sonya answered, "Well, it all depends on what she said about us." And when the film about the Center had brought it a measure of fame, causing membership to swell, Rachel remarked stoically, "Now that the Center is all of a sudden blooming, everyone wants to come and smell the flowers."

In their present life, men and women were cut loose from all the usual ties and obligations—economic, kinship, and ritual—

and this freedom was an opportunity for them to do things in their own way; for most women it was the first such chance in their life. None of them would have chosen the losses that made independence a possibility, but since this was an unalterable fact of their situation, they dealt with it. The men responded to their freedom by resting and waiting, the women by shaping their life, exerting themselves, and molding their world.

I sat in Basha's kitchen thinking about how ingenious and resourceful these old women were, and they thought so, too, it was clear. "Basha, darling," Olga said, "you will be all right wherever you are. Above all, when you get to the new home you should adapt yourself. The worst part will be having a roommate. If you're lucky you won't end up with someone who snores all night. Try to be cheerful. And you could do like I do in the Guest House. Whenever I want a snack, I got into the kitchen and make jokes with the girl there. If you get people to laugh, they help you and they won't pity you neither. Last week I went to the doctor. They put on me one of those foolish paper robes. I had everybody in stitches. I told them if they would give me a broom I would fly away to the Witches' Sabbath. If people see you're a person and not a ghost, they do nice little things for you. You've seen how I am on the boardwalk. Everybody knows me and calls me 'Grandma.' I can walk anywhere I want without getting hurt. Now I have no husband, and a woman needs a male escort, so I tell everyone I'm out for a stroll with my boyfriend. My cane is my boyfriend, best one I ever had. He is faithful, strong, and never talks back to me. Between him and my smile, I feel safe wherever I go."

"That's right. Adapt and have a sense of humor about you," said Hannah. "When I was to go to the hospital I spent two days cooking. My neighbor comes in and says, 'Hannah, what are you doing? Are you planning on having a party or going for an operation?' 'I'll tell you, dear,' I says, 'I'm going to cook all this food and freeze it. If I come back, I'll have what to eat, nourishing food to recover on. If I don't, my friends should have all the best food to eat for my wake, just the way I would cook it myself.' She got a kick out of that."

The women were describing some of the strategies they had cultivated for coping with their circumstances—growing old, living alone and with little money. Each in a different way, with a different specialization had improvised techniques for growing old with originality and dedication. For these women, aging was a career, as it had been for Jacob, a serious commitment to surviving, complete with standards of excellence, clear, public, long-term goals whose attainment yielded community recognition and inner satisfaction.

When middle-aged or young people look at the situation of the elderly, inevitably they compare it with their own. Then aging seems only a pathetic series of losses—money, freedom, relationships, rōles, strength, beauty, potence, and possibilities. Aging is usually discussed from this point of view; whether compassionately or patronizingly, this stance is *external*, describing aging as it appears to one who is not old. We are rarely presented with the views of old people about themselves and given an opportunity to hear how aging is experienced by them, "from inside the native's head," so to speak. This approach, basic to anthropology, yields the "aging as a career" concept, to replace the usual "series of losses" notion that results when younger people regard the elderly from their own perspective. Another advantage accrues to the study of aging from an anthropological point of view: attention to the correspondences—or lack of them—between action and ideas, or real and idealized conduct. For example, many of the Center people's verbal statements about aging were as grim as anything said or written about them by younger people, but their behavior often belied their words. Even those who stated flatly that old age was a curse, with no redeeming features, could be seen living engaged lives, passionate and original. Nearly every person in the Center community—men and women—had devised some career, some activity or purpose to which he/she was committed. They had provided themselves with new possibilities to replace those that had been lost, regularly set new standards for themselves in terms of which to measure growth and achievement, sought and found meaning in their lives, in the short run and the long.[12]

The elders were not deluded and knew quite well the difference between careers in aging and those in the outside "real world of work." Thus, Sadie, whose career was composing and singing her songs, said, "Myself, when I sing I am in glory. My only regret is I never had the chance for a real career. I had talent but I had to sacrifice. I had to choose between myself and my children. But now when I sing I try to get better all the time, and then I really lose myself." There were many other careers: Basha's ceaseless efforts on behalf of Israeli causes; Gita's passion for dancing; the involvement of many of the women with the philanthropic work; Hannah's devotion to the pigeons she fed every day, gathering huge bags of crumbs from neighbors, stores, and restaurants. Olga told and retold a cycle of highly polished, nearly invariant stories about herself that showed how she handled hostility and indifference with courage and dignity; these tales become her special lifework.

With considerable pride she recounted a story we had all heard many times:

"One Saturday afternoon near Christmas, it was very dark, and as usual, I was out walking. All of a sudden about ten big boys about fifteen, sixteen years old, surrounded me. 'Hi, Grandma,' they said. 'How do you do? It's not a very nice day,' I answered them real polite. 'Spread out, guys,' one of them told the others and they surrounded me. 'Are you Jewish?' he asks me, looking real mean. 'Yes,' I say. 'Do you believe in Jesus?' 'It all depends,' I answer. 'Do you believe he is here walking with us?' he asks. 'No, I don't,' I say. 'How do you know he isn't here with us?' he asks me real menacing. 'Because if he would be here, he would come up to me and say, "Hello, Olga, how are you?" After all, he was my cousin before yours.' After that they laughed and separated to let me go on my way. That's how I handle people."

It was one of her favorite stories, sanctified and validated by use and intent, and everyone nodded appreciatively.

Sonya was just as proud of the neat, well-spelled minutes that she kept so faithfully for Center meetings. And she made truly elegant dresses out of scraps and castoffs that she bought in rummage sales, her self-satisfaction doubled because the money she laid out for materials went to Israel.

And for all of them, getting up each morning, being independent, living up to their goals, despite incredible odds, managing for themselves, whether it was only dressing, cooking, shopping, demanding and getting satisfaction from a hardhearted or indifferent doctor or welfare official—these, too, should be counted as successful examples of the lifework of aging.

"Even though Sonya is mad at me for leaving, she should know that I wouldn't let myself sink into a vegetable," sighed

Basha, pouring tea into our glasses. "I wouldn't pretend to you it's all easy. The home took all my savings. All right, what would I do now with three thousand dollars? They charged my children five hundred dollars each, even my son-in-law who doesn't like me. They take my monthly check from now on. I wouldn't complain about it. My books I gave to the Center, there's no room for anything in that place. My clothes, I sent almost everything to Israel. A few little things I have saved." None of us felt like asking Basha what she would do with the samovar. "I gave my children strict orders to burn all my writings, letters, poems, everything. I make a finish of all that. It's time to begin now a different life. In this I'm prepared. But I'll tell you what worries me. It isn't going to be so easy to make new friends. My hearing and eyes aren't so good anymore. If I don't go soon, I wouldn't recognize a new friend if I could find one. I'll tell you what is the worst that could happen. If no one speaks Yiddish, I don't know how I'll manage. Somehow, no matter how bad things are, when I hear Yiddish, something in me goes free, and everything changes around. Without this I think I would just dry up."

"Basha," Sonya said, "where do you think you could go and find not even one old Jew? We're the world's best wanderers. We turn up everywhere. Maybe you'll be lucky. Your roommate knows Yiddish, she doesn't snore, and she's not Litvak either."[13] We all laughed and raised our tea glasses, making a toast to Basha and to life.

The next day was Friday, the day the Sabbath was celebrated in the Center. It always seemed to me to belong especially to the women, even though the men dominated the ceremony and directed the women's participation for that event. Perhaps I had this impression because the Sabbath was so completely associated with home and family for the old people. After Yom Kippur, the Sabbath is the most sacred of Jewish holidays. On Sabbath, for one day, a Jew may enter Paradise. The baleboosteh, in lighting the candles, brings the foretaste of Paradise into her home. When she offers the challah, her kitchen is the Temple, she is the priestess, and her ordinary oven the altar for her sacrifice.[14] On Sabbath, some say, the Jew has an extra soul.[15] Certainly something special was in the air on Fridays at the beach. Everyone was always especially excited, the women in particular.

The Oneg Shabbat ceremony was a perilous venture, the Center's most ambitious undertaking and the only regular, traditional, religious event attempted. Always, cynical and dissident voices were heard, complaining about variations pressed upon the people by necessity: The service was held midday instead of at twilight as was proper; it followed instead of preceded the meal; there was too much Hebrew for some, too little for others. Always there was the danger that the confusion and contentiousness that were normally acceptable, even functional in Center affairs would destroy the delicate mood and the event would collapse in a rubble of broken spirits and empty forms. But it never did. Somehow each week, for the space of less than an hour, the essential religious experience occurred in the Center—a true hierophany, when the sacred shows itself to us, breaking through the secular plane, and allows us a moment of contact with a wholly different reality.[16] The Center folk never found the ideal Sabbath of peace, but they reached their religious climax in flashes of genuine and intense unity with each other and continuity with the past, most conspicuously when the women lit the candles.

Center people's memories of the Sabbath always returned to the theme of the Jewish homemaker. "We sat at the table with such dignity and happiness. No matter how poor, Mama always managed to find somehow a fish or a chicken, even if she had to hock her pearls. On this night only would she sit down with us to eat. Only this night, my father would not lose his temper, no matter what. Everything was transferred into a different realm. The papa was king, the mama was queen and we were the luckiest people in the world." This was Moshe's description of Sabbath in his childhood. He concluded sadly, "All this here beauty didn't do us any good. We could give to our American children nice clothes, good food, education, but we couldn't give them what our fathers and mothers gave us. It all went out from us, all that respect for the mama and the papa, the love of the home. American children didn't receive that memory."

Basha did not agree with him. "Whether you give it out or not, on Friday there's still something special in the air. Because American children don't take it in, don't mean it isn't still the Sabbath, like it always was."

Elderly women of the Center, without their own households had no access to the three religious duties enjoined on them. Postmenopausal, they did not attend the ritual bath. They no longer baked, so could not prepare or offer the Sabbath loaf. And having neither home nor family, they did not light candles, though technically it would have been possible to do so, alone in their rooms. But this was probably too painful a reminder of their isolation and none of the women lit candles outside of the Center. At the Oneg Shabbat on Friday, the Center became home and the members family. For all the old people at the Center, memories of their mother fulfilling the blessed obligations of the Sabbath held the greatest personal and religious significance.

Every week, before a woman was called to the candles by the president, there was a hesitation in the ceremony. Which woman would receive the honor? Normally, only one woman lights the candles. In the Center the honor was shared by two or sometimes three women. In the silence before the names were called, there was a faint rustling in the room. It was the women who knew the prayer quietly fluttering their scarves in their lap, wordlessly signaling their readiness. This week Basha, Faegl, and Olga were named. They approached the table together. Olga began. In a strong alto voice, she sang a song of her own composition, a Yiddish blessing, belting it out like a torch singer, then stepped back. Faegl struck the match and lit the candles, then barely audible, Basha chanted the traditional Hebrew prayer, encircling the flames three times with open hands, drawing their holiness to her face, covering her eyes with her hands, finishing with her own private prayer as tears spread through her fingers down her cheeks. She removed her hands, looked about as though surprised, smiled fully and wished everyone a "Gut Shabbes," turned and kissed Olga and Faegl. Slowly, the women returned to their seats, stopping to shake hands, embrace their special friends, wishing everyone "a gute woch," a good week, while Moshe helplessly implored them to sit down so the ceremony could continue. Reluctantly they did so, still clasping the outstretched hands of their friends who thanked and complimented them.

Basha rarely said the blessing. She was very pleased that Moshe had honored her in recognition of her impending departure. She hadn't expected to be so moved. The candle blessing was a powerful and complex event in Basha's life, in which she experienced a unification with her mother, and with herself as a child. Such rare moments of personal integration may happen when early memories stored in the body are triggered by the enactment of ancient long-known ethnic ritual gestures. Later Basha said, "Do you know what it meant to me when I was called to the candles last Friday? I'll tell you. When I was a little girl, I would stand this way, beside my mother when she would light the candles for Shabbat. We were alone in the house, everything warm and clean and quiet with all the good smells of the cooking food coming in around us. We were still warm from the mikva. My braids very tight, to last through Shabbes, made with my best ribbons. Whatever we had, we wore our best. To this day, when the heat of the candles is on my face, I circle the flame and cover my eyes, and then I feel again my mother's hands on my smooth cheeks."

Basha's description of how the Sabbath ritual affected her and stayed with her, preserving intact with complete freshness the original context in which she acquired it, seemed to me a striking example of what Rachel had called "Domestic Religion." It had the same features she described, acquired in early childhood, completely associated with family and household, blending nurturance and ethnic specificities, and it was this blend that gave hearth-based religion such endurance and depth. Rachel's concept of Domestic Religion corresponded to what Shmuel called Jewish culture, distinguishing it from nationalism and religious doctrine, and it was what most Center people would have called Yiddishkeit if they were asked about it. Robert Redfield's distinction between Little and Great Traditions points to a similar interpretation. The latter, referring to the abstract, eternal verities of a culture, are usually controlled by literati from a distance, interpreted and enforced by official institutions. The Little Tradition, in contrast, is a local, folk expression of a group's beliefs; unsystematized, not elaborately idealized, it is an oral tradition practiced constantly and often unconsciously by ordinary people without external enforcement or interference. Domestic Religion, Little Tradition, folk culture ethnicity—whatever term one prefers—have in common the potential of providing a sacredness that issues from its being thoroughly embedded in a culture. Its authority comes from the fact that it is completely internalized within the psyche of a people, permeating every institution and relationship. More a matter of customs than ideas, it is mostly enacted rather than discussed, it is often evoked by rituals, triggered by certain symbols that usually pertain to the family, the home, and the immediate community.

Indeed, in the shtetl the distinctions between Great and Little Tradition were exceptionally clear. Great scholars of Judaism represented the Great Tradition and in their practices the tradition was exalted, pure and perpetual. Their studies were devoted to systematizing, scrutinizing, reading, and writing about enormous ideas, in the language of the Great Tradition, Hebrew. But Yiddishkeit was a matter of everyday life and mundane concerns, no less authentically Jewish because more homely. The Jews were "One People" insofar as they participated in the Great Tradition, sharing the literate history and language, practicing scholarship and prayer, but most shtetl folk and almost all Center folk were not able to participate in the Great Tradition, fully or consistently. It was mediated to them through their leaders, teachers, and sages. The more direct version of Judaism, diffuse and concrete, came in the form of Yiddishkeit.

Victor Turner has suggested that sacred symbols have two opposite poles, one abstract, ideal, normative, the other concrete, physiological, affective. An exchange of these properties may occur in rituals, and then their abstract dimension fuses with the concrete, so that the abstract pole is made vital and personal, while the particular and physiological pole becomes ennobled and equated with the highest ideals of the collectivity. Thus does duty become desire. It is the physiological pole that is most basic, acquired earlier, in the preverbal experiences of the infant in relation to those who nurture him or her; it is survival, existence itself.[17]

Survival comes in cultural inflections. The infant is fed particular foods, lulled with particular words and songs, wrapped in particular garments. Desire, appetite, fundamental feelings are inflected in local, household idioms that once acquired are not interchangeable. These forms precede ideas or words. They become expressible later in the child's life, and then their meanings may be overtly taught, but this teaching is an overlay that rarely penetrates the very ground of being in the same way that the first inexpressible meanings do. When sacred symbols are employed in rituals, when the poles fuse, a single experiential reality is created and the individual becomes the embodiment of certain of the collectivities' beliefs. The beliefs are laid upon and empowered by the original mixture of household odors, habits, gestures, sounds, tastes, and sentiments, the accumulation of historical moments—perhaps no longer consciously remembered but nonetheless effective. These first experiences of domestic life, transmuted into Domestic Religion, are permanent and powerful, for their roots have been set down in the deepest layers of the heart. It is no wonder then that Basha felt she could face any difficulty, bear any loss except that of no longer being able to speak to someone in Yiddish.

On leaving the Sabbath ceremony at the Center one afternoon not long after Rachel expounded her views about Domestic Religion, I stopped by the Ocean Beach Kosher Guest Home. What I encountered there might have been designed by her if she had wanted to provide proof for her theory. Services were held once a week at the Guest Home, begun by the devout old men who had been praying together for years. Previously it was their custom to circulate among the several small synagogues in the neighborhood. As the community had dwindled in size, all but four of the shuls had closed, two on the boardwalk, and two within walking distance. A Jewish charitable organization had purchased the mortgages on those remaining and agreed that as long as a *minyon* (ten men required for prayer) held services in them once a week, the synagogues would be kept open. The shrinking circle of devout old men became known as the "marching minyon." Each Friday they strode along the boardwalk, picking up extra men whenever they could. Recently they had become too frail to continue making the circuit and had retrenched, using the lounge in the Guest Home instead. The home was a drab plaster one-story duplex converted into a facility for about sixty people, all of whom were Center members. Once a week, the "lounge" served as shul, and the television set became a bima. On Friday afternoons the broken Naugahyde chairs and ragged couches were pushed against the walls. The room smelled of mold and disinfectant. It reminded me of a bus station waiting room in northern Mexico. The women had moved into the corridor, where they leaned patiently against the walls, peering into the lounge. Many of the men were Orthodox and would not pray with women. About half the men wore fringed blue and white prayer shawls. All had covered their head in one way or another—with golf caps, berets, paper yarmulkes, jeweled and beaded yarmulkes, and one man had borrowed a woman's scarf that he had tied up like a turban. Two men stood before the bima leading the prayers. They were blind but preserved the appearance of reading, as required by Jewish law. A third man stood nearby and prompted them from time to time. Eighteen men were in the room, all praying with great *kavannah,** swaying deeply, stepping forward and back, bowing, striking their chest with clenched fists. I had never seen the Center men so energetic and forceful. The faintest of them now seemed to fill up and throb with vitality, and their hymns rang out powerfully. Outside, the women moved their lips with the men's chants. I was sad and resentful watching them there, trying to follow the prayers. I remembered a story Basha once told me about how as a small girl she had been indignant at having to stay with her mother in the women's gallery over the main body of the synagogue where the men prayed. She had leaned out as far as she dared to try to catch a glimpse of her father and brothers below. She resented being cooped up with the women, some so ignorant they held their prayer book upside down. The gallery had been terribly hot and crowded. Basha thought she was going to faint and had to run outside, weeping in outrage and humiliation.

As I stood watching the women, I noticed Sylvia, standing apart in a dark, little niche in the hall. She was "on the other side," as people said about those they regarded as senile. Usually remote and disoriented, Sylvia seldom spoke. She did not wear glasses. Her eyes were bright but glazed and unseeing. She wore a faded cotton washdress and her feet bulged over her broken, shapeless shoes. I was puzzled seeing her now, for she was very animated. I could not hear her from where I stood, but I saw her lips moving. She bobbed up and down, from one foot to another, almost dancing, waving her hands upward, weeping, laughing, shaking her finger, head, and shoulders, seeming to scold or argue with an invisible antagonist. On her head was an odd white patch. So bizarre was her behavior that I wondered if she was hallucinating or if somehow she had had a head injury and the patch was a bandage. I moved closer and stood next to her. She was reciting the prayer for the dead, "El Moley Rachamim," engaged in an intense, prolonged debate with God, conducting her own private Sabbath service.

The white patch on her head was a piece of folded toilet

* Religious fervor; inner intention of a prayer.

paper, pinned precisely in place. Beneath it her hair was damp. She had combed it neatly with water. Following Orthodox custom, she had covered her head to say the prayers. I was very close to her, but she didn't see me. When she finished I said her name. She regarded me without expression and was silent. I took her hand and wished her a good Sabbath. The physical contact was startling. Something suddenly flew open, as though a window shade had snapped up. For a moment I felt as though I was standing inside a membrane with her. She smiled and clutched me so fervently that her hard, yellow nails raised red welts on my forearm.

"Look, darling, how beautiful it is today," she said. "I am rejoicing in the Sabbath, like always. This I must do because if you wouldn't rejoice in the Sabbath in this world, you wouldn't know what to do in the world to come. These are the same, '*Ot hi le olam*, the Sabbath is a token of eternity.' So on Sabbath, I get all dressed up, the best what I can, and let my heart rise up, like in the psalm:

> "*Come forth from thy ruins,*
> *Long enough have you dwelt in the vale of tears.*
> *Shake off your dust. Arise*
> *Put on your glorious garments, my people.*
> *Be not ashamed.*
> *Your God will rejoice over you*
> *As a bridegroom rejoices over his bride.*
> *Come my beloved, meet the Sabbath bride* . . ."

Sylvia reached her hand to her hair and shyly, vainly, smoothed it beneath the head covering. The gesture bespoke a sense of inner beauty on this Sabbath eve. Truly she had come forth from the ruins and put on glorious garments.

"On Sabbath, darling, there is only joy. You shouldn't cry." She reached up and with great gentleness wiped away my tears. "Shabbat shalom, you should have peace.

"You see, darling, I still know all my prayers. I still got all the sounds in my heart. It comes back to me every week like this, like the Sabbath soul, *neshoma yetera*. All the prayers, the psalms, the hymns. My Jewish heart is lasting long." Sylvia was *here*, on this side, connected and present, tied by a band of memory to God and the day, and for that instant, to me.

Driving home, I thought about the day and the praying of the afternoon. I remembered how often I had been utterly unmoved by beautiful temple services held in lavish halls, the women dressed in finery, fully included as participants in the ceremonies, sitting in dignity and comfort with the men, the rich sounds of well-trained choirs surrounding the sermons of erudite and subtle rabbis. I had avoided synagogues ever since adolescence, for I never found in them the kind of religious experience I wanted. But I would return to the Ocean Beach Kosher Guest Home on Friday afternoons as often as I could, even though as a woman I would have to stand outside. I had never been to so religious a service, nor had I ever beheld an object so sacred as the covering on Sylvia's head.

Women in the shtetl (and some writers say, women in all cultures) were emotional leaders in their family and community. They were responsible for nurturance, for interpersonal relations, and for what might be called in contemporary parlance "quality-of-life" concerns. Some sociologists have called this dimension of behavior "expressive" and contrasted it to more goal-directed, problem-oriented, focused activities called "instrumental."[18] In charge of expressive concerns, women have often been responsible for the general well-being of others, especially their family members, and for creating an emotional ambience in the home. In contrast, men, particularly in relation to their family, have had the task of providing for the family's worldly state. In the shtetl and elsewhere, the husband-father in the family was usually thought of as more emotionally neutral than his wife, oriented to external needs and problems, more in and of the public world. In this view, women's lives are thought of as more concerned with processes—emotional and biological—and men's with products. The former is diffuse and repetitive, the latter more purposive and directed to outcome. Some psychologists have suggested that male and female psychology and cognitive styles correspond to this distinction between instrumental and expressive.[19]

The expressive/instrumental distinction is useful and comes into play in the area of aging as well as sexual difference, for at present, roles allocated to the elderly are predominantly of the expressive kind. Retired people in our society—men and women—are expected to spend their time socializing, taking care of themselves, passing the days pleasantly, attending to quality-of-life and interpersonal concerns. If the expressive domain expands, the instrumental contracts with time. All the links to the instrumental dimension of life are lost to the men with the loss of work. This costs the retired man not only his ability to earn money, but impairs his sense of worth and autonomy, attached as these are to our current ideas about mastery, achievement, problem-solving, and accomplishing clear-cut goals. The expressive concerns that men are expected to devote themselves to after retirement are usually areas in which they have had little experience, and often which they regard as demeaning, being associated with female ("not serious") concerns. This state of affairs gives older women an enormous advantage over men, for their earlier expressive specialization continues to be viable in later years. No wonder many women appear to be better at being old than men, for the male's lifelong involvement with instrumental activities is not viable after retirement.

Other factors may also contribute to the Center women's seeming advantage over the men. They are marginal people on every count: Jews, old, poor, and female. The men's lot was not completely consistent, however; they were regarded as superior to the women of their own community, and thus they were caught in a conflicting set of hierarchies, exalted within their immediate group, but disdained outside of it. In contrast, the status of the Old World women was unambiguous: They were on the bottom. Perhaps the simplicity and consistency of this arrangement made it easier for women to work out personal solutions. Certainly, it gave those who failed to do so every excuse necessary, all in terms of social definitions, rather than individual shortcomings.

Compared to the women, Center men were less connected and less needed by each other, by the women and children. They had not been as accustomed to accepting or even recognizing their need for others, except in economic terms, which were no longer applicable. The old men were less enmeshed in social and kinship networks, less engaged in even superficial interpersonal relations than the women. Always expressive leaders, the Center women by contrast were experts in human relationships.[20]

Roles based on nurturant functions are durable and expandable. They can last as long as life and enlarge as needed, for there is always someone around who needs taking care of. The nurturance role has two added advantages: putting the caretaker "one up" in terms of never being the worst-off person in the world and arousing obligations and sentiments in the cared-for that may develop into deep and long-lasting associations. By definition, expressive roles take account of people's emotions, and thus are more likely to expand than more narrowly construed instrumental transactions.

Another part of the nurturant role advantageous to old women is its provision of experience in self-maintenance. If one's basic biological requirements have always been attended to by others, it can come as a shock to tend these things oneself. For the Center women, getting rid of their garbage, doing their laundry, mending, shopping, cleaning, cooking were not troublesome. On the contrary, this work was a steady source of satisfaction. Sofie, for example, mentioned that her arthritis was growing worse. She was resigned when she was no longer able to carry heavy objects or hold a paint brush, even though she loved her art classes. But when she realized that she could no longer make her own bed, she wept. The adage, "A woman's work is never done" calls attention to the continuity of woman's tasks on a daily basis, but it applies no less to the continuity over a lifetime. In those instances where the Center men needed to perform maintenance tasks for others, often their ailing or incapacitated wives, they were distressed and inept. But incontinent or invalid husbands presented no surprises to the women. Changing diapers was not a shocking affair to them, whether done for an infant or old person.[21]

Since childhood, the Center women have been *bricoleurs*. They have long known how to devise entire though miniature worlds out of their secondary status and tasks. Their worlds were made of smaller and commoner materials but built with proportion, as complex and compelling as the external, male-dominated realm. In her own world, the woman was in charge, using time and energy according to her own lights. Within the structured points of her day in the household, she did a great many highly diverse tasks, all at the same time, always expecting to be interrupted, never finding full closure, but hastening from one activity to the next, watching her work come undone as soon as it was completed. Her standards for performance had to be flexible and individually administered.

Men in the public sector did not usually work in isolation, and thus were not as self-regulating as the women. The loss of the world of work for Center men meant they lost the activity that had always dictated their use of time and energy. Within the household, it was true that women were often tightly tied to biological rhythms of small children and had to respond also to the outside scheduling of other family members. But within this framework there was considerable choice and discretion. As the children matured, these constraints gradually eased up. The nearest equivalent to male retirement is the mother's "empty nest" when her youngest child moves out. But this phenomenon is always less abrupt and irreversible than a man's retirement from a job. Her children need her less by small increments. And even after they have physically left the home, they may return for services, favors, meals, advice, baby-sitting, care of clothing, and the like. Before and after the "empty nest" a woman has more time to adjust, to establish her independence and then accommodate to the changes.

Let us consider biology, too. Perhaps women in general are more prepared for the inevitable infirmities of old age by a lifetime of acceptance of their bodily limits and changes. Initially, the little girl observes herself to be physically weaker than her brothers and nothing she does can alter that. With the onset of menstruation, again, she finds her body intrudes itself on her wishes and must be taken into account in her plans. Soon after, the cycle of childbirth and nursing begins, and once more her projects must take her bodily limits into account. Finally, menopause interrupts her activities and her fantasies. She must regularly acknowledge her biological base in making choices, decisions and interpreting her nature. All this is good schooling for what lies ahead.

By contrast, old men of the Center have been able to indulge in more independent self-conceptions. Among the most agonizing of the difficulties they faced was their daily awareness of being physically limited, and ultimately, dominated by "forces outside themselves," beyond their control. Old age is a brutal check on omnipotence fantasies. The discovery of dependence and weakness later in life, it seemed, shocked the male ego more severely than the female. Women in the Center—and perhaps women everywhere—had always known that the body had "a life of its own." They knew about dependence and interdependence, while the men (assisted by mothers and wives) were able to overlook or gloss their own corresponding limits. All the Center women found it easier to accept help from others; what was etiquette to them was "weakness" to the men. When I performed small courtesies for the women—helping them on with coats, finding someone a chair, taking someone's arm to step up a high curb—I received an easy and warm response. Such amenities offered to the Center men, even if much needed and perhaps desired, aroused embarrassment, a frown, averted eyes.

One of the tasks and pleasures for the elderly is the life review—so often used as an opportunity for "taking stock," recounting what was done well, what could have been better, what is left of their efforts, and what really matters in the end. All Center men had devoted most of their efforts to "chasing Parnassus," making a living before retiring. A few had also been concerned with religious devotion or study. Now, in later life, neither of these concerns "counted." The money—in all but a few cases—had been used to keep the family afloat. Nothing of it remained. And religion was a problematic matter, even before emigration to the secular New World, certainly more difficult after. The handful of men who managed to accumulate some savings found themselves in a strange position, for the norms of Center people did not permit them to spend their money in any conspicuous fashion. It was not possible to translate it into a superior standard of living or social prestige and remain an accepted member of the group. Indeed, the well-off were generally suspect and resented. They themselves were ambivalent and rather guilty about their wealth, for nearly everyone still had some commitment to Socialist principles. Whom had they exploited to gain their wealth? And why had they not been more generous with Jewish charities? These questions others asked of them and they asked themselves. Further, those with money were not able to engage in one of the most challenging and prestigious group activities: bargain-hunting. When Leah appeared in a fine gown and announced that she had found it in a thrift shop she was much admired, as much for her resourcefulness as her appearance. When Mr. Weidman, known to have a sizable nest egg in the bank, did the same he was derided as being foolish.

Why would someone rummage in the trash who didn't have to? It didn't make sense. When Sonya found a day-old bakery within walking distance of the Center, she was much applauded for acumen, and, too, this benefited the entire group. When Mr. Weidman gave a large sum to Israel, no one was very impressed. He was only doing what was expected. But a smaller donation from one who was really hard pressed was widely appreciated.

What did "count" then for these people, in reviewing their accomplishments? Above all, the rearing of children who were well-educated, well-married, good citizens, good parents in their own right, children who considered themselves Jews and raised their children as Jews, and who respected their elderly parents. Here again, the old women had the deck stacked in their favor. Nearly always, they had maintained closer ties with their children than the men, and fairly or not, it was they who were considered most responsible for "how the children turned out." The men had been outside of the home for so much of their time during the children's formative years, working to support the family while the women stayed home, that finally the woman was considered as the one to whom praise or blame went for the children. Since few women regarded their children as total failures, they always gained more satisfaction than grief by considering their children the important accomplishment of their life. It seemed that the men had got short shrift. Their work had cost them the satisfactions of intimate relationships with friends and family, more often than not. And in their old age, when some now sought these satisfactions, they often found it was too late. Their children were strangers or resentful, and they didn't really know how to sustain intense friendships with their peers. And it was not unusual for their elderly wives to turn away their attempts to participate in household routines. Sofie refused to let her husband help in the kitchen when he expressed a desire to cook; it was *her* territory and no one was going to encroach on it.

There is a final comment to be made concerning the different bases for evaluating lifework, in comparing old men and women. It is often said that the contingent nature of woman's work makes it intrinsically less satisfying, and that this is why it is consistently and permanently devalued by societies all over the world.[22] Women are identified as responsible for the work of "nature," while "culture," it is said, is officially the work of men. Many writers feel that women concur with men in viewing cultural projects as more valuable an activity than their "natural" enterprises. A woman's projects are described as transient, pure process compared with the lasting, transforming products of men's work. Her tasks are mundane, concrete; his are abstract, elevated; hers involve subjectivity, personalism, and particularism; his are objective, general, lofty, and so on. Says Simone de Beauvoir:

> . . . in her heart of hearts [a woman] finds confirmation of the masculine pretensions. She joins the men in the festivals that celebrate the successes and victories of the males. Her misfortune is to have been biologically destined for the repetition of Life, when even her own Life does not carry within itself its reasons for being, reasons that are more important than life itself.[23]

Is it really true that women consider their work lesser "in their heart of hearts"? The work of traditional women—women of the Center and my grandmother—is very complex and subtle, not made of the kinds of victories and successes celebrated in war dances and hunting parties. The work is not clear-cut; unequivocal successes and failures are relatively rare. Every realistic mother is reminded continually as to how much of her "product" is beyond control. In child-rearing, she is facilitator and mediator, not "maker." *Outcome* is not an accurate term in reference to human beings who as long as they live provide surprises and demonstrate potentiality.

Perhaps it is true that women are kept humble by the nature of their everyday activities. They spend so much time immersed in unglamorous stuff—the mess of life itself, bodily excretions and necessities, transient and trivial details that vanish and reappear to be done again the next moment. But does this necessarily mean that a woman is not fully aware of the enormous importance of offering food, producing and raising children, shaping the atmosphere of the home? Considering again my grandmother and the Center women, I suggest there is a set of understandings shared among women, concerning the meaning and value of their conventional functions. These are often communicated but in a form not always easy to recognize.[24] Because their tasks are particularized, concrete, embedded, and subjective, there is less urgency (not to mention little opportunity) to make them into platforms, public festivals, ideological treatises. They are known as part of living rather than discussions about living, and their very form makes it an inconsistency to formulate them as enduring, collective principles. These understandings are a kind of underground culture, quietly transmitted in situations, no less essential than the starkly evident, grandiose cultural productions we customarily attend. Real but rather easy to overlook, they continue through the life cycle, and may reemerge as essential aids in later life. The old women I have described communicated a quiet conviction and satisfaction with themselves, perhaps because they did what had to be done, did it as well as it could be done, and knew that without what they did there would be nothing and no one. This is not scant comfort at looking back at one's lifework.[25] Perhaps these Center women are the exemplars to whom we should look when seeking visible models for retirement. In domestic religion, in caring for others, in serious, dedicated friendships, in constructing individual careers made of personally discovered projects, in arranging lives of self-care and attentiveness to others who are needy, they present us with possibilities for our future. For surely all of us—men and women, young and old—must attend these irreducible human tasks. They are concerns that apply to everyone who would fully experience and express the ample range of human possibilities. Who of us can afford to overlook the lessons of heart, the lessons concerning which the old women of the Center showed themselves to be such worthy teachers?

EPILOGUE

It is Easter week, 1978. Shmuel has been dead for four years, Jacob Koved for three. Basha, Kominsky, Sylvia, Sonya, Sofie, Jacob Weidman, and Nathan are dead. Hannah has taken up residence at the Ocean Beach Kosher Guest Home. After a stroke Olga "crossed over" and moved away to a convalescent hospital. Rebekah comes into the Center from time to time. She has a male companion who obviously adores her. "He's a nice enough person," she whispered to me. "As long as I don't allow myself to compare him to Shmuel, I enjoy him." In spite of all the deaths, the Center does not seem depleted. Leah, Moshe, Heschel, Anna, Sadie, Faegl, Gita, and Abe the director are hearty and active as ever. ("Kana hora"). New members continue to appear at the Center and there is no further talk of its closing. But the community is still in peril. A large apartment in the neighborhood that houses about one third of the Center members is owned by a man of eighty, long sympathetic to his tenants. He has just had a heart attack. If he dies, his son will inherit the property and is expected to renovate and raise the rents. There is talk of another rent strike.

Some young Jews, fervent Hasids, have come in a body to "bring new life" to the boardwalk shul. The old people who still use it are worried about these young people: "They're fanatical. That's OK, I wouldn't interfere," said Moshe, "but they put up a cloth in the middle, the women on one side, the men on the other. This is out of the Old Country." "I am offended," Rachel announced. "Do they expect me to lie beside my husband at night and shut my face away from him during the day when I pray? This is too much hypocrisy." "Rachel, when was the last time you prayed?" Moshe asked. "That's not the point. Even atheists got principles," she replied. Anna was so angry that in a mood of great indignation she took the cloth down and threw it in the ocean. Later she remarked, "It was not dignified to have such a thing. Besides, it was a shmatte. It looked terrible. At least they should put up a nice piece of cloth." The young Hasids were baffled. They had expected their elders to have "more respect for Torah." Abe was weary but encouraged by the incident. "These young men have a lot to learn." "All right, we will take them in," said Moshe. "We need the next generation, but they got to learn to be more open-minded about these here practices of theirs."

Heschel was a broken man. His only relative remaining after the Holocaust, his daughter whom he had hidden, then rescued in Belgium, had had him declared her ward and taken over his savings account. He was wounded and humiliated by this; he would not tell her that he needed new dentures. He was unwilling to try to explain to her what this meant to him. "I am a simple man," he said. "I couldn't bring out my own inner workings in the right way. If this is how she wants to do it, I have to leave it this way. But I will say to you that after what we went through together, I never would believe such a thing could happen."

It is spring now. Soon there will be a fine Passover at the Center. On Sunday, Jacob Koved's third birthday-commemoration party will take place. How can I finish this book and say good-bye to all these people, so alive in these pages? Like Shmuel, I feel I am making an end of them by ending the telling. I am making inconsequential changes in the manuscript, what Kominsky would have called "davening" over it. The day I finish is dreary and unsatisfying. That night I attend a performance of Bach's B Minor Mass. Easter week was the time of greatest fear in Shmuel's town in Poland, when anti-Semitism was at its most virulent. How is it possible that the same event that inspired such divine music brought the Jews such extremities of terror? Surely that is part of its mournfulness. The "Crucifixus" is the most grief-stricken statement conceivable. What human situation corresponds to it? The Christian referent does not serve me. A picture is taking shape in my mind as I listen, in a deepening reverie. A dream or a memory, I cannot be sure what it is; I see that I am floating through an empty city in Poland. It may be the Warsaw ghetto or Lodz, or perhaps Shmuel's little town.

There are no signs of violence here, but also no signs of life. Remnants testify to life having been torn out in midcourse—a toy, a simmering kettle, a broom left in the middle of the room, an open book. I hear the music and Shmuel's voice:

"Even with all that poverty and suffering, it would be enough if the place remained; even old men like me, ending their days, would find it enough. But when I remember the way they lived is gone forever, wiped out like you would erase a line of writing, then it makes another thing altogether for me to accept leaving this life. If my life goes now it means nothing, but if my life goes with my memories, and all that is lost, that is something else to bear."

Then if it is remembered, if the stories are still told and retold, does everything change? Is it made bearable? This was suggested in so many ways throughout this work—in the bobbemyseh, the grandmothers' stories, in the hearth tales that are the application of domestic religion, in the reminiscences, and by the wonder rabbis who "knew how to bring Torah to light with a story that showed how it went into your ordinary life." It is reechoed in the Holocaust survivors' fierce determination to "bear witness," to return from hell and tell what they had seen. It barely mattered if there was someone listening. Few survivors were so optimistic as to think people would listen and improve from hearing their reports. If none listen, nevertheless the tale is told aloud, to oneself, to prove that there is existence, to tame the chaos of the world, to give meaning. The tale certifies the fact of being and gives sense at the same time. Perhaps these are the same, because people everywhere have always needed to narrate their lives and worlds, as surely as they have needed food, love, sex, and safety.

The Jews have always been intensely literate, but just as they loved scholarship and the written word, they treasured the spoken word. For the Hasids, the highest form of religious expression is in song. And they were always the great storytellers. Stories are a renewal of the word, made alive by being spoken, passed from one to another, released from considerations of correctness and Law. Rabbi Yohanan Ben Zakkai said, "He who reads without melody and repeats without song, concerning him the scripture says, 'Therefore I [give you] statutes which [are] not to your advantage.' " Rabbi Nachman of Bratzlav ordered that all written records of his teachings be destroyed. His words must be passed from mouth to mouth, learned by and in heart. "My words have no clothes," he said. "When one speaks to one's fellows, there arises a simple light and a returning light."[26]

Generations later the great storyteller Elie Wiesel also understood this. He knows that storytelling can be a link to oneself, to one's fellows or to God. He says this in the dedication of his book on Hasidism:

> *My father, an enlighted spirit, believed in man.*
> *My grandfather, a fervent Hasid, believed in God.*
> *The one taught me to speak, the other to sing.*
> *Both loved stories.*
> *And when I tell mine, I hear their voices.*
> *Whispering from beyond the silenced storm.*
> *They are what links the survivor to their memory.*[27]

The one who believes in God tells Him the story. The one who does not must tell it to progeny, to humankind, and to oneself. *Homo narrans*, humankind as storyteller, is a human constant.

Floating through the Polish town, surely a journey through the underworld, I am accompanied by my two spirit guides: the great German musician, religious Lutheran, on my right; the anonymous Jewish agnostic tailor from Eastern Europe on my left. I am filled unexpectedly with serenity and relief. So this is how it ends. "Very well, Shmuel, I am in Poland. You see, it is not gone. You told me and I shall tell it. I still don't know Hebrew or Aramaic or Yiddish or Torah or Talmud. Neither do I know the prayer, nor can I light the fire or find my way to the place in the forest. But now I have been told about these things and perhaps this will be sufficient."

NOTES

Editor's Note

Yiddish presents some transliteration problems. Customary usage often varies greatly from the scholarly, standardized system suggested by YIVO (Institute for Jewish Research and Max Weinrich Center for Advanced Jewish Studies). In this book, as much as possible, we have been phonetically faithful to the speech of the people involved, even when this has deviated from YIVO's recommendations.

CHAPTER ONE

pages 1–39

1. It is necessary to pause here to clarify some terms that I use. Technically, Center life is a part-culture or subculture, surrounded as it is by a larger, overlapping dominant outside society in which Center members also participate. The term "culture" is used to refer to Center life, however, because it is less cumbersome and because it emphasizes the uniqueness, the intensity, and significance of the Center members' common attitudes and practices, developed out of a shared past, common language, and religion.

The term *shtetl* is surrounded by considerable confusion. Some writers have used it to refer to the territorial units in which Jews lived outside of cities in nineteenth-century Eastern Europe. Of those who stress the territorial dimension, some refer to shtetls as villages, settlements, and towns. Others, Irving Howe for example, prefer that it be preserved for units smaller than towns. Some writers mean shtetl to refer to the legally organized communities in Eastern Europe governed by Jewish regulatory organs known as *kehilla*. Many use it to signify a particular way of life or state of mind, equating shtetl with Yiddishkeit. Much of the confusion stems from the fact that the most widely read work on the subject, *Life Is With People: The Culture of the Shtetl* by Mark Zborowski and Elizabeth Herzog, is a valuable though seriously flawed work, as Barbara Kirshenblatt-Gimblett has pointed out. The book is an ethnography based on reconstructed materials rather than first-hand observations, and is generally agreed to be overly general, idealized, and static. Since its appearance three decades ago, many authors have used the term shtetl very broadly: to signify contemporary Jewish ghettoes in the New World, life in the Pale of Settlement in the Old World, and all manifestations of immigrant cultures historically based on Eastern European life, regardless of enormous regional and national variations.

Center old people also used the term shtetl to refer to their childhood culture, whether they had lived primarily in cities in Eastern Europe or not. They too idealized these memories and generalized about them, minimizing internal and external variations in the culture. Nevertheless, I have adopted their usage, employing the word to mean their childhood experiences, memories, and the culture of Yiddishkeit. To distinguish between the elders' recollections and actual experiences was not my purpose, nor was it possible. Rather I wished to render their interpretation of their past and present lives.

"Shtetl life" or Yiddishkeit are terms that can and often have been equated with Robert Redfield's concept of *folk culture*. In this notion, Redfield points to a small community that is isolated, stable, homogeneous, and in which members share a strong sense of identity with each other and the community. Their behavior is highly personalized and their world is dominated by the family. In outlook their attitudes are more sacred than secular. Local traditions are strong and cherished. The Center people's life in the present, and in the past, resembled Redfield's folk culture in all the features just mentioned, and is applicable with a few exceptions: Most notably, Redfield had a non-literate group in mind and these people are certainly literate. And unlike people in a folk society as Redfield understands it, Center folk had extensive contacts with outsiders; intellectual, economic, and legal. But in terms of the importance of intimate relationships, strong common identity, and possessing its own language, religion, values, social institutions, and shared common identity, one may speak of Center life and Yiddishkeit—in the Old and New World—as constituting a valid example of a folk culture.

2. Irving Howe, *The World of Our Fathers*, p. 8.

3. Claude Lévi-Strauss, *The Savage Mind*, p. 17.

4. Will Herberg, *Protestant-Catholic-Jew: An Essay in American Religious Sociology*.

5. In doing fieldwork, an anthropologist "becomes the phenomenon" being studied, by taking on the reality of the observed peoples. But some part of oneself is usually held back for self-protection, and

justified methodologically as providing the objectivity necessary for scientific observation. Hugh Mehan and Houston Wood, in a discussion of the paradox of belonging and not-belonging to an observed culture, lament this "methodological aloofness," stating that it is unacceptable because it prevents the fieldworker from effectively knowing the people being studied by preventing the researcher from "becoming one of them." They urge a greater involvement. "The researcher cannot hold back. The researcher who holds back in the name of objectivity never comes to respect [the] reality [being studied] or be respected by its practitioners." "Membership," they insist, "cannot be simulated." See *The Reality of Ethnomethodology*, p. 227.

6. See the author's *Peyote Hunt: The Sacred Journey of the Huichol Indians.*

7. For further discussion of the complex question of survivor's guilt, see the following in particular: Robert Jay Lifton, *Death in Life: Survivors of Hiroshima;* Terrence Des Pres, *The Survivor: An Anatomy of Life in the Death Camps;* Dorothy Rabinowitz, *New Lives: Survivors of the Holocaust Living in America;* Bruno Bettelheim, "Reflections: Surviving," *The New Yorker*, August 2, 1976, pp. 31–52.

8. Elie Wiesel and Bruno Bettelheim point out that survivors and all those who have "borne witness" are ultimately an embarrassment to a world that would find it much easier if they simply weren't around. See Bettelheim, "Reflections," p. 52. Says Des Pres, we protect ourselves by discrediting the unbearable tales told by survivors. "The survivor, then, is a disturber of the peace. He is a runner of the blockade men erect against knowledge of 'unspeakable' things." Des Pres, *Survivor*, p. 45. "Thus we undermine the survivor's authority by pointing to his guilt. If he is guilty, then perhaps it is true that the victims of atrocity collaborate in their own destruction; in which case blame can be imputed to the victims themselves. And if he is guilty, then the survivor's suffering . . . is deserved; in which case a balance between *that* pain and our own is restored." Ibid., p. 44.

9. Himself a survivor, Bettelheim points to what he considers one of the deepest lessons learned from having lived through the concentration camps, not that life is meaningless but that it is the very opposite–full of meaning. The discovery of one's humanity can occur through the experience of survival guilt. He says, "And our feeling of guilt for having been so lucky as to survive the hell of the concentration camp is a most significant part of this meaning–testimony to a humanity that not even the abomination of the concentration camp can destroy." Bettelheim, "Reflections," p. 52. Viktor E. Frankl's classic work, *Man's Search for Meaning*, makes the same point.

10. Lifton, *Death in Life*, p. 526.

11. Des Pres, *Survivors*, p. 43.

12. *Enemies, A Love Story*. For further discussion of difficulties experienced by Jews in writing about themselves—and other Jews—see Philip Roth, "Writing About Jews," *Reading Myself and Others*, pp. 135–153.

13. The film, also entitled *Number Our Days*, is a thirty-minute 16mm color sound documentary, produced and directed by Lynne Littman for KCET, Community Television of Southern California, Los Angeles. It received many awards, including an Academy Award for Best Short Documentary in 1977.

14. Victor Turner, *Dramas, Fields and Metaphors: Symbolic Action in Human Society*.

15. The interpretation of culture as a reflecting surface, part of the developing area of reflexive anthropology, was explored by Barbara Babcock, Victor Turner, and others who attended a conference entitled "Cultural Frames and Reflections: Ritual, Drama and Spectacle," held in August 1977 at Burg-Wartenstein, Austria, sponsored by the Wenner-Gren Foundation for Anthropological Research, convened by Turner, Babcock, and myself. I am indebted to Barbara Babcock who introduced me to this subject. Her dissertation presents an excellent summary.

16. Sally F. Moore and Barbara G. Myerhoff, "Introduction: Forms and Meanings" in *Secular Ritual*, pp. 3–24. Also, Roy A. Rappaport, "Ritual Sanctity and Cybernetics," *American Anthropologist* 73 (1): pp. 59–76.

17. Lifton, *Death in Life*, p. 534. In fact many of the Center folk had spent only part of their childhood in shtetls. But even those who had not resided within them for most of their early life had come to regard the shtetl as their place of origin and were inclined to use the shtetl as a symbol for Yiddishkeit, a cultural form that did indeed embrace everyone.

18. Freud, *Death, Grief and Mourning*.

19. Andrew Ehrlich is presently exploring the therapeutic functions of story-telling among the elderly. His forthcoming dissertation will present the results of his study. Robert Butler (1969), Barbara Myerhoff, and Virginia Tufte (1975) have published articles on the benefits of autobiographical work among the elderly. Kenneth Koch's work with the elderly, using a collective poetry writing class, seems to have many similarities with the discourse and emotions aroused in these Living History classes. See his *I Never Told Anybody: Teaching Poetry in a Nursing Home*. For works that give evidence of the significance of storytelling as a powerful and necessary human activity, see Reynolds Price, *A Palpable God: Thirty Stories Translated from the Bible with an Essay on the Origins and Life of Narrative*. I am especially indebted to Jerome Rothenberg's collections of poetry and essays that emphasize the

importance of orally transmitted tales, "in which the word is renewed by being re-sounded." These ideas are set forth in *A Big Jewish Book: Poems and Other Visions of the Jews from Tribal Times to Present* and in an unpublished essay entitled "The Poetics of Performance," delivered at the Burg-Wartenstein Conference, Austria, 1977. One of the greatest practitioners and appreciators of the significance of oral traditions among the Jews is Elie Wiesel, especially in *Souls on Fire: Portraits and Legends of Hasidic Masters*.

20. Hasidism was a form of popular Judaism, an intensely personal, often mystical revitalization movement influential in Europe in the eighteenth and nineteenth centuries. Because of the fervor of its expression and emotional appeal to the poor and uneducated, it was opposed by the established rabbinate in many communities who regarded it as a threat to orthodoxy, order, and authority. Among the Hasidim, ". . . Torah took the form of an inexhaustible fountain of storytelling," according to Gershom G. Scholem whose work *Major Trends in Jewish Mysticism* is a definitive study of the subject.

CHAPTER THREE

pages 79–112

A longer version of this chapter was presented at a Burg-Wartenstein Conference entitled "Secular Rituals Considered: Prolegomena toward a Theory of Ritual, Ceremony and Formality," organized by Max Gluckman, Victor Turner, and Sally F. Moore, sponsored by the Wenner-Gren Foundation for Anthropological Research, Austria, 1974. The papers from this volume, including another version of this chapter appear in *Secular Ritual*, edited by Moore and Myerhoff.

1. The danger underlying rituals, that they will be seen to be artificial, is developed in Moore and Myerhoff's "Introduction: Forms and Meanings," in *Secular Ritual*. In the same essay the order-endowing properties of ritual, regarded as in part due to the morphological characteristics of ritual, are analyzed.

2. "Learning" here corresponds to what Sherry Ortner in her article "On Key Symbols" calls a "key scenario," a symbol that is also a method for attaining a valued cultural goal.

3. Clifford Geertz emphasizes the capacity of ritual to contain conflict and contradiction, especially in his essay "Religion as a Cultural System."

4. This distinction loosely follows that suggested by Robert Redfield whose term "Great Tradition" refers to the abstract, literate, often impersonal and formal set of usages often associated with civilizations. The "Little Tradition" is the local, oral, often more concrete set of ideas and practices, which is authoritative because it is ancient and indigenous; it is what might be called the folk culture, associated with community rather than civilized social forms. Also

germane is Julian Pitt-Rivers's concept of infrastructure corresponding to the Little Tradition, in *The People of the Sierra.*

5. Kenneth Burke analyzes the functions of proverbs in his essay on the subject in *The Philosophy of Literary Forms: Studies in Symbolic Action.*

6. James Fernandez has an insightful discussion of performance and emotion in his study, "Persuasions and Performances: Of the Beast in Everybody . . . and the Metaphors of Everyman," and in his article, "The Mission of Metaphor in Expressive Culture."

7. The sense of personal continuity often occurs in ritual settings that allow for enactments that may re-arouse and release earlier memories. Some of the reasons that ritual has the capacity for releasing stored experiences are suggested by Susanne K. Langer's discussion of dance, where she describes what might be called *body memory*. Dancers, like participants in ritual, create and behave in a "virtual image of a different world," where one may "with his own body feeling . . . understand the gestic forms that are its interwoven, basic elements. He cannot see his own form as such, but he knows his appearance . . . . He sees the world in which his body dances." So too, the Center elders, in certain ritual enactments, were able to see themselves at earlier periods of their lives, and the world in which those earlier experiences took place. See "The Magic Circle," in Langer's *Feeling and Form*, pp. 200ff.

8. Lucy Dawidowicz (1977) discusses the profound emotional associations to Yiddish that occasionally merge into sentimentalization. Certainly this is often the case, particularly among second- and third-generation Jews of this background. Among these people, however, the entire childhood experience is maintained and condensed through the power of their mother tongue.

9. This is not to deny that the childhood world was beginning to change, responding to major social and political currents. But these internal changes were dwarfed compared to the enormity of the rupture in continuity caused by the emigration experience, and the movement from the Old to the New World.

CHAPTER FOUR

pages 113–152

1. The special uses of a stranger to a group is discussed by Max Gluckman in *Politics, Law and Ritual in Tribal Society*. A fine study of the role of the stranger as scapegoat in situations of irresolvable social conflict is presented by Ronald Frankenberg, *Village on the Border: A Social Study of Religion, Politics and Football in a North Wales Community*. The classic work is G. Simmel, "The Stranger."

2. The operation of politics in intimate settings (called "micropolitics" by Victor Turner) has been widely and well studied; most

useful to me were works by F. G. Bailey, Max Gluckman, John Middleton, Sally F. Moore, I. Schapera, Mark Swartz, Arthur Tuden, and Victor Turner.

3. Some of these notions concerning the manifestations of honor were explored in a seminar held at the University of Southern California on "Controlled Peoples," Department of Anthropology, 1976; participants whose ideas were particularly valuable in my work included Sally F. Moore, Andrei Simic, and William Partridge. See also J. Pitt-Rivers (ed.), *Mediterranean Countrymen*, and Abner Cohen, *Two-Dimensional Man: An Essay on the Anthropology of Power and Symbolism in Complex Society*, concerning elaborations of the themes of shame and honor in particular societies.

4. The cases of internally generated values and standards of worth, opposed to those of a hostile, external, more powerful society are abundant and sometimes controversial, shading into the complex questions concerning Oscar Lewis's concept of a "Culture of Poverty." The arguments are well and sensibly analyzed and many studies summarized by Ulf Hannerz in *Soulside: Inquiries into Ghetto Culture and Community*. My attention to the manner in which honor and power are manipulated was informed by Peter M. Blau's *Exchange and Power in Social Life*. The significance of exchange among the elderly was first brought to my attention by James J. Dowd in a paper entitled "Aging as Exchange: A Preface to Theory," and Gordon F. Steib's article, "Are the Aged a Minority Group?"

5. See Sally F. Moore for a discussion of the significance of aging within a stable cohort of age mates, in connection with her distinction between "life-term" and "limited-term social arenas," in *Life's Career-Aging: Cultural Variations on Growing Old*, Myerhoff and Simic (eds.).

6. Attention in this group was definitely a "limited good," in the sense that the term is used by George Foster to characterize the outlook found in many peasant societies.

7. The work of Erving Goffman is basic to this interpretation, especially concerning visibility (his *Presentation of Self in Everyday Life*), social ritual (*Interaction Ritual*), and the processes of "framing" (*Frame Analysis*).

8. Victor Turner suggested that a norm may be violated by being "overfulfilled." Personal communication, 1977.

CHAPTER FIVE

pages 153–194

1. The classic study of witchcraft is E. E. Evans-Pritchard's *Witchcraft, Magic and Oracles Among the Azande of the Anglo-Egyptian Sudan*. See also Max Gluckman's *Custom and Conflict in Africa*; Mary Douglas, *Purity and Danger*; M. J. Field, *Search for Security*; Lucy Mair's *Witchcraft*.

2. Max Gluckman's article "Gossip and Scandal" is particularly useful. Several of the studies in Moore and Myerhoff's collection, *Symbol and Politics in Communal Ideology: Cases and Questions*, illustrate the processes of informal, often unconscious devices used to maintain social control in intimate settings.

3. Word-magic is treated by numerous writers; most helpful to me were Gershom A. Scholem, *On the Kabbalah and Its Symbolism;* Joshua Trachtenberg, *Jewish Magic and Superstition;* Ernst Cassirer, *Language and Myth;* and Kenneth Burke, *The Rhetoric of Religion.* Conversations with Roy Rappaport on the subject were also useful and suggestive.

4. For a highly interesting discussion of "privileged information" and its manipulations, see Samuel C. Heilman's *Synagogue Life.*

5. Lewis Coser ably discusses the uses of conflict and anger in his study *The Functions of Social Conflict.*

6. I am obliged to Riv-Ellen Prell-Foldes and Steven Foldes for a probing discussion of this kind of social drama. Dr. Prell-Foldes analyzes some similar episodes in her dissertation, *Strategies in Conflict Situations: Ritual and Redress in an Urban Jewish Prayer Community.*

7. The ensuing interpretation of myth and ritual performances, in particular my views on the attitudes underlying enactments, are influenced by Kenneth Burke, *Philosophy of Literary Form: Studies in Symbolic Action;* Susanne K. Langer, *Philosophy in a New Key* and *Feeling and Form;* and Mircea Eliade, *The Sacred and Profane.*

CHAPTER SIX

pages 195–231

An earlier, variant interpretation of this episode appears in Myerhoff and Simic's *Life's Career–Aging: Cultural Variations in Growing Old.* Several people with whom I discussed this chapter were particularly generous and helpful, including Andrew Ehrlich, Rabbi Laura Geller, Walter Levine, John MacAloon, Beryl Mintz, Morris Rosen, Rabbi Chaim Seidler-Feller, and Dyanne Simon.

1. For further discussion of the concept of aging as a career, see Myerhoff and Simic, *Life's Career–Aging: Cultural Variations on Growing Old.*

2. Rituals and symbols pertaining to death in Jewish tradition are discussed by Leo Jung, S. H. Dresner, J. Zashin, and others in Jack Riemer's *Jewish Reflections on Death.* Also useful are Maurice Lamm, *The Jewish Way in Death and Mourning;* Joshua Trachtenberg, *Jewish Magic and Superstition: A Study in Folk Religion;* and Gershom Scholem, *Kabbalah and its Symbolism* and *Magic Trends in Jewish Mysticism.*

3. A provocative discussion of the role of luck in aging well is given by Andrei Simic in his article, "Winners and Losers: Aging

Yugoslavs in a Changing World," in *Life's Career–Aging: Cultural Variations on Growing Old.*

4. Melvin Seeman considers the relativistic perspective acquired as a result of social marginality under certain circumstances, as leading to the ability to accept ideological conflict, and thus to creativity. See "Intellectual Perspectives and Adjustment to Minority Status." Margaret Clark and Barbara Anderson have noted a similar necessity for creative solutions to aging, including the ability to find suitable substitutions for inappropriate goals and activities, and occasionally a certain aggressive or eccentric approach that enables the old person to wrest from society a legitimate place. David Gutmann also observed that grouchiness and anger may be survival assets in later life. A related notion is implicit in Louis Wirth's *The Ghetto* and "Urbanism as a Way of Life."

5. James Olney, *Metaphors of Self: The Meaning of Autobiography*, pp. 4 and 6.

6. "The Mission of Metaphor in Expressive Culture."

7. Robert N. Butler was one of the first gerontologists to emphasize reminiscence as a necessary and valuable enterprise among the elderly. See also Myerhoff and Tufte, "Life History as Integration: Personal Myth and Aging," *The Gerontologist*, 1975, pp. 541–543.

8. Susanne K. Langer emphasizes the theme repeatedly, most prominently in *Philosophy in a New Key*, drawing on philosophers Alfred North Whitehead and Ernst Cassirer. In the same tradition, the work of Clifford Geertz is outstanding, particularly "Religion as a Cultural System" and his essays in *The Interpretation of Cultures.*

9. *See* Joseph Zashin, "The Fraternity of Mourners," in *Jewish Reflections on Death.*

10. Langer, *op. cit.*

11. *Time and Experience*, p. 137. Many writers have treated this collapsing of time, especially Marcel Proust, also Eliade in his distinction between "temporal duration" and "sacred time," the latter being "by its very nature . . . reversible . . . indefinitely recoverable . . . and repeatable," hence eternally present, transcending history and change (*The Sacred and the Profane*, p. 68). Richard Schechner refers to this experience of the simultaneous presence of the past as "bunching time," personal communication, Los Angeles, 1978. Robert Ornstein's discussion of the subject in *On the Experience of Time* is exceptionally helpful.

12. Essential to the religious experience is some sense of wonder, what Rudolph Otto calls the sense of "awe-inspiring mystery" (*mysterium tremendum*), and an awareness of the "perfect fullness of being" . . . aroused by an experience of the fascinating mystery (*mysterium fascinans*), presented in *The Idea of the Holy.*

13. Peter Freuchen, *Book of the Eskimos.*

14. Philippe Ariès, *Western Attitudes Toward Death: From the Middle Ages to the Present.*

CHAPTER SEVEN

pages 232–268

An earlier version of this chapter appears in Judith Hoch-Smith and Anita Spring (eds.), *Women in Ritual and Symbolic Roles.* The paper was written in the course of the research project, "Ethnicity and Aging," conducted at the Andrus Gerontology Center of the University of Southern California, principal investigator, Vern L. Bengtson; Barbara Myerhoff, project director, supported by grants from the National Science Foundation's RANN program (#ARP 21178) and by the 1907 Foundation of the United Parcel Service. Conclusions are those of the author and do not necessarily reflect the views of the NSF or the 1907 Foundation.

1. Charlotte Baum, "What Made Yetta Work," *The Economic Role of Eastern European Jewish Women in the Family.*

2. Cited by Paula Hyman in "The Other Half: Women in the Jewish Tradition," p. 112.

3. Mark Zborowski and Elizabeth Herzog, *Life Is with People: The Culture of the Shtetl.*

4. Paula Hyman, "The Other Half: The Woman in Jewish Tradition"; also Saul Berman, "The Status of Women in Halakhic Judaism"; and Rachel Adler, "*Tumah* and *Taharah:* Ends and Beginnings" and "The Jew Who Wasn't There: *Halacha* and the Jewish Woman."

5. Mark Zborowski and Elizabeth Herzog, *Life Is with People.*

6. See Elizabeth Koltun's Preface to her collection entitled, The *Jewish Woman: New Perspectives.* A related argument is developed by Michelle Z. Rosaldo in "Women, Culture, and Society: A Theoretical Overview," and in many of the essays in Judith Hoch-Smith and Anita Spring's *Women in Ritual and Symbolic Roles,* especially in "Part I: Women and Divinity," and the editors' introductory essay.

7. This theme is described in Mark Zborowski and Elizabeth Herzog, *Life Is with People,* and appears in much Yiddish literature, especially the humorous and satirical writings of Sholom Aleichem, Mendele Mokher Sforim, and I. B. Singer. The same theme is sounded in the ethnographic and folkloristic descriptions of shtetl life, especially by Barbara Kirshenblatt-Gimblett and many of the stories anthologized by Irving Howe and Eliezer Ginzberg.

8. Andrei Simic, referring to Latin and Baltic cultures, personal communication, Los Angeles, 1977.

9. This observation occurs often in Charlotte Baum, Paula Hyman, and Sonya Michel's collection.

10. The pattern of women socially subordinate in highly patri-

archal societies becoming more powerful than men in the latter part of life was noted also among elderly Yugoslavs by Andrei Simic and among aging Mexicans by Carlos Veléz-I, cited in *Life's Career—Aging*.

11. Similar song-duels, or contests in verbal skills, cursing, exchanging insults, and the like are noted by anthropologists among peoples who are expected and often by circumstances required to live harmoniously and eschew overt conflict; the Eskimo and Bushmen of the Kalahari Desert are well-known examples; see Peter Freuchen and Elizabeth M. Thomas.

12. At various times I discussed some of the theories about aging with the Center people. I was especially curious about their reaction to "disengagement theories" (Elaine Cumming and W. E. Henry, *Growing Old*, 1961) that suggest the elderly gradually withdraw from social relationships and activities toward the end of life as they prepare to die. The Center people had mixed responses to this idea. A number of them indicated that they were more socially active and engaged in exploring personal interests now than at any other time of life. Some of them were unwilling to define themselves as old, much less disengaged. But of course the truly withdrawn individuals stayed away and did not come to the Center. One can only conclude the obvious, then, that disengagement is not a universal phenomenon.

13. Jews of Lithuania spoke a Yiddish dialect, Litvish, and had a regional sense of identity and distinctiveness, expressed in food preparations, vocabulary, singing styles, and other minor cultural variations. Between the Jews from Galicia, the *Galitzianers*, and the Litvaks a kind of joking relationship existed, made up of a sense of simultaneous identity and distinctiveness, and overstated disdain to imply nonseriousness. An amusing discussion of this relationship is in the charming book by Diane K. and David G. Roskies, *The Shtetl Book*, p. 42.

14. Riv-Ellen Prell-Foldes, "Coming of Age in Kelton," p. 79.

15. Abraham Joshua Heschel, *The Sabbath*, p. 42.

16. Mircea Eliade uses the term *hierophany* to describe this breakthrough of the sacred into the secular in his book, *The Sacred and the Profane: The Nature of Religion*, p. 11.

17. Victor Turner, *The Forest of Symbols*, p. 30.

18. Morris Zelditch, Talcott Parsons, and other American sociologists have suggested that this instrumental-expressive dichotomy is a universal arrangement in the allocation of family roles to men and women, respectively. It is found in many cultures, though several scholars question its universality.

19. Psychologists, David Bakan and Nancy Chowdorow among others, describe male-female differences in cognitive style in a fashion that corroborates and reflects the Zelditch/Parsons dichotomy.

20. The cases by Andrei Simic and Carlos Veléz-I in which older women became more dominant than they were in their middle years were consistent with observations of the Center women; among these cases, increased power was based on women's abilities to exploit familial roles, which had proved stronger in advanced age for them than for the men. The ethnographic literature is filled with examples where postmenopausal women in tribal and peasant societies are given great license and freedom—in ritual, in the marketplace, and in politics. They often enjoy privileges that are not available to men of any age, and many of these have nothing to do with kinship roles. David Gutmann provides an excellent review of "androgyny" in men and women during later life. Role reversal by sexes is found among the elderly in many societies.

21. This suggests yet another reason—preparation for old age—that may be offered in favor of encouraging men to participate more fully in child-rearing and other nurturant roles, a case made with great force by Adrienne Rich in *Of Woman Born*.

22. *See* Sherry Ortner, "Is Female to Male as Nature to Culture?" in *Woman, Culture and Society*.

23. Simone de Beauvoir, *The Second Sex*, p. 59.

24. Deena Metzger describes these activities and understandings as "Women's Culture."

25. To use a Jungian model, it might be said that the women more than the men had moved beyond the external, willfull projects of an ego-dominated existence and toward a more fully developed, integrated expression of the Self.

26. I am indebted to Jerome Rothenberg for this conception of the "renewal of the word by sounding." See also Martin Buber, *The Tales of Rabbi Nachman*.

27. Elie Wiesel, *Souls on Fire: Portraits and Legends of Hasidic Masters*. See also Martin Buber's *Tales of Hasidim* and Jerome R. Mintz, *Legends of the Hasidim: An Introduction to Hasidic Culture and Oral Tradition in the New World*.

Many students and colleagues contributed helpful ideas and much pertinent information in the course of this study, especially the anthropologists with whom I worked on the "Ethnicity and Aging Project," Sally F. Moore and Andrei Simic. Several students undertook projects or research papers, particularly in a seminar conducted at the University of Southern California Department of Anthropology and Sociology in "The Age Factor in Human Societies," 1974. These and other students with whom I worked include Joanne Altschuler, Renee Cronenwalt, Neil Daniels, Davida Earlix, Andrew Ehrlich, Deanne Honeyman, Andrea Port, Elizabeth Thompson, and Wendy Zacuta. I would like particularly to thank Professor Tzvee Zahavy, Department of Near and Middle Eastern Studies, Program in Ancient Near Eastern and Jewish Studies, University of Minnesota, for reading and checking the complete manuscript.

REFERENCES

ABARBANEL JAY S. "Prestige of the Aged and Their Control Over Resources: A Cross-Cultural Analysis." Presented at annual meeting of the Gerontological Society, Portland, Oregon, 1974, symposium on "Cross-Cultural Perspectives on Aging."

ADLER, MORRIS. *The World of the Talmud*. 2d ed. New York: Schocken Books, 1963.

ADLER, RACHEL. "The Jew Who Wasn't There: Halacha and the Jewish Woman." *Response: A Contemporary Jewish Review*, vol. 8, no. 18 (1973): 77–83.

———. "*Tumah and Taharah;* Ends and Beginnings." In *The Jewish Woman: New Perspectives*, edited by Elizabeth Koltun. New York: Schocken Books, 1976.

AIN, ABRAHAM. "Swislocz: Portrait of a Shtetl." In *Voices from the Yiddish: Essays, Memoirs and Diaries*, edited by Irving Howe and Eliezer Greenberg. Schocken Books: New York, 1975.

ALEICHEM, SHOLOM. *Inside Kasrilevke*. New York: Schocken Books, 1948.

———. *Old Country Tales*. Translated by Curt Leviant. New York: Paperback Library, 1969.

ALTSCHULER, JOANNE. "Cultural Perspective on Aging: A Case Study of a California Beach Community." Unpublished Student Paper. Hebrew Union College, Los Angeles, California, 1974.

ANDERSON, BARBARA G. "The Process of Deculturation–Its Dynamics Among United States Aged." *Anthropological Quarterly* 45 (1972): 209–216.

ARIÈS, PHILIPPE. *Western Attitudes Toward Death: From the Middle Ages to the Present*. Translated by P. M. Ranum. Baltimore: Johns Hopkins Press, 1966.

AYALTI, HANAN J., ed. *Yiddish Proverbs*. New York: Schocken Books, 1949.

Babcock, Barbara. *Mirrors, Masks and Metafiction: Studies in Narrative Reflexivity.* Doctoral dissertation. Department of English, University of Chicago, 1975.

Bailey, F. G., ed. *Gifts and Poison: The Politics of Reputation.* New York: Schocken Books, 1971.

———. *Stratagems and Spoils: A Social Anthropology of Politics.* New York: Schocken Books, 1969.

Bakan, David. "The Quality of Human Existence: Isolation and Communication in Western Man." In *Woman, Culture, and Society,* edited by Michelle Z. Rosaldo and Louise Lamphere. Stanford: Stanford University Press, 1974.

Banton, Michael, ed. *The Social Anthropology of Complex Societies.* London: Tavistock Publications, 1966.

Barth, Fredrik, ed. *Ethnic Groups and Boundaries: The Social Organization of Cultural Difference.* Boston: Little, Brown and Company, 1969.

Baum, Charlotte. "What Made Yetta Work: The Economic Role of Eastern European Jewish Women in the Family." *Response: A Contemporary Jewish Review,* vol. 8, no. 18 (1973): 32–38.

Baum, Charlotte; Hyman, Paula; and Michel, Sonya. *The Jewish Woman in America.* New York: Dial Press, 1976.

Becker, Ernest. *The Denial of Death.* New York: The Free Press, 1973.

Bellow, Saul, ed. *Great Jewish Short Stories.* New York: Dell Publishing Company, 1963.

Benet, Sula. *Abkhasians: The Long-Living People of the Caucasus.* New York: Holt, Rinehart and Winston, Inc., 1974.

Berman, Saul. "The Status of Women in Halakhic Judaism." In *The Jewish Woman: New Perspectives,* edited by Elizabeth Koltun. New York: Schocken Books, 1976.

Bettelheim, Bruno. "Individual and Mass Behavior in Extreme Situations." *Journal of Abnormal and Social Psychology,* vol. 38, no. 4 (October, 1943): 417–452.

———. "Reflections: Surviving." *The New Yorker* (August 2, 1976): 31–52.

Blau, Peter. *Exchange and Power in Social Life.* New York: John Wiley and Sons, 1964.

Blau, Zena Smith. *Old Age in a Changing Society.* New York: New Viewpoints, 1973.

Blumenthal, Albert. "The Nature of Gossip." Sociology and Social Research 22 (1932).

Britchto, Herbert C. "The Problem of 'Curse' in the Hebrew Bible." *Journal of Biblical Literature,* vol. 13. Philadelphia: Society of Biblical Literature and Exegesis, 1963.

Buber, Martin. *Tales of the Hasidim: The Early Masters.* New York: Schocken Books, 1975.

———. *Tales of Rabbi Nachman*. Translated by Maurice Friedman. New York: Avon Books, 1956.

Burke, Kenneth. *The Philosophy of Literary Form: Studies in Symbolic Action*. New York: Vintage, 1957.

———. *The Rhetoric of Religion: Studies in Logology*. Berkeley: University of California Press, 1970.

Butler, Robert N. "Aspects of Survival of Adaptation in Human Aging." *The American Journal of Psychiatry* 123 (April 1967): 1233–1243.

———. "How to Grow Old and Poor in an Affluent Society." In *Issues in American Society*, edited by Joseph Boskin. Encino, California: Glencoe Publishing Company, Inc., 1978.

———. "The Life Review: An Interpretation of Reminiscence in the Aged." In *Middle Age and Aging*, edited by Bernice L. Neugarten. Chicago: Chicago University Press, 1968.

Butler, Robert N., and Lewis, Myrna I. *Aging and Mental Health: Positive Psychosocial Approaches*. St. Louis: The C. V. Mosby Company, 1973.

Cahan, Abraham. *The Education of Abraham Cahan*. Leo Stein, ed. Philadelphia: Jewish Publication Society of America, 1969.

———. *The Rise of David Levinsky*. New York: Harper & Row, 1917.

Calhoun, Craig Jackson. "Continuity and Change: The Meaning of Time in the Organization of Experience." Unpublished student paper. Horace Mann-Lincoln Institute, Columbia University, New York, 1973.

Campbell, J. *Honour, Family, and Patronage*. Oxford: Clarendon Press, 1964.

Cassirer, Ernst. *An Essay on Man*. New Haven: Yale University Press, 1944.

———. *Language and Myth*. Translated by Susanne K. Langer. New York: Dover Publishing, Inc., 1946.

Chagall, Bella and Marc. *Burning Lights*. Translated by Norbert Guterman. New York: Schocken Books, 1972.

Chodorow, Nancy. "Family Structure and Feminine Personality." In *Women, Culture, and Society*, edited by Michelle Z. Rosaldo and Louise Lamphere. Stanford: Stanford University Press, 1974.

Choron, Jacques. *Death and Modern Man*. New York: Collier Books, 1964.

Chown, Sheila M., ed. *Human Ageing: Selected Readings*. Middlesex, England: Penguin Books, 1972.

Clark, Margaret M. "The Anthropology of Aging: A New Area for Studies of Culture and Personality." *The Gerontologist* 7 (1967): 55–64.

Clark, Margaret and Anderson, Barbara G. *Culture and*

Aging: An Anthropological Study of Older Americans. Springfield, Illinois: Charles C Thomas, 1967.

———. "Cultural Values and Dependency in Later Life." In *Aging and Modernization*, edited by D. O. Cowgill and L. D. Holmes. New York: Appleton-Century-Crofts, 1972.

CLEUGH, M. F. *Educating Older People*. London: Tavistock Publications, 1962.

COHEN, ABNER. *Two-Dimensional Man: An Essay on the Anthropology of Power and Symbolism in Complex Society*. Berkeley: University of California Press, 1974.

COSER, LEWIS A. *The Functions of Social Conflict*. New York: The Free Press, 1956.

COWGILL, D. O., and HOLMES, L. D., eds. *Aging and Modernization*. New York: Appleton-Century-Crofts, 1972.

COX, B. A. "What Is Hopi Gossip About? Information Management and Hopi Factions." *Man: Journal of the Royal Anthropological Institute*, vol. 5, no. 1 (March 1970): 88–98.

CRONENWALT, RENEE. *With Torch Held High: A History of the Emma Lazarus Federation of Jewish Women's Clubs, and a Portrait of 'Emma', Annie Krupkin*. Unpublished M.L.A. thesis. Los Angeles: University of Southern California, 1977.

CUMMING, ELAINE, and HENRY, W. E. *Growing Old: The Process of Disengagement*. New York: Basic Books, 1961.

CURTIN, SHARON R. *Nobody Ever Died of Old Age*. Boston: Little, Brown and Company, 1972.

DANIELS, NEIL. "The Role of Religion and Theology in the Lives of the Jewish Elderly in a California Beach Community." Unpublished student paper. Hebrew Union College, Los Angeles, California, 1973.

DAVID, JAY, ed. *Growing Up Jewish*. New York: Pocket Books, 1969.

DAVIS, RICHARD H., and NEISWENDER, MARGARET, eds. *Aging: Prospects and Issues: A Monograph from the Ethel Percy Andrus Gerontology Center*. Los Angeles, 1973.

DAWIDOWICZ, LUCY S., ed. *The Golden Tradition: Jewish Life and Thought in Eastern Europe*. New York: Holt, Rinehart and Winston, 1967.

———. *The Jewish Presence: Essays on Identity and History*. New York: Holt, Rinehart and Winston, 1977.

DE BEAUVOIR, SIMONE. *The Coming of Age*. Translated by Patrick O'Brian. New York: G. P. Putnam's Sons, 1972.

———. *The Second Sex*. Translated by H. M. Pashley. New York: Alfred A. Knopf, 1953.

DES PRES, TERRENCE. *The Survivor: An Anatomy of Life in the Death Camps*. New York: Pocket Books, 1977.

Douglas, Mary. *Natural Symbols: Explorations in Cosmology.* New York: Pantheon, 1970.

———. *Purity and Danger: An Analysis of Concepts of Pollution and Taboo.* London: Penguin Books, 1966.

Dowd, James. "Aging as Exchange: A Preface to Theory." Unpublished student paper. Los Angeles: University of Southern California, 1976.

Dresner, Samuel H. *The Jew in American Life.* New York: Crown Publishers, Inc., 1963.

Dubow, S. M. *History of the Jews in Russia and Poland . . . Until the Present Day.* Philadelphia: Jewish Publication Society of America, 1916–1920.

Durkheim, Emile. *The Division of Labor in Society.* Translated by G. Simpson. Glencoe, Illinois: Collier-Macmillan Ltd., 1964.

———. *The Elementary Forms of Religious Life.* Translated by J. W. Swain, New York: Collier, 1961.

Earlix, Davida. "A Study of Life Perceptions and Organization: Three Life Histories." Unpublished student paper. University of Southern California, Los Angeles, California, 1973.

Eliade, Mircea. *Images and Symbols: Studies in Religious Symbolism.* Translated by Philip Mairet. New York: Sheed and Ward, 1961.

———. *The Sacred and the Profane: The Nature of Religion.* Translated by Willard R. Trask. New York: Harcourt, Brace and World, Inc., 1957.

———. *The Two and the One.* Translated by J. C. Cohen. New York: Harper and Row, 1965.

Epstein, A. L., ed. *The Craft of Social Anthropology.* London: The Tavistock Publications, 1967.

Evans-Pritchard, E. E. *Witchcraft, Oracles, and Magic Among the Azande.* Oxford: Clarendon Press, 1965.

———. *Theories of Primitive Religion.* Oxford: Clarendon Press, 1965.

Fernandez, James. "The Mission of Metaphor in Expressive Culture." *Current Anthropology*, vol. 15, no. 2 (1974): 119–133.

———. "Persuasions and Performances: Of the Beast in Everybody . . . and the Metaphors of Everyman." In *Myth, Symbol and Culture*, edited by Clifford Geertz. New York: W.W. Norton, 1971.

Field, M. J. *Search for Security: An Ethno-Psychiatric Study of Rural Ghana.* Chicago: Northwestern University Press, 1966.

Finkelstein, Louis, ed. *The Jews: Their History.* New York: Schocken Books, 1972.

Fischer, David Hackett. *Growing Old in America.* Oxford: Oxford University Press, 1977.

FOSTER, GEORGE. "Peasant Society and the Image of Limited Good." *American Anthropologist* vol. 67 (1965): 293–315.

FOX, SUSAN. "The Jewish Family in the Shtetl at the Turn of the Century: Cultural Contingencies and Parental Goals." Unpublished student paper. University of Southern California, Los Angeles, California, 1975.

FRANKENBERG, RONALD. *Village on the Border: A Social Study of Religion, Politics and Football in a North Wales Community.* London: Cohen and West, 1957.

FRANKL, VICTOR E. *Man's Search for Meaning: An Introduction to Logotherapy.* Translated by Ilse Lasch. New York: Pocket Books, 1973.

FREUCHEN, PETER. *Book of the Eskimos.* Cleveland: World Press, 1961.

FREUD, SIGMUND. *Death, Grief and Mourning.* New York: Doubleday, 1965.

GEERTZ, CLIFFORD. "Ethos, World-View and the Analysis of Sacred Symbols." *Antioch Review* 17 (1957–1958): 421–437.

———. "Thick Description: Toward an Interpretive Theory of Culture," In *The Interpretation of Cultures*, edited by Clifford Geertz. New York: Basic Books, 1973.

———. "Religion as a Cultural System." In *Anthropological Approaches in the Study of Religion*, edited by M. Banton. New York: Praeger 1965.

GLATZER, NAHUM, N. ed. *Hammer on the Rock: A Midrash Reader.* Translated by Jacob Sloan. New York: Schocken Books, 1962.

———, ed. *On Judaism by Martin Buber.* New York: Schocken Books, 1972.

GLATZER, NAHUM. N. ed. *Hammer on the Rock: A Midrash Jews.* New York: Jewish Education Committee Press, 1965.

———. *American Judaism.* Chicago: University of Chicago Press, 1957.

GLUCKMAN, MAX. *Custom and Conflict in Africa.* New York: Barnes and Noble, 1964.

———. *Essays on the Ritual of Social Relations.* Edited by Max Gluckman. Manchester: Manchester University Press, 1962.

———. "Gossip and Scandal." *Current Anthropology* Vol. 4, no. 3 (1963): 308–315.

———. *Politics, Law and Ritual in Tribal Society.* New York: The New American Library, 1965.

———. "Psychological, Sociological, and Anthropological Explanation of Witchcraft and Gossip: A Clarification." *Man: Journal of the Royal Anthropological Institute*, vol. 3, no. 1 (March 1968): 20–34.

GOFFMAN, ERVING. *Interaction Ritual: Essays on Face-to-Face Behavior*. New York: Anchor Books, 1967.

———. *Frame Analysis: An Essay on the Organization of Experience*. Cambridge: Harvard University Press, 1974.

———. *Presentation of Self in Everyday Life*. Edinburgh: University of Edinburgh, 1956.

GOLDIN, HYMAN E. *Hamadrikh, the Rabbi's Guide: A Manual of Jewish Religious Rituals, Ceremonials and Customs*. New York: Hebrew Publishing Company, 1939.

GOODY, JACK. "Death and the Interpretation of Culture: A Bibliographic Overview." *American Quarterly*, vol. 26, no. 5 (December 1974).

———. "Religion and Ritual, the Definitional Problem." *British Journal of Sociology*, vol. 12 (1962): 142–146.

GRAVES, ROBERT, and PATAI, RAPHAEL. *Hebrew Myths: The Book of Genesis*. New York: McGraw-Hill, 1966.

GREENBERG, LOUIS. *The Jews in Russia: The Struggle for Emancipation*. New York: Schocken Books, 1976.

GUBRIUM, JABER F. *Living and Dying at Murray Manor*. New York: St. Martin's Press, 1975.

GUTMANN, DAVID. "The Cross-Cultural Perspective: Notes Toward a Comparative Psychology of Aging," In *Handbook of the Psychology of Aging*, edited by James Birren. New York: Van Nostrem, 1977.

HANDLIN, OSCAR. *Adventure in Freedom: Three Hundred Years of Jewish Life in America*. New York: McGraw-Hill, 1954.

———. *The Newcomers: Negroes and Puerto Ricans in a Changing Metropolis*. Garden City, New York: Doubleday Anchor Books, 1962.

———. *The Uprooted*. New York: Grosset & Dunlap, 1951.

HANNERZ, ULF. *Soulside: Inquiries into Ghetto Culture and Community*. New York: Columbia University Press, 1969.

HANSEN, MARCUS LEE. "The Third Generation in America." *Commentary*, vol. 14 (November 1952): 492–500.

HAPGOOD, HUTCHINS. *The Spirit of the Ghetto*. New York: Schocken Books, 1966. (first published 1902.)

HEILMAN, SAMUEL C. *Synagogue Life: A Study in Symbolic Interaction*. Chicago: University of Chicago Press, 1976.

HERBERG, WILL. *Protestant-Catholic-Jew: An Essay in American Religious Sociology*. New York: Anchor Books, 1955.

HERMAN, SIMON N. *Jewish Identity: A Social Psychological Perspective*. Beverly Hills, California: Sage Publications, 1977.

HESCHEL, ABRAHAM J. *The Earth Is the Lord's: The Inner World of the Jew In Eastern Europe* and *The Sabbath*. New York: Harper and Row, 1966.

———. *God in Search of Man: A Philosophy of Judaism.* New York: Farrar, Straus and Giroux, 1955.

———. *The Prophets,* vol. 1. New York: Harper and Row, 1955.

HOCH-SMITH, JUDITH and SPRING, ANITA, eds. *Women in Ritual and Symbolic Roles.* New York: Plenum Press, 1978.

HONEYMAN, DEANNE E. "An Exploration of the Communication Patterns of the Aged in a Modern Urban Setting." Dissertation proposal. University of Southern California, Los Angeles, California, 1977.

HOWE, IRVING. *World of Our Fathers.* New York: Harcourt, Brace, Jovanovich, 1976.

HOWE, IRVING and GREENBERG, ELIEZER, eds. *A Treasury of Yiddish Stories.* New York: Schocken Books, 1973.

———. *Voices from the Yiddish.* New York: Schocken Books, 1975.

HYMAN, PAULA. "The Other Half: Women in Jewish Tradition." *Response: A Contemporary Jewish Review,* vol. 8, no. 18 (1973): 67–76.

Institute of Gerontology. *No Longer Young: The Older Woman in America.* The University of Michigan, Wayne State University, 1975.

JACOBS, JERRY. *Fun City: An Ethnographic Study of a Retirement Community.* New York: Holt, Rinehart and Winston, 1974.

JACOBS, LOUIS. *Jewish Ethics, Philosophy and Mysticism.* New York: Behrman House, 1969.

JUNG, LEO. "The Meaning of the Kaddish." In *Jewish Reflections on Death,* edited by Jack Riemer. New York: Schocken Books, 1974.

KASTENBAUM, ROBERT, ed. *New Thoughts on Old Age.* New York: Springer Publishing Company, 1964.

KATZ, JACOB. *Exclusiveness and Tolerance: Studies in Jewish-Gentile Relations in Medieval and Modern Times.* New York: Schocken Books, 1961.

KENDIG, HAL. "Neighborhood Conditions of the Aged and Local Government." Presented at annual meeting of the Gerontology Society, Portland, Oregon, 1974.

KIRSHENBLATT-GIMBLETT, BARBARA. "Bibliography." *The Yiddish Folktale.* New York: Columbia University, 1973. Unpublished ms.

———. "The Concept and Varieties of Narrative Performance in East European Jewish Culture." In *Explorations in the Ethnography of Speaking,* edited by Richard Bauman and Joel Sherzer. Cambridge: Cambridge University Press, 1974.

———. "The *Shtetl* Model in East European Jewish Ethnology," paper presented at the American Anthropological Association meeting, Washington, D.C., November, 1976.

KOCH, KENNETH. *I Never Told Anybody: Teaching Poetry Writing in a Nursing Home*. New York: Random House, 1977.

KOLTUN, ELIZABETH, ed. *The Jewish Woman: New Perspectives*. New York: Schocken Books, 1976.

KRAMER, JUDITH R., and LEVENTMAN, SEYMOUR. *Children of the Gilded Ghetto*. New Haven: Yale University Press, 1961.

KÜBLER-ROSS, ELISABETH. *On Death and Dying*. New York: The Macmillan Company, 1969.

LA FONTAINE, J. S., ed. *The Interpretation of Ritual: Essays in Honour of A. I. Richards*. London: Tavistock Publishers, 1972.

LAMM, MAURICE. *The Jewish Way in Death and Mourning*. New York: Jonathan David, 1969.

LANGER, SUSANNE K. *Feeling and Form: A Theory of Art*. New York: Charles Scribner's Sons, 1953.

———. *Philosophy in a New Key*. Cambridge: Harvard University Press, 1960.

LEACH, E. R. "Ritual." In *International Encyclopedia of the Social Sciences*, vol. 13, edited by D. Sills. New York: Macmillan and The Free Press, 1968.

LEVINE, NAOMI and HOCHBAUM, MARTIN, eds. *Poor Jews: An American Awakening*. New Brunswick, New Jersey: Transaction Books, 1974.

LÉVI-STRAUSS, CLAUDE. *The Elementary Structures of Kinship*. Translated by J. H. Bell and J. R. von Sturmer. Edited by Rodney Needham. Boston: Beacon Press, 1969.

———. *The Savage Mind*. Translated by G. Weidenfeld and Nicolson Ltd. Chicago: University of Chicago Press, 1966.

———. "The Story of Asdiwal." In *The Structural Study of Myth and Totemism*, edited by E. Leach. Translated by N. Mann. London: Tavistock Publications, 1967.

———. *Structural Anthropology*. Translated by Claire Jacobson and Brooke Grundfest Schoepf. New York: Basic Books, 1963.

LEWIS, OSCAR. *Five Families*. New York: Basic Books, 1959.

LIFTON, ROBERT JAY. *Death in Life: Survivors of Hiroshima*. New York: Simon and Schuster, 1967.

LIPMAN, EUGENE J., ed. *The Mishnah: Oral Teachings of Judaism*. Translated by Eugene J. Lipman. New York: Schocken Books, 1974.

MADISON, CHARLES A. *Yiddish Literature: Its Scope and Major Writers*. New York: Schocken Books, 1971.

MAIR, LUCY. *Witchcraft*. New York: McGraw-Hill, 1969.

MALINOWSKI, BRONISLAW. *Magic, Science and Religion*. New York: Doubleday, 1955.

MANNEY, JAMES D., JR. *Aging in American Society: An Examination of Concepts and Issues.* Ann Arbor, Michigan: The Institute of Gerontology, The University of Michigan–Wayne State University, 1975.

MARSELLA, JOAN F. "Portraits from the Sunny Side: Scenes and Dreams of Senior Jewish Women Residents of South Miami Beach Hotels." Unpublished manuscript. Smithfield, Rhode Island: Bryant College, 1977.

MEHAN, HUGH and WOOD, HOUSTON. *The Reality of Ethnomethodology.* New York: John Wiley and Sons, 1975.

MENDILOW, ADAM A. *Time and Experience.* London: Peter Nevill, 1952.

METZGER, DEENA. "In Her Image." *Heresies: A Feminist Publication on Art and Politics,* vol. 2 (May 1977): 2–11.

METZKER, ISAAC, ed. *A Bintel Brief: Sixty Years of Letters from the Lower East Side to the Jewish Daily Forward.* New York: Ballantine Books, 1971.

MIDDLETON, JOHN. *Lugbara Religion: Ritual and Authority Among an East African People.* London: Oxford University Press for International African Institute, 1960.

MIDDLETON, JOHN and TAIT, DAVID, eds. *Tribes without Rulers: Studies in African Segmentary Systems.* London: Rutledge and Kegan Paul, 1958.

MINTZ, JEROME R. *Legends of the Hasidim: An Introduction to Hasidic Culture and Oral Tradition in the New World.* Chicago: University of Chicago Press, 1968.

MOORE, SALLY F. and MYERHOFF, BARBARA G. "Introduction: Forms and Meanings." In *Secular Ritual,* edited by Sally F. Moore and Barbara G. Myerhoff. Amsterdam: Van Gorcum, 1977.

MOORE, SALLY FALK. "Old Age in a Life-Term Social Arena: Some Chagga of Kilimanjaro in 1974." In *Life's Career–Aging: Cultural Variations in Growing Old,* edited by Barbara G. Myerhoff and Andrei Simic. Beverly Hills, California: Sage Publications, 1977.

———. "Selection for Failure in a Small Social Field: Ritual Concord and Fraternal Strife on Kilimanjaro, 1968–69." In *Symbol and Politics in Communal Ideology: Cases and Questions,* edited by Sally F. Moore and Barbara G. Myerhoff. Ithaca: Cornell University Press, 1975.

———. Uncertainty in Situations: Indeterminacies in Culture." In *Symbol and Politics in Communal Ideology: Cases and Questions,* edited by Sally F. Moore and Barbara G. Myerhoff. Ithaca: Cornell University Press, 1975.

MYERHOFF, BARBARA G. *Peyote Hunt: The Sacred Journey of the Huichol Indians.* Ithaca: Cornell University Press, 1974.

———. "Return to Wirikuta: Ritual Reversal and Symbolic

Continuity Among the Huichol Indians." In *The Reversible World*, edited by Barbara Babcock. Ithaca: Cornell University Press, 1976.

———. "We Don't Wrap Herring in a Printed Page: Fusions and Continuity in Secular Ritual." In *Secular Ritual*, edited by Sally F. Moore and Barbara G. Myerhoff. Amsterdam: Van Gorcum, 1977.

MYERHOFF, BARBARA G. and SIMIC, ANDREI. *Life's Career—Aging: Cultural Variations in Growing Old*. Beverly Hills, California: Sage Publications, 1977.

MYERHOFF, BARBARA G., and TUFTE, VIRGINIA. "Life History as Integration: Personal Myth and Aging." *The Gerontologist*, 1975.

NAHMAD, H. M., ed. *A Portion in Paradise and Other Jewish Folktales*. New York: Schocken Books, 1974.

NEEDHAM, R. "Percussion and Transition." *Man*, vol. 2 (1967): 606–614.

NEUGARTEN, BERNICE L., ed. *Middle Age and Aging: A Reader in Social Psychology*. Chicago: The University of Chicago Press, 1968.

———. "Personality and Aging." In *Handbook of the Psychology of Aging*, edited by James Birren. New York: Van Nostrem, 1977.

NEUGARTEN, BERNICE and BENGTSON, VERNE. "Cross-National Studies of Adulthood and Aging." In *Methodological Problems in Cross-National Studies of Aging*, edited by Ethel Shanas. Basel: Karger, 1968.

NOY, DOV, ed. *Folktales of Israel*. Translated by Gene Baharov. Chicago: The University of Chicago Press, 1963.

OLNEY, JAMES. *Metaphors of Self: The Meaning of Autobiography*. Princeton, New Jersey: Princeton University Press, 1973.

OLSVANGER, IMMANUEL, ed., *Royte Pomerantsen or How to Laugh in Yiddish*. New York: Schocken Books, 1965.

ORNSTEIN, ROBERT E. *On the Experience of Time*. Middlesex, England: Penguin Books, 1969.

ORTNER, SHERRY B. "On Key Symbols." *American Anthropologist*, vol. 75, no. 5 (1973): 1338–1346.

———. "Is Female to Male as Nature Is to Culture?" In *Woman, Culture, and Society*, edited by Michelle Z. Rosaldo and Louise Lamphere. Stanford: Stanford University Press, 1974.

OTTO, RUDOLF. *The Idea of the Holy: An Inquiry into the Non-Rational Factor in the Divine and Its Relation to the Rational*. Translated by John W. Harvey. New York: Oxford University Press, 1958.

PETERMAN, DONALD J. "A Study of Interaction in a Jewish Multi-Generational Celebration—The Ha-Kesher Project," Unpublished master's thesis. Hebrew Union College, Los Angeles, California, 1975.

PITT-RIVERS, JULIAN A., ed. *Mediterranean Countrymen.* Paris: Mouton, 1963.

———. *The People of the Sierra.* Chicago: University of Chicago Press, 1961.

The Pittsburgh Section National Council of Jewish Women, under the direction of Ailon Shiloh. *By Myself, I'm a Book! An Oral History of the Immigrant Jewish Experience in Pittsburgh.* Waltham, Massachusetts: American Jewish Historical Society, 1972.

POLL, SOLOMON. *The Hasidic Community of Williamsburg: A Study in the Sociology of Religion.* New York: Schocken Books, 1962.

POWERS, JAMES L. "Two Jewish Women." Unpublished student paper. University of Southern California, Los Angeles, California, 1974.

PRELL-FOLDES, RIV-ELLEN. "Coming of Age in Kelton: The Constraints on Gender Symbolism in Jewish Ritual." In *Women in Ritual and Symbolic Roles,* edited by Judith Hoch-Smith and Anita Spring. New York: Plenum Press, 1978.

———. "Strategies in Conflict Situations: Ritual and Redress in an Urban Jewish Prayer Community." Doctoral dissertation. Department of Anthropology. University of Chicago, 1978.

———. *The Unity of Oneness: Unity and Opposition in Jewish Ritual.* M.A. thesis. Chicago: University of Chicago, 1973.

PRESS, IRWIN and MCKOOL, JR., MIKE. "Social Structure and Status of the Aged: Toward some Valid Cross-Cultural Generalizations." *Aging and Human Development,* vol. 3, no. 4 (1972): 279–306.

PRICE, REYNOLDS. *A Palpable God: Thirty Stories Translated from the Bible with an Essay on the Origins and Life of Narrative.* New York: Atheneum, 1978.

RABINOWITZ, DOROTHY. *New Lives: Survivors of the Holocaust Living in America.* New York: Avon Books, 1976.

RAPPAPORT, ROY. "Ritual Sanctity and Cybernetics." *American Anthropologist,* vol. 73, no. 1 (1971): 59–76.

REDFIELD, ROBERT. *The Little Community and Peasant Society and Culture.* Chicago: The University of Chicago Press, 1960.

———. *The Primitive World and Its Transformations.* Ithaca: Cornell University Press, 1953.

RICH, ADRIENNE. *Of Woman Born.* New York: W.W. Norton, 1976.

RIEMER, JACK, ed. *Jewish Reflections on Death.* New York: Schocken Books, 1974.

RIESSMAN, FRANK, ed. *Older Person: Unused Resources for Unmet Needs.* Beverly Hills, California: Sage Publications, 1977.

RIIS, JACOB. *How the Other Half Lives.* New York: C. Scribner's & Sons, 1890.

RISCHIN, MOSES. *The Promised City: New York's Jews, 1870–1914*. Cambridge: Harvard University Press, 1962.

ROSALDO, MICHELLE Z. "Women, Culture, and Society: A Theoretical Overview," In *Women, Culture and Society*, edited by Michelle Z. Rosaldo and Louise Lamphere. Stanford: Stanford University Press, 1974.

ROSE, ARNOLD M. "The Subculture of the Aging: A Topic for Sociological Research." In *Middle Age and Aging: A Reader in Social Psychology*, edited by Bernice Neugarten. Chicago: University of Chicago Press, 1968.

ROSE, PETER I., ed. *The Ghetto and Beyond: Essays on Jewish Life in America*. New York: Random House, 1969.

ROSEN-BAYEWITZ, PASSI and NOVEK, MINDA. *Shiloah: Discovering Jewish Identity Through Oral/Folk History; A Source Book*. New York: Institute for Jewish Life, 1976.

ROSKIES, DAVID G. and ROSKIES, DIANE K. *The Shtetl Book*. Ktay (no place given), 1975.

ROSTEN, LEO. *The Joys of Yiddish*. New York: Pocket Books, 1968.

———. *Leo Rosten's Treasury of Jewish Quotations*. New York: Bantam Books, 1972.

ROSS, JENNIE-KEITH. *Old People, New Lives: Community Creation in a Retirement Residence*. Chicago: University of Chicago Press, 1977.

ROTH, CECIL. *A History of the Jews: From Earliest Times Through the Six Day War*. New York: Schocken Books, 1970.

ROTH, PHILIP. "Writing About Jews," *Reading Myself and Others*. New York: Bantam Books, 1977.

ROTHENBERG, JEROME. *The Big Jewish Book: Poems and Other Visions of the Jews from Tribal Times to the Present*. New York: Doubleday, 1978.

———. "The Poetics of Performance." Paper delivered to the Burg-Wartenstein Conference on "Cultural Frames and Reflections: Ritual, Drama and Spectacle," sponsored by Wenner-Gren Foundation for Anthropological Research. Austria, 1977.

SAMUEL, MAURICE. *In Praise of Yiddish*. Chicago: Cowles Book Company, 1971.

———. *Prince of the Ghetto*. New York: Schocken Books, 1973.

———. *The World of Sholom Aleichem*. New York: Schocken Books, 1965.

SANDERS, RONALD. *The Downtown Jews: Portraits of an Immigrant Generation*. New York: New American Library, 1969.

SAPIR, EDWARD. "Symbolism." In *Encyclopedia of the Social Sciences*, vol. 14. New York: Macmillan.

SCHAPERA, I. *Government and Politics in Tribal Societies*. London: C.A. Watts and Company, 1956.

SCHECHNER, RICHARD. *Essays on Performance Theory 1970–1976*. New York: Drama Book Specialists, 1977.

SCHOLEM, GERSHOM G. *On the Kabbalah and Its Symbolism*. Translated by Ralph Manheim. New York: Schocken Books, 1969.

———. *Major Trends in Jewish Mysticism*. New York: Schocken Books, 1961.

———. *The Messianic Idea in Judaism and Other Essays on Jewish Spirituality*. New York: Schocken Books, 1971.

SCHRIRE, T. *Hebrew Amulets: Their Decipherment and Interpretation*. London: Routledge and Kegan Paul, 1966.

SEEMAN, MELVIN. "Intellectual Perspective and Adjustment to Minority Status." *Social Problems*, vol. 3 (January 1956): 141–153.

SHANAS, ETHEL et al. *Old People in Three Industrial Societies*. New York: Atherton Press, 1968.

SHNEIDMAN, EDWIN S. *Deaths of Man*. Baltimore, Maryland: Penguin Books, 1973.

SHULMAN, ABRAHAM. *The Old Country: The Lost World of East European Jews*. New York: C. Scribner's & Sons, 1974.

SIMIC, ANDREI. "Winners and Losers: Aging Yugoslavs in a Changing World." In *Life's Career–Aging: Cultural Variations in Growing Old*, edited by Barbara G. Myerhoff and Andrei Simic. Beverly Hills, California: Sage Publications, 1977.

SIMMEL, GEORG. "The Stranger." In *Sociology of Georg Simmel*, edited and translated by Kurt H. Wolf. Glencoe, Illinois: The Free Press, 1950.

SIMMONS, LEO W. *The Role of the Aged in Primitive Society*. New Haven: Yale University Press, 1945.

———. "Aging in Preindustrial Societies." In *Handbook of Social Gerontology*, edited by Clark Tibbitts. Chicago: University of Chicago Press, 1960.

SIMOS, BERTHA GOLDFARB. "Intergenerational Relations of Middle-Aged Adults with Their Aging Parents." Unpublished student paper. University of Southern California, Los Angeles, California, 1969.

SINGER, ISAAC BASHEVIS. *Enemies, A Love Story*. Greenwich: Fawcett Crest, 1973.

SKLARE, MARSHALL. *Conservative Judaism*. Glencoe, Illinois: The Free Press, 1965.

SKLARE, MARSHALL, ed. *The Jews: Social Patterns of an American Group*. Glencoe, Illinois: The Free Press, 1958.

SLEEPER, JAMES A. and MINTZ, ALAN L., eds. *The New Jews*. New York: Vintage Books, 1971.

SMITH, BERT KRUGER. *Aging in America*. Boston: Beacon Press, 1973.

SONTAG, SUSAN. "The Double Standard of Aging." In *No Longer Young: The Older Woman in America*. Occasional Papers in Gerontology, No. 1. University of Michigan Institute of Gerontology, 1975.

STANNARD, DAVID E. "Growing Up and Growing Old: Dilemmas of Aging in Bureaucratic Society." Human Values and Aging Project. Case Western Reserve University, 1976.

STREIB, GORDON F. "Are the Aged a Minority Group?" In *Middle Age and Aging: A Reader in Social Psychology*, edited by Bernice L. Neugarten. Chicago: University of Chicago Press, 1968.

SWARTZ, MARC J.; TURNER, VICTOR W.; and TUDEN, ARTHUR, eds. *Political Anthropology*. Chicago: Aldine Publishing Company, 1966.

TAMBIAH, S. J. "Form and Meaning of Magical Acts: A Point of View." In *Modes of Thought*, edited by Robin Horton and Ruth Finnegan. London: Faber and Faber, 1973.

———. "The Magical Power of Words." *Man* vol. 3, no. 2 (1968).

THOMAS, ELIZABETH M. *The Harmless People*. New York: Vintage Books, 1959.

TIBBITS, CLARK, ed. *Handbook of Social Gerontology: Societal Aspects of Aging*. Chicago: University of Chicago Press, 1960.

TRACHTENBERG, JOSHUA. *Jewish Magic and Superstition: A Study in Folk Religion*. New York: Atheneum, 1970.

TURNER, VICTOR W. *Dramas, Fields and Metaphors: Symbolic Action in Human Society*. Ithaca: Cornell University Press, 1974.

———. *The Drums of Affliction: A Study of Religious Processes Among the Ndembu of Zambia*. Oxford: Clarendon Press and the International African Institute, 1968.

———. *The Forest of Symbols: Aspects of Ndembu Ritual*. Ithaca: Cornell University Press, 1967.

———. "Forms of Symbolic Action: Introduction." In *Proceedings of the 1969 Annual Spring Ethnological Society Meetings*. Seattle: University of Washington Press, 1969.

———. *The Ritual Process: Structure and Anti-Structure*. Chicago: Aldine, 1969.

VANSINA, JAN. *Oral Tradition: A Study in Historical Methodology*. Translated by H. M. Wright. Chicago: Aldine, 1961.

VAN VELSEN, J. "The Extended-Case Method and Situational Analysis." In *The Craft of Social Anthropology*, edited by A. L. Epstein. London: Tavistock Publishers, 1967.

VELEZ-I, CARLOS. "Youth and Aging in Central Mexico: One Day in the Life of Four Families of Migrants." In *Life's Career—Aging: Cultural Variations on Growing Old*, edited by Barbara G. Myerhoff and Andrei Simic. Beverly Hills, California: Sage Publications, 1977.

WEINER, HERBERT. 9½ *Mystics: The Kabbala Today*. New York: Collier Books, 1969.

WIESEL, ELIE. *Messengers of God: Biblical Portraits and Legends*. Translated by Marion Wiesel. New York: Pocket Books, 1976.

———. *Souls on Fire: Portraits and Legends of Hasidic Masters*. Translated by Marion Wiesel. New York: Vintage Books, 1973.

WILLIAMS, RICHARD H. and WIRTHS, CLAUDINE G. *Lives Through the Years: Styles of Life and Successful Aging*. New York: Atherton, 1965.

WILLS, DEBORAH. "Case Study on Two Aging Eastern European Jews. Unpublished student paper. University of Southern California, Los Angeles, California, 1974.

WILSON, MONICA. *Rituals of Kinship among the Nyakyusa*. Oxford: Oxford University Press, 1957.

WIRTH, LOUIS. *The Ghetto*. Chicago: The University of Chicago Press, 1928.

———."Urbanism as a Way of Life." *American Journal of Sociology*, vol. 64 (July 1938): 12–22.

YAFFE, JAMES. *The American Jews: Portrait of a Split Personality*. New York: Paperback Library, 1969.

ZASHIN, JOSEPH. "The Fraternity of Mourners." In *Jewish Reflections on Death*, edited by Jack Riemer. New York: Schocken Books, 1974.

ZBOROWSKI, MARK and HERZOG, ELIZABETH. *Life Is with the People: The Culture of the Shtetl*. New York: Schocken Books, 1952.

ZELDITCH, MORRIS. "Role Differentiation in the Nuclear Family: A Comparative Study." In *Family, Socialization and Interpretation Process*, edited by Talcott Parsons and Robert F. Bales. Glencoe, Illinois: The Free Press, 1955.

INDEX